OTHER BOOKS BY JAMES F. T. BUGENTAL

Psychological Interviewing

The Search for Authenticity:
An Existential-Analytic Approach to Psychotherapy

Challenges of Humanistic Psychology (Editor)

Processes of Communication

The Human Possibility

The Search for Existential Identity:
Patient-Therapist Dialogues in Humanistic Psychotherapy

The Search for Authenticity
(Enlarged Edition)

Psychotherapy and Process:
The Fundamentals of an Existential-Humanistic Approach

The Art of the Psychotherapist

Intimate Journeys

JAMES F. T. BUGENTAL

Intimate Journeys

Stories from Life-Changing Therapy

Jossey-Bass Publishers

San Francisco • Oxford • 1990

INTIMATE JOURNEYS
Stories from Life-Changing Therapy
by James F. T. Bugental

Copyright © 1990 by: Jossey-Bass Inc., Publishers
350 Sansome Street
San Francisco, California 94104

Jossey-Bass Limited
Headington Hill Hall
Oxford OX3 0BW

James F. T. Bugental

Library of Congress Cataloging-in-Publication Data

Bugental, James F. T.
    Intimate journeys : stories from life-changing therapy / James
F.T. Bugental.
      p.   cm. — (Jossey-Bass social and behavioral science series)
    Includes index.
    ISBN 1-55542-274-8
    1. Psychotherapist and patient—Case studies. 2. Existential
psychotherapy—Case studies. 3. Humanistic psychotherapy—Case
studies. 4. Identity (Psychology)—Case studies. I. Title.
II. Series.
RC480.8.B83 1990
616.89'14—dc20   90-53091
                         CIP

Manufactured in the United States of America

The paper in this book meets the guidelines for
permanence and durability of the Committee on
Production Guidelines for Book Longevity of
the Council on Library Resources.

JACKET DESIGN BY CHARLOTTE KAY

REVISED EDITION

Code 9077

The Jossey-Bass
Social and Behavioral Science Series

Contents

Preface   xi

The Author   xix

1. "I Don't Feel Fifty."   1

2. "You've Been Blindfolded Since Childhood."   16

3. "I Need to Get into Therapy."   37

4. "Blame Is All I Have Left."   62

5. "And No One Came. No One."   79

6. "If I Ever Gave Up My Misery . . . "   103

7. "I'm Nothing but a Warming Machine."   126

8. "Show Me Your Legs."   145

9. "I Felt Motherly!"   167

10. "What Is Death?"   187

11. "I Am God!"   207

12. "I'll Kill Her. I'll Kill Her!"   233

13. "We Traded a Lot of Punches, Didn't We?"   258

14. "There's a Riot in Me, Too."   277

15. "We Had an Affair."   295

     Postscripts on the Clients   322

     Lessons Clients Teach Therapists   325

     Index   329

Preface

For nearly a half-century, men and women have been telling me about their lives. They have told me their secret and public stories, their loves and hates, their dreads and hopes, and all the concerns that make up our human histories. Executives, homemakers, secretaries, students, nurses and doctors, nuns, cab drivers, ministers and priests, engineers, police officers, lawyers, prostitutes, teachers and professors, actors, and still others have invited me to be with them as they searched deeply within themselves to discover what they sought most dearly, as they struggled through agony and soared on joy, as they confronted fears and mustered courage for their intimate journeys.

There is much that these, my teachers, have taught me — much that powerfully changed my own life. Changing too is my view of human nature. My formal education, valuable as it was, is pallid and partial when contrasted with the sum of lived experience these women and men have offered.

This discrepancy is sharply evident when I read academic and "scientific" psychology's views of human nature and speculations about the fundamental driving force of life: homeostasis, drive reduction, sexuality, power, individuation, spiritual growth — all, indeed, important — yet each ultimately falls short.

The rock bottom concern of each human being is the simple but profound fact of being alive. Life is the question we all face; living is the answer each of us gives.

xi

Who has not felt unrealized potentials sleeping within? That intuition is absolutely accurate. The most important point in this book, the one most easily overlooked or too little appreciated, is this: Each of us is subtly crippled, lacking access to this potential. I believe quite literally that each person is a handicapped person and thus diminished in vitality, in fullness of living.

In this book six people reclaim their lives, take more than usual charge of their own experience and actions. They are able to do this because they learn to use more fully their inner (existential) sense. This is a learning dearly come by, and their journeys to its attainment are instructive for us all.

I am one of the six, and I am also privileged to be designated helper to the other five. As their therapist, I come to know them intimately, probably more so than anyone else. Yet my knowing of each is always limited when contrasted with the immensity of a human life. The small perspective provided by even two or three hundred hours of deep conversation is but a set of snapshots, not a full-length documentary.

I do not intend to produce an objectively factual record. Rather, I undertake the more demanding task of attempting to portray a composite subjective experience. This experience is, of course, basically and inescapably my own. It cannot be otherwise. My experience, however, is always — and equally inescapably — compounded of my relations with others.

Detached, objective reporting of human experiences of the kind herein related is a kind of betrayal of those experiences, even as it is a parody of "scientific" statement. A science that misses the very essence of that which it purports to study is no science at all but sophistry in the service of the small minded. It is akin to an "art" that attempts to convey Mozart's *Requiem* by giving the vibrational frequencies of the notes the instruments play.

Just as each lived human life is an artistic product, each psychotherapy journey is an artistic product, whether pleasing or not. That is the very point: The Mozartian frequencies are objectively present, and a musical craftsman might well use them to construct instruments that ultimately could produce great beauty. But the objective study only describes the vehicle of the art, not its process or the artistic product. Psychotherapy, of course, also has its objective understructure. It has many important dimensions — interview skills, knowledge of psychopathology, and similar matters — but these are neither the art of psychotherapy nor its product.

What all this means is that to achieve my goal of writing a subjectively valid account of the work of my clients and myself I need to make every effort to convey my own inner experiences while that work is in progress. In *Intimate Journeys,* I recreate, as best I can, the often implicit interactions, going beyond objective reporting. This means further that I am more self-disclosing than is usually discreet (or altogether comfortable), since only in this way can the reader truly share in our experiences.

In simplest terms this is the story of my journey. It is a movement from seeing human lives chiefly in terms of their outward manifestations to the explosive recognition that life is truly invisible to our usual ways of seeing. Life is a subjective experience, and the subjective lies beneath the surface of usual language and concepts.

Writing explicitly about subjective matters is donning a diver's helmet and slowly lowering into the depths. In that world our vision must penetrate murkiness, and what we bring to the surface to report inevitably is changed in the transit and is different in the light of objective examination. Only when we are in the subjective can we recognize the subjective.

To tell the total subjective truth objectively and explicitly is impossible. Whatever I say can only point clumsily toward the endless more that is beyond verbalization. I point, not with a precise single index finger but with an awkward elbow — or perhaps, with my right buttock. And that necessary but inexact appendage always directs attention back of where we are currently looking. Not only can I not say all; neither can I say what we are immediately recognizing. Words lag behind vision.

So these pages are reconstructions of my experience, not mechanical recordings. I have freely changed objective elements to bring out, as best I could, the more subjective and usually hidden struggles, defeats, and triumphs of being human as these are disclosed in the life and work of one psychotherapist.

A word of warning: The issues the people in this book confront are issues of living — that is to say issues in the subjective realm. The violence they encounter is subjective. Their stories have less overt violence than most of us today are familiar with — even addicted to — from exposure to our popular media. As our inner, subjective life has become anesthetized, this addiction has reached a point at which each new offering must provide a bigger shock if it is to gain our attention and deliver the jolt our jaded sensitivity now demands. If you wish to gain for your own life from these accounts, you will have the difficult task of recalibrating your emotional sensitivity.

About the Form in Which This Work Is Presented

I have written this book in the first person and the present tense to make the experiences in it as available as possible. The immediacy of speaking about myself is valid; the immediacy of time is not. The time of the actual interviews was chiefly 1965 to 1975. I have rearranged the dates of interviews and omitted most of the work with other clients during this period to create a more integrated narrative. I have adjusted factual details about my own life to make them fit the time when I was seeing these clients.

Those were the years of *Hair* and *Woodstock,* of encounter groups and nude marathons, of Students for a Democratic Society and Vietnam, of mass demonstrations and streaking (running naked in public), of love beads and meditation, of civil rights marches and police dogs, of freer sex and spiritual awakenings, and of personal and group experimentation in many forms.

There are many differences between the mid 1960s and the early 1990s, between Jim Bugental in those days and today; but in the course of preparing this book I have come to realize how much continuity, even sameness, exists. The things I write today, when I am seventy-five, were as true in most respects when I was fifty, at the time of these experiences.

Note: Intimate Journeys is based in part on an earlier account of my work with these people: *The Search for Existential Identity,* published by Jossey-Bass in 1976. The present book has been largely rewritten from a different perspective, with considerable material added and some deleted.

Acknowledgments

One of the most frustrating and most satisfying tasks in writing a book is, for me, this one of acknowledging those who have contributed to the work. I have, as always, the limitations of my own memory, consciousness, conscience, good manners, indebtedness, sense of propriety, ethical obligations and restrictions, and energy. But beyond these limitations is the recognition of how many and how subtle are the varied resources I've drawn on and how tangled and interwoven with so many other considerations are the lines along which I might try to trace aid received.

At this fragile instant in my awareness's time, I want to say thank you to John Levy, always my friend, my compassionate critic, and my advocate. Thank you Jean Elsa Sloss and Cecily Beckwith, for providing a hideout for me when I needed to focus my energies. Thank you Molly Sterling and David Young, for support both overt and visible and subtle and pervasive. Thanks too to those in my workshops, classes, consultation groups, and courses at the California School of Professional Psychology. Your case presentations, questions, and fresh perspectives have enriched my work.

A special note of appreciation to Gracia A. Alkema, my editor at Jossey-Bass, for this and an earlier book. Her belief in what I was trying to do, her steady support of my efforts to bring the work to a wider audience, and her intelligent and sympathetic professional skills have constituted precisely the critical agency to bring this book into being. Thank you, Gracia.

To Karen Marie Bugental, my lovely and loving daughter and general gofer and office maintainer, a big hug and kiss of appreciation for very practical aid but even more for being such a joy to me.

Finally but foremost, Elizabeth Catherine Keber Bugental, what you give me is far beyond specification — yet of course, being a writer, I will try to specify: patience and impatience, clinical wisdom, a challenging difference of viewpoint, a heartening convergence of values and perspective, the wonder of being truly known and loved nevertheless, and — ultimately just your own healing presence in my life.

To My Clients

You have been my teachers, my companions, and my clients (to use a term that is now current but wasn't when we were together). Those characterizations are all true, but they seem, when set forth explicitly, partial and cool. Robert Frost says, "Any eye is an evil eye that looks in on . . . a mood apart." To look in on our relation and our work together from a detached position is to see with an evil eye — evil in the sense that it mistakes the surface for the depth. I do not want you to think that I would ever so look at our shared and intimate journeys.

Yet I want to pass along what you have taught me through your hope, pain, dread, and courage. Though years have passed since those days, I have repeatedly been brought to recognize that what we learned is as vital today as ever — perhaps even more so.

Our species at this point in history knows so little about the mystery of being human and alive. We have studied that which is outside of ourselves with so much greater care and thoroughness. And our world is paying the fearful price of this neglect. We are long overdue to expend the same effort on our true homeland, our inner living.

The most promising avenue for such study is depth psychotherapy. This enterprise, properly conducted, lays bare dimensions of experience seldom given full attention otherwise. Each of you has contributed to this study with your living being.

The five clients in the following pages are fictional to the extent that I have created them as carriers for accounts of your personal experiences in psychotherapy. You, my very real clients, may each recognize some of those events as your own experiences. If so, you will also find other events of the same composite client are not from your experience. By reconstructing our work in this form, I protect you from embarrassment while making as accessible as possible what our experiences have demonstrated about what it means to be alive.

The one exception to this practice is "Jim," my own story. Despite some real misgivings, I choose to be fairly candid in describing my own history and experience. This decision grows out of my conviction that our psychotherapy is above all an engagement between two humans, both of whom are struggling with the miracle of life itself. Thus to tell only the client's story is to distort the account, to pretend to an omniscience I do not have, and to give the reader a misleading sense of the very process this book seeks to describe.

I believe the notion of "therapeutic detachment" is an oxymoron, a self-deception, and a seduction for the faint-hearted. I am much encouraged by the warm response my disclosures have received by those who read them in other settings.

I have taken liberties with the details of our sessions in order to make them more understandable to others. Thus I have omitted the long periods of repetitive work that are always necessary; I've condensed interactions that spread over a number of interviews; and I've portrayed myself as more active than was generally my practice. These changes, I trust, preserve the spirit and meaning of our work by making it more accessible in written form.

Finally, I hope you will recognize my caring for you, my appreciation of what you went through and achieved, and my salute to the untapped potentials within all of us — potentials you pursued and actualized more than most.

Novato, California   James F. T. Bugental
August 1990

The Author

James F. T. Bugental is Visiting Distinguished Professor at the California School of Professional Psychology, Berkeley-Alameda. He is also emeritus professor of the Saybrook Institute and emeritus clinical faculty member of the Stanford University School of Medicine. He received his B.S. degree (1940) from West Texas State Teachers College in education, his M.A. degree (1941) from George Peabody College in sociology, and his Ph.D. degree (1948) from Ohio State University in psychology.

Bugental's chief contributions have been in the development of the humanistic perspective in psychology and in enunciating an existential-humanistic approach to intensive psychotherapy. He lectures and conducts workshops in many settings in this and other countries. He is past president of the Association for Humanistic Psychology and of the California State Psychological Association. For some years he was director of Inter/Logue, a training and service psychotherapy agency. In 1987 he was the recipient of The Mentor Society's Rollo May Award for "contributions to the literary pursuit," and in 1986 he was recognized by the Division of Clinical Psychology of the American Psychological Association for "distinguished contributions."

Bugental's books include *The Search for Authenticity* (1965, enlarged 1981), *Challenges of Humanistic Psychology* (editor, 1967), *The Search for Existential Identity* (1976), *Psychotherapy and Process* (1978), and *The Art of the Psychotherapist* (1987).

From the years up to this, the year of my three-quarters century of being, I have the well-fed feeling of having learned much about life, and I have an eager appetite to learn much more. One of the cornerstone learnings thus far — and one that I feel sure will endure — is how enriching, challenging, growth-evoking, and reassuring it is to have companions along the way. This book tells of those whom I accompanied on their intimate journeys. On this page I want to celebrate the wealth of such companionship that has been my privilege and to embrace some of those who have accompanied me on my own intimate journeys:

Elizabeth, Jane, JO, Karen, and Mary Edith
Al, Art, Bill, Bob, Gerry, Jim, and Tom
George, John, and Margot
Adele, Bill, Conn, Fran, Jean Elsa, John, Louis, and Mondi

Intimate Journeys

One

"I Don't Feel Fifty."

Friday, November 12

Jim. Driving to the office this morning is a descent into the sea. Our home sits on the top of the hills in western Los Angeles, and we can see across the San Fernando Valley, already bathed in sunlight. But going south into Westwood means dropping down into the sea fog that has come in during the night. It isn't heavy today; sometimes it adds a bit of danger and excitement to the familiar drive. Traffic is stacked up on Veteran waiting to cross Wilshire, but that's normal.

I feel smug as I pull into my private parking place beneath the overhang of our big second-floor group room. Every day parking is getting to be more of a problem around Westwood Village, but we have a lease that establishes my rights so no one can take my space. (I'm also a little embarrassed by these thoughts.)

Our suite takes the rear half of both sides of the upper floor of the two-story office building and includes offices for five therapists, two secretaries, two group rooms, and a library-staff room. My embarrassment doesn't keep me from savoring the sense of achievement that all this represents. The Depression boy likes to review his defenses against ever again being out of work, out of money, out of luck. The house on the hill, the prosperous professional practice are assurances that I've made it, that I can be who I am at last. Or nearly so.

1

I'm thinking about the big blackout on the East Coast day before yesterday. Nine states and two Canadian provinces — around 25 million people — were left in the dark. The power failed because there was too much drain on it. It seems like a metaphor for so much in life — too much dependence on any source of power makes us very vulnerable, whether as individuals or as societies. I have relied so much on being bright and effective; it scares me to think what could happen if I push it too far.

I'm the first here this morning, and I walk through the suite savoring the books in our library that tell of the work that I love; the rooms of my colleagues whom I value; the sense of a place, a time, and a vocation that so fulfill me. Entering my own office brings a subtle relaxation as I take in the chairs where my clients and I sit; the couch some of those clients use; the books, pictures, and travel souvenirs.

The sun is starting to break through as I go to the windows to admire the view — of the alley and garages. Really, it's not that bad. When you're seated you only see trees — and a telephone pole and wires.

I turn on the lights, unlock the desk, pull out my clipboard. Geting set for the day, I leaf through the sheets I keep on the back of the clipboard — a list of clients' names and file numbers (all records are identified only by number to additionally protect client privacy), a list of resources to which I can refer, jottings of ideas that hit me while I work and that I want to note down so they won't intrude on my attention, and four pages of my "doodles."

I don't know whether other therapists have found the benefits I get from doodling, making relatively random marks on paper while I listen. This seems to get me into a subjective space where I get less caught up in the words and tune in better to the "music" of the client's use of our time.

I don't understand just how my doodling works, and I don't intend to figure it out. I'm protective of this aid. The few times I've tried to analyze it or let friends speculate about it proved disruptive. When next I began to doodle I was too self-conscious, watching what I was producing. I had to give it up for a while, and I felt handicapped during the interval.

It's just another place where I'm leery of cognitive interpretations of subconscious processes. I feel the same caution about figuring out my clients' dreams or my own. Our larger consciousness (that includes what the analysts call the conscious, the preconscious, the personal unconscious, and the collective unconscious) is to be trusted. If understanding of doodles or dreams doesn't come readily, then I'm inclined to wait and do more unlayering rather than blast through with intricate scenarios or hypnosis.

I learned from my own experience of psychoanalysis that everything need not and cannot be made focally conscious or explicit, that we have to trust that larger self at times. This is not an either-or matter, but one of degree.

Naturally, when I'm doodling, clients sometimes question what I'm doing at my clipboard (I also make brief notes during the hour); and so I explain and sometimes let them see my doodles (or my notes). Most get used to these activities, but a very few still find them distracting after a few sessions. When this is the case, we have to work out mutually agreeable plans — these vary with the individuals.

Today, I look at my doodles and enjoy the feeling they give me. I'm no artist; I always wished I could draw as my dad could. Still, I enjoy doing these.

Ten to eight, time for a cup of coffee before my first interview, a new client. Feels luxurious, didn't arrive in my usual last-minute dash; so to the staff room for the coffee — only to find that someone left the pot on all night. It's dry and very likely may be burned out again. Damn! This shouldn't happen to such a well-established and successful professional. So I'll settle for a cup of water from the hall dispenser.

But no one has put a fresh bottle of water on the stand; so it's up to me. By now it's time for my intake, so I decide to skip the water after all. My mood of satisfaction is somewhat deflated when I finally do go to pick up the new client.

Louise. As I open the door between my office and the waiting room and look in at the two people there, a subtle perfume of femininity reaches me from the attractive woman. (In the back of my mind: How could that happen so fast?)

Instantly alert to my entry and quickly apologizing to the man, with whom she's been talking, the woman turns to me expectantly. I pick up a hint of annoyance from him as I ask, "Miss Gowan?" and he relinquishes her.

"Yes. Dr. Bug-*en*-tall?" She comes to her feet quickly with a bright smile.

"That's right. I usually make it '*Byew*-jen-tall,' but it gets all kinds of pronunciations." I'm pleased; this new client seems so attractive and responsive. As I motion her ahead of me into my office, I give the abandoned male a reassuring nod.

"Oh, I'm sorry! *Byew*-jen-tall. There. Did I get it right?" Such a cheery voice!

"Just fine. Try that chair, why don't you?"

She sits in my big client chair, poised, proper, yet, remarkably, still sending out that female fragrance. I realize now that it's not an actual physical odor to be sensed with the nose or mouth; rather, it is a psychic essence she exudes. I'm intrigued. How does she do it? Is it conscious? With everyone? Every man? And what in the world is "a psychic essence"?!

We exchange the usual conversational filler about the weather and the traffic. It gives her an opportunity to glance about the room, look at me again, and get better settled in the chair. This transition time is essential, and it's always a guess just how much a new client may require. She seems to be reasonably "here." Let's see.

"Why don't you tell me how I may be helpful to you?"

She hesitates, "Well, I. . . . " She looks down at her lap, marshals her determination, and raises her head. "It's hard to just start out, you know."

"Of course. Take your time. You don't have to get it all out at once or just right."

"Yes. Thank you. That's helpful."

"Mm-hmmm."

"I don't know how to say this . . . or whether it will make much sense to you. . . . " She pauses, looks to me for encouragement. I nod, and she goes on. "I mean, I have the feeling I'm hollow or. . . . " She stops, looks confused, embarrassed.

"Some way you feel hollow inside?"

"Yes, I·. . . I can't seem to find out what I stand for, or what I. . . . It's really vague, I know, but. . . . "

"So often the most important inner feelings don't easily come out in words. Just say it any way it comes to you."

"I'll try. I guess what I'm trying to say is . . . is that I feel . . . sometimes I feel as though I haven't any core inside. Like I don't know who I really am."

She goes on, haltingly, but eventually making clear her feeling of lacking substance, not having meaning or purpose. She links this hollowness to her repeated times of loneliness and unhappy moods. Then she says, "Being a social worker, I think I ought to give you my history. Is that all right?"

"If it would help me understand you, by all means do so." I'm not much for case histories, but I want her to take responsibility for her own participation; so I'll go along.

Her story is sad and anything but erotic: Father dead in an auto accident before she is ten, her mother and herself seriously injured. Mother's efforts to provide. . . . As I listen, one part of my mind is observing: articulate, intelligent, somewhat detached (usual this soon, of course). Dress conservative but in good taste; body not flaunted but not denied either. Where is that feral hint coming from?

"After the accident, for nearly a year, I couldn't go to school. My mother, recovering from her own injuries and from Dad's death, tried to teach me at home, but mostly I was on my own. It was such a lonely time (wistfully). I'd look out the window at the kids playing and wish I could go out."

"A lonely time."

"Yes." A quick, grateful smile. A little too grateful for such a simple response. Does she overrespond? Yes, she does, and it does detract from the invitingness.

"And then, in the spring, Mother found out she had cancer. She tried to be brave, I know, but I could hear her crying in her room. I tried to keep her from knowing that I heard her, and I did my best to make her happy." Tears starting in her eyes. "She was in such pain, you know, and she just seemed to dwindle away. Right after Labor Day she died, and. . . . "
She is weeping quietly now.

"Hard for a young girl just regaining her own strength."

She nods. I wait quietly as she dries her eyes, blows her nose, and looks up at me with a little rueful smile. "I'm sorry to be such a baby."

"Really, that's not the way I see you."

"That's nice of you to say." Oh, blah! I find her too sweet, too proper. Where's the erotic perfume now? I'll be damned, it's still here! Seems paradoxical to be put off by her cloying sweetness even as some other part of my mind wants to pet her. Ah, well, take note of it, but don't get sidetracked.

"I went to live with my mother's brother and his wife, Uncle Bennett and Aunt Julie. But it didn't work out well. Aunt Julie resented me. She tried to be understanding, I know, but at night I could hear them arguing and my name being said. Finally, one evening. . . . " Another pause as the tide of tears returns. She cries so quietly.

"It's painful to recall what happened, eh?"

"Yes, but it is silly of me, don't you think?" An appealing smile clearly invites me to say it isn't silly. How often she needs reassurance! Makes me want to say that she's right, it is silly. Wow! This woman really gets to me. "Well, anyway, one evening my uncle asked me to go for a walk with him. He said he was really sorry, but it just wasn't working out for me to live with them. Aunt Julie was going through the menopause and was very nervous. So he'd arranged for me to go live with a cousin on a New Hampshire farm."

"Um-hmm."

"I felt just awful . . . so scared." Tears coming more strongly now. "At least I had known Uncle Bennett and Aunt Julie before the accident, but I'd never even heard of these New Hampshire cousins. I wanted to run away, but I was so scared."

She cries in earnest now, and I realize that for the first time since she entered the room I don't feel the focus of her attention. Mostly I've been the center of her awareness no matter what she talked about. That attention combined with her "female scent" has a subtle but heady impact.

"The fright and lost feeling you knew then are in you right now." It's clear she's no longer just reporting; she's very present to the emotions in her right now. It is this vital immediacy — so in contrast to her previous focus on me — that I want to reinforce.

"Oh, yes. Yes." Her head comes up instantly, and the appealing look, now mixed with gratitude for my understanding, shines on me. The sarcasm in my thought tells me that I'm embarrassed by my response to her. But I am also genuinely moved by her tragic story and . . . and by her unspoken appeals . . . and by that erotic quality as well. Well! This *is* going to be interesting.

"How did it go in New Hampshire?"

"Well, all right at first. The Coltens were older and really good people. They tried to make me feel at home and to teach me the right things. Their children were all grown with children of their own. Sometimes we had big family picnics and parties at the holidays, just like in stories, but then. . . . "

"Then?"

"Then, well . . . Mr. Colten was getting kind of old, I guess, and . . . and I. . . . This is embarrassing for me." Again she gives me a sweet, appealing smile; but she is really uncomfortable, not just looking for my response.

"It's hard to talk about what happened?"

"Yes. You see, I had matured while I was with Uncle Bennett and Aunt Julie, you know. I mean, I matured rather early and had a rather full figure when I was twelve or thirteen. Oh, this is. . . . " She looks down at her hands twisting in her lap.

"It's difficult to talk about your body and its sexual maturing, eh?"

"Yes, but . . . but I don't know why. I'm not a child. I'm thirty-seven years old, but . . . but I guess I'm rather inexperienced. . . . " Her voice fades, and now genuine embarrassment is compounded with her subtle pull for encouragement. I'll resist for the moment, at least.

We are quiet for a minute or so, and she regains her poise rather promptly. Interesting.

"I gradually realized Mr. Colten was trying to see me when I took a bath and he wanted me to go for walks alone with him. One time when I did, he led me down to the creek and said this was his old swimming hole, where they used to swim nude. Then he wanted me to take off my clothes and go in right then. He said he'd watch to be sure nobody came so I'd be all right.

"I was scared and said I didn't want to, but he kept insisting, and so I started to do it. Then just as I got out of my dress and brassiere, Mrs. Colten came through the bushes, shouting at us both. I think she thought I was trying to lure him on or something. I just cried and cried and tried to explain, but it seemed as though nobody would believe me. And the old man got all mixed up trying to protect me and himself and denying the whole thing, so that it just was a terrible time. Anyway, after about a week, they sent me back to Uncle Bennett."

"What was that like for you?"

"I really don't know now. I just remember that I felt kind of numb and terribly ashamed. I didn't want to see anyone who had heard anything about the whole thing." She cries quietly, avoiding letting our eyes meet — the old shame is revived. "Well, then, of course, I couldn't stay there. So, in a month or so, they arranged for me to live with an elderly lady and to help take care of her in exchange for my board and room. That was Mrs. Davis, and I stayed with her until I was sixteen."

So Louise tells me of her troubled, insecure childhood. Losing her parents early, thereafter, she is constantly in situations in which she must meet others' wishes just to continue to live in what is temporarily her home.

Toward the end of the hour I want to explore how aware she is of her impact on others.

"One thing that has impressed me as we talked, Miss Gowan, is the extent to which you seem concerned with being pleasing and continually return to smiling, even when you are telling me of unhappy events. It will be useful if I know to what extent you are aware of this pattern."

"Oh, that embarrasses me again." She is embarrassed; yet there is a subtle coy quality as well. "Well, I think I know some about it. I have sometimes been aware that I want so much to . . . to . . . I don't know how to say it. I remember one time after a movie I thought, 'I've had a Bette Davis life, but I cover it up with Shirley Temple.'"

And that says it very well, I think to myself, except I'd add, "Shirley Temple and Marilyn Monroe."

Jim. Louise's impact is so pronounced that she lingers in my thoughts, coming back again as I drive home that evening. She is so totally focused on me (or on whomever she is with, I'd guess) that I feel her presence as though it were a constant physical touch. This happens with other clients too, of course; but combined with the erotic female quality, it is really potent.

There's a certain irony in how her focus on me affects me: This is exactly what we therapists often do and what adds significantly to our power in the interviews. Having someone set aside everything else just to attend to you is potent in any circumstance.

Nearing home, I make a mental note to think more about my response to Louise. Got to keep that conscious. I'm not immune to the "charms" of a desirable woman, and she certainly is that. And I need to keep aware of all those thoughts about her and her body and her attractiveness — especially when I'm with her.

Friday, December 10

Hal. Hal is a fellow psychologist but one who adheres to a perspective quite different from my own. Though we have met a few times at professional meetings, our paths seldom cross otherwise. Thus I am surprised — and a bit flattered — when he calls for an appointment with me.

At this, his first session, after brief, waiting-room greetings, he enters my office with an intense, preoccupied manner, takes the chair I offer, and immediately launches into why he is here.

"The thing is this: I'm out of my head with my kid — my son, Tim. He's sixteen, a junior in high school, and a —. All right (belligerently), I'll say it the way it comes: He's a goddamn hippie. The whole stupid bit: long hair, trying to grow a beard, doesn't bathe, hates school, probably cuts so many classes he'll bust out, likely into pot or worse. . . . God! I hope nothing worse."

"Hal, let me interrupt for a minute."

"Yeah, sure, go ahead."

"I don't see adolescents in treatment. I find that I don't have the temperament to. . . . "

"Oh, wait, Jim. Sorry to interrupt, but that's not why I'm here. I wish we could get him to come to you or someone, but I don't think there's a chance in hell he'd even consider it. No, it's not Tim who's the problem, it's me! I just go kind of nuts with that kid. I rage at him, try to scare him. Scare myself is more what happens. So I figure I better get someone to look under my hood and see what's going on. That's why I'm here. Do you want to take me on?"

So we begin our work. Hal is bluff, boisterous at times, but he's also very much in pain. As he tells of his relation with his son and then fills me in on his own background, I am curious — but decide not to ask — about the meaning of his choosing me.

Hal is big. He is big physically: at least six-feet-four and two hundred twenty-five pounds, I'd guess. He's no musclebound jock, though, for he's big mentally too. I've noticed the Phi Beta key he earned at an Ivy League school before taking his doctorate, also at a top university.

He's big as well in his professional life. From what he tells me now, and what I know otherwise, he has some private practice in addition to a post at a research and development institute. He is on the part-time faculty at a local college, is active in professional societies, and puts out professional papers. A big schedule indeed!

And before this session ends, it is very evident that Hal's bafflement is big too. He has tried all the devices of rational attack on his own ungovernable temper, on his overreacting (as he himself terms it) to his son, and he realizes he has been unable to bring about the change he feels desperately he must make in himself.

We set up a schedule of two visits a week. I recommend three, but he insists his commitments just won't permit it.

Generally I try to see my clients three or four times a week at the outset. It means we both know we are undertaking a major task, and clients experience a significant impact on their usual round of affairs. It also means that I become much more fully caught up in the work than if I were to see more clients, each less frequently. Later we may reduce the frequency. Our sessions are forty-five minutes in length, and, as a general rule, I start and stop quite promptly.

Although there are marked differences, in general, my clients use the chair at first, trying out the couch after we've gotten under way together. Some then use the couch all the time, some only occasionally, and some practically never. For the most part, the choice is up to them.

Jim. Hal's training emphasized experimental psychology and objective, "scientific" methodology. His teachers held that external behavior alone provides sufficient basis for understanding human beings, without recourse to the murky realms of subjective experience. Thus it surprises me that he wants to enter therapy with me. There's a message here, whether or not Hal is conscious of sending it. He is looking for something that I represent for him and that, evidently, he feels he can't find in his own perspective.

In addition to being pleased, though, I have to recognize that I am also challenged. As much as I want to help him, I know myself well enough to know I need to be alert to see Hal, the person, rather than react to his philosophic orientation.

I'm alternately angry and sad that the behaviorist perspective — Hal's training — is currently dominating American psychology. This is due to its persistent claim to being a "science" in the field. I have no quarrel with that goal, only with the narrow and outdated conception of science that is accepted as dogma. Years of talking with people have demonstrated to me beyond question that the simplistic formulations of behaviorism are only helpful in a limited range of conditions. The behaviorist view is not so much wrong as it is radically limited, yet it proclaims itself to be a universal revelation. I think of it as "crawl psychology": The behaviorist looks on the whole range of human locomotion — crawling, walking, running, jumping, and all the

aids we've developed — and still insists that they're all only forms
of crawling.

In all fairness, my own existential outlook also seems to
me to have universal implications. But I think this is redeemed
by its recognition of the contributions of most other views —
including the behaviorist. To me, being existential means putting the fact of life itself — that is, existence — as the foremost matter for psychological attention. The humanistic adjective (that
is, existential-humanistic) attests to our putting human well-
being and the actualization of human potential as our highest
value.

Well, Hal must have his reasons for coming to me. We'll
see what they are. Meantime, I'll bet our differences are going
to be stimulating — and, at times, frustrating.

I have time now to sit back and chew on the feelings Hal
raises in me. I get a cup of coffee and let the thoughts run. Hal
is such a winner in so many ways — the right academic background, sports star, well recognized professionally. Yet it isn't
all working out right for him either. It doesn't *all* work out for
anyone, does it?

Sure doesn't work out for the poor guys in Vietnam. What
in God's name are we doing there? And when will we get out?
It makes me sick that our country is in yet another war, and
so soon. I ought to be more active in the antiwar effort, but
I have excuses: My clients need me to be dependably available;
my family needs me to keep our finances coming in; what can
one individual do? These excuses don't satisfy me. Then I think,
I'm too old; the young people are carrying the peace effort.

Too old? How old? And what does that mean? I'm fifty
years old this month. What a strange statement that is! I don't
feel fifty. Fact is, I don't feel forty-nine, or any other age. How
old am I? Damned if I know. Sometimes I feel young, sometimes old; no age really feels true.

But the official, mathematical verdict is that I'll have completed fifty years in a couple of weeks. What is "fifty"? Men who
are fifty are at the peak of middle age (and starting down the other
side?). They're heading toward being "older" men (a long way

from "old men"). Before I get to "old," I've got a lot I want to do yet. I'm trying to find out how to be a person, a professional man, a husband, a father. Those are big orders, I've discovered.

It's all happening so fast. I hurry along, trying to do things right, trying to enjoy the good things I have, trying to learn — always trying to learn — trying to be more the way I want to be. What is that? How do I really want to be?

For fifty years I've been trying to get ready to live the *real* life. For fifty years I've been getting prepared to live — as soon as I find out how, — as soon as I make enough money, — as soon as I have enough time, — as soon as I become more a person I can trust. Lately I feel as though I know a little more about how to live, how to be a friend, how to be real with people, how to face things within myself. Lately I feel more hopeful for me. Yet here I am, more than halfway along, and I know damned well I've not arrived yet. Will I ever?

I have always wanted to be one of the "right" people — as Hal seems to be; but the definition of *right* keeps changing. The only constant is that "right" is always different than I am. Over time, though, I'm gaining on it. Right people live in a house on a hill, and now I have such a house. Of course, they have lived in their house for generations, and we moved into ours when it was new. Still, it's something; and so is getting my doctorate and being on the faculty at UCLA. (My students there loved it when I told them I couldn't get in as a student myself because of my erratic high school and junior college grades!) New-found confidence in my capacities and a war-created need for psychologists helped me move up. Am I doing it right at last? Still the shadow, the sense of something wrong, is there.

From my mother's view, I'm probably "bad," since I'm just back from the Esalen Institute where I ran a weekend workshop. Esalen is a remarkable place. It's daring to innovate in ways that our more staid colleges and universities should be but aren't. And not just in ways that cause raised eyebrows.

Of course, I can't quite imagine a university that would have the hot baths for which Esalen is famous. I really enjoy those — though I was shy about them at first. The idea of mixed

nude bathing was titillating, fascinating, and . . . scary. Once
I was there, though, it was much more matter-of-fact and much
less erotic than I'd anticipated (hoped?).

One thing hit me that first time — it's not news, but the
actual experience of it was surprising nevertheless — the totally
naked woman is less exciting than one who is partially nude.
Of course, that's what the whole youth culture is teaching us
all over again. *Hair's* first-act finale with the cast standing naked
and facing the audience is interesting — and a letdown.

Closing and locking my desk and files, I pause in my
reflections. All of these thoughts and feelings are very much part
of me. I can't discard them, and they can get in the way when
I'm with Louise, who excites my libidinal response. I've got to
keep aware. So easy to say that; so hard to do. Yet, since my
own psychoanalysis, I'm better able to manage it. But, of course,
there's always more. That's the reason this is such a fascinating
business, such a necessary enterprise, and such an impossible
profession.

After so many years of trying to find what I wanted to
do with my life — years of study and preparation, of discovering clinical psychology as an army psychologist, of graduate
school, of university teaching, of getting started in practice and
pursuing further training — after all of this, here I am: a full-
time psychotherapist. Sometimes that surprises me still. Yet I
know and enjoy that reality now with a new quiet I've never
had before. I'm not the best therapist, but I'm getting to be a
really good psychotherapist.

So what does it mean to be a psychotherapist? To give
more than a superficial answer is difficult. Take the words that
are linked with the profession, for example: I really wish I could
discard terms such as *psychotherapy, doctor, patient, treatment, symptoms,* and *diagnosis.* Though the word *patient* is getting displaced
now by *client,* I can't see that as much of an improvement.
They're all honorable words and come from a humane tradi-
tion, but they carry a lot of excess baggage that doesn't fit what
goes on in my office.

Talking with two new people — Hal and Louise — about

entering therapy, I'm reminded of how my way of doing this work has changed. No longer do I "take a history," painstakingly getting all sorts of objective information about a potential client. Histories have value in clinics, public agencies, and research; yet, when I'm just beginning work with someone, I don't want to make fact-gathering their first experience of our partnership.

That's not the only change. I seldom collect symptoms or try to "establish a diagnosis," except as insurance companies (which sometimes pay for therapy) require it. These tasks are, to my mind, relics of the supposed medical history of psychotherapy. To be frank about it, I think that history has seriously handicapped the development of truly life-changing work.

The reason I don't take histories, collect symptoms, and work out diagnoses is simple: I'm not engaged in healing illnesses or repairing injuries.

When Hal comes complaining of his inability to govern his temper with his son, and when Louise speaks of feeling "hollow inside," I hear these as evidencing their wanting to grow larger. They want to be more alive, which is to say, more able to have charge of how their lives go.

They don't tell of suffering an injury or a disease. Our work soon makes clear that they've not lost some former state of well-being. Rather, they have come to the edges of their prior ways of living and want more power in their lives. I'm sure Hal has often known troubling impulses and Louise has never felt solid and secure in herself. Neither has had a loss that must now be corrected.

So if this isn't a kind of medical treatment, what is it? And what's the work all about? The answer is easy: This is life-growth consultation. This is life-expansion school. We need it to make up for the poor preparation we've had for the job of creating our lives.

We're poorly prepared because much of our preparation was about how to be children, how to get set for adult life; but so little was about how to *be* adults. *What we call intensive therapy is really a crash educative process that seeks in two or more years to catch up on the maturation stunted by twenty or more years of trying to live out a child's view of life.*

Two

"You've Been Blindfolded Since Childhood."

Monday, February 7

Kate. When Dr. Kate Margate first comes to see me, she looks like the Hollywood stereotype of a prim governess. She wears no makeup, a nondescript but neat tweed suit, and "sensible" shoes. Her face is composed, intelligent, and completely unreachable. By that I mean that she smiles or frowns appropriately to what is being said but shows few, if any, of the small changes of expression that usually animate a face in interaction with another person. She responds in a restrained way to the content of what I say but not at all to me as a person in conversation with her. What iron determination such a mask must require!

"I'll be candid with you, Dr. *Burg*-gan-thal; I do not like being here. I am annoyed with myself for requiring psychological help. Nevertheless, I am here, and I am here because of my sense of professional responsibility."

"Professional responsibility?"

"Professional responsibility." Flatly, not inflected, only a factual announcement. "I am a physiologist, a research scientist. I come because I realize that I have not been functioning in my work as well as my employers have a right to expect — indeed, as well as I expect of myself. In past years I was much more productive and efficient."

"You've seen yourself change."

"Yes, yes." A hint of annoyance. Restatements that might help most people clearly seem to her only irrelevant interruptions. I'll keep out of the way for the time being.

"I have changed. It is obvious to me, and it will soon be obvious to my colleagues, if it is not already. It is for this reason that I come to you. I want your help so that I can regain my former competence."

She goes on, telling of a life devoted to the intellect and stripped of emotion. She made an exceptional scholastic record and, on finishing her doctorate, joined the research staff of a large pharmaceutical corporation, where she now holds a responsible position. She married a colleague, but the marriage was short, its ending cold and abrupt.

As she talks I note that her controlled face does not fully conceal traces of sadness around the corners of her eyes and mouth. In her lap, her hands, initially clenching her handbag, have loosened to some extent and now make small aborted gestures with her words. I am a bit surprised to discover that, despite her steely grip on herself, I have an impulse of warmth toward her. She needs comforting, I think, but I'm certain she would be furious if it were offered.

"I have a number of acquaintances, although there is no one currently in my life whom I would think of as a close friend." She pauses, reflecting.

"Do you miss having a 'close friend'?"

"Oh, I'm sure it would be nice to have such a relation, but for the most part I much prefer to live a more solitary life." Yes and no, eh? Let it be, for now.

What is manifest is that coming to see me is repugnant to her. As a consequence, Kate-with-me acts as though she were a messenger from Kate-the-person. She tells me about that person, but she is determined that person — herself — will not come into my office or be seen directly by me. It's going to take some careful work to help her risk being really in this room with me.

Jim. How we all learned to make ourselves into objects to be moved about, reported on, or otherwise dealt with! Thus, though her way of being here exaggerates it, Kate's standing apart from herself is by no means unusual. In their own unique ways, Louise and Hal try the same self-defeating maneuver.

The lesson was: *objectivity* is virtue, *subjectivity* is sin. Incredible! Subjectivity — being the live, animate center of one's own life, rather than an object in it — is considered a sin, a manifest disgrace! No wonder our lives are not as we want.

So if subjectivity isn't a sin, what is it? It is *the only site* in which we can effect fundamental change in our lives. That's one of the biggest secrets about life. How few of us — even psychotherapists — really seem to know this!

Changes enforced from the outside, whether by others or by one's self, are undependable and often lead to more trouble. Every dictatorship carries the seeds of its own eventual overthrow.

We all know that making satisfying and lasting life changes is difficult at best. Why? Kate's unwillingness to be truly present in therapy is a partial answer. It's virtually impossible to bring about changes if we're not truly in our lives; if we're trying to be critics, not authors, of the drama of our lives.

A client of mine once described the problem succinctly: "I don't live my life; I tell myself about it."

What we all need, what Kate has not yet experienced, what Hal complains of, what Louise has still to discover, and what others avoid, is that life management requires that we truly *be* in our lives. To have charge of life requires that we come out of the audience and take up our tasks of being the authors and actors of our own lives.

Frank. During my break, I take a phone call.

"Dr. Burg-in-*thale?*" He sounds gruff — or defensive.

"Yes. Byew-jen-tal, I usually say."

"Yeah. Well, how much do you charge?" No wasted time here!

"Who is this? I'll be glad to answer you when I know to whom I'm talking."

"I'm Frank Connelly. I want to get into therapy, but I don't know whether I can afford you. Now will you tell me?"

"Right. I charge $30 an hour, Mr. Connelly. If you like we can have a first appointment just to see how we each feel about working together. But I charge for that hour also."

"Yeah, okay. Can I come in tomorrow?"

"I'm sorry, but the first opening I have is next Tuesday at 2:00 in the afternoon. How's that?"

"Naw, I gotta work then."

We have to make several bids back and forth before we find a time. I have the feeling Mr. Connelly does not like taking a time I offer but wants to have me meet his proposal. That's okay, and eventually I am able to do so.

I wonder what this Frank Connelly will be like. He's pretty gruff on the phone, and he seems easily displeased. Wonder what brings him in? Well, every intake is the first chapter of a mystery story.

Jim. In the few minutes I have before Hal's appointment, I reflect on what a frightening business it is for most of us to call a psychotherapist for the first time. I remember two weeks of postponing calling my analyst for an appointment even after I learned he would see me. Daily I meant to call, and equally frequently I "forgot" until it was "too late" to dial his number.

The apprehension is partly the fear of what we may have to disclose, the gray or black secrets everyone carries, but I think it is even more a shapeless, content-less dread of being seen, being naked before anonymous eyes, being discovered. It has little if anything to do with what we know or suppose about the therapist as a particular living person; it has nearly everything to do with our own self-mistrust and the seemingly instinctual fear of being helpless before what may be a powerful watcher.

Yet, for many of us, there is also a fascination, a yearning for the experience of being wholly open to someone, of being — for once and at last — truly known.

Two new people who want to change their lives — Kate Margate and Frank Connelly. What a contrast! One formal, restrained, proper, reluctant. The other rough, direct, eager. Yet both are beginning the quest for better, more fulfilling living.

It seems strange to think in terms of being more or less alive, but there's a big payoff to doing so. A wide range of human experiences are called "being alive."

- At a state mental hospital, I occasionally saw a middle-aged, catatonic woman. She never left her crib-like bed, was fed intravenously, and soiled and wet herself as an infant does. She responded neither to her own body nor to any visitor — not to mother, husband, or daughter. Was she alive?
- George Bannerman is thirty-four years old when his parents, with whom he has always lived, bring him to see me. He has no real friends, has never dated, has never been away from home overnight. He works occasionally as a handyman for sympathetic neighbors or for his father's construction firm. He is not mentally deficient or psychotic. He is extremely undeveloped socially, and he has no motivation to change. Is he alive in an existence more suitable to a fourteen year old?
- Barbara Meyer is an office manager for the central office of a grocery chain. She is the first woman in this position. She works ten-hour days at the office, often brings work home, is determined to demonstrate her qualifications for further promotion. She has discontinued relations with men, seldom sees her relatives, and rarely takes time out for recreation. She is certainly busy, alert, productive, but how alive?
- What of Georgia O'Keefe, painting with a youthful eye when well into her eighties? What of Pablo Casals, practicing diligently at eighty-six? Of Marc Chagall painting his glowing "Lovers" series in his nineties? What of Vladimir Horowitz in his last years, laughing joyously as he played the piano? Watching them was watching vitality in action in later years.
- Then I look in the mirror: Is he really alive? How much? How much more might he be? Can I claim more of the aliveness I feel yearning inside me?

Is there a key difference separating these people? One characteristic does so above all others: the degree to which we are in touch with our inner sensing.

Minilives come from having too little access to our vital existential sense. The woman in the crib, the middle-aged child, and the office manager were crippled people, unable to draw on and realize their own vitality. The artists appeared to be bursting with their own aliveness.

The difference is not inevitable or irreversible. We tap into and increase that aliveness as we recover the talent that is latent in each of us. That is the point: For most of us, this crucial capacity is at least partially a "lost sense." Just as a blind or deaf person is limited, so are we handicapped in expressing our potential to the extent we are separated from our living cores. Then we have to deduce what we could know intimately.

Q_1:   Are you hungry?
A_1:   Huh? Oh, it's almost one o'clock! Gosh, yes.

Q_2:   What do you want to do this weekend?
A_2:   I always love to sail; let's go sailing.

Q_3:   How are you feeling?
A_3:   Well, I noticed that I was frowning a lot this morning. I think something must be bugging me.

Do these exchanges sound familiar? Probably. We all play both Q and A in such talk. And in both roles we fail to notice that A seldom answers Q from any real inner awareness. A could just as well be talking about B or X instead of A. How different if the answers had been:

A_1:   Mmm? No, my mouth and stomach say not now.

A_2:   When I really tune in, it turns out I mostly want to read this weekend, not sail as I usually do.

A_3:   I've been so busy I haven't really checked my feelings, but now that I do, I find I'm uneasy and restless for some reason. I need to take time to feel into that now.

The sad truth is that most of us are accustomed to thinking about ourselves just as when we consider other persons. We infer inner intents from outer cues or actions, but we find it difficult to directly access those intents as they are alive within us.

Oversimplifying: My work is principally to uncover the patterns that have grown up to choke off inner knowing, to help my clients recover this existential sense. Once clients fully grasp the nature of this work, our sessions become alive and nourishing adventures. They are energized by the process itself and the vision of greater fullness of being that it discloses.

Monday, February 14

Jim. How is it that some women can set a man's sexual yearning afire just by the way they walk or sit or look at him? Nothing so overt as a revealing blouse or skirt or a come-hither look. Louise is such a woman. From our first meeting I knew I wanted her — and that I couldn't have her. Or I thought I knew it.

I look forward to Louise's hours. The cloying sweetness is less frequent or less apparent — or I am more accustomed to it. Though the erotic hint is always there, I'm surprised to discover that she is largely without sexual experience. Indeed, she seldom dates men. I don't know yet what that means.

Louise is supervisor of social work trainees in a large community agency, and from what I can gather she is effective and well liked. The agency itself is known in the professional community to be overworked and understaffed, as are so many of our public efforts to serve the needy.

I am concentrating on helping Louise become more aware of her lack of inward vision and the sense of identity it brings. She says she knows this; but it is a kind of abstract, academic knowing that is more an obstacle than an aid.

When a new client begins work with me, our first task is to help her recognize her own subjectivity and its importance. Then we work to help her gain ready access to this vital resource.

Sadly, I am unable to help every person who comes to me to find her lost sense in this way.

The effort to help the client open up the blocked roads to her own inner center requires me to use my own inner center as well. It's ironic to recognize that my training taught me to try to deny or suppress feelings such as I have with Louise — they might lead to undesirable actions. After all, one can't be sexual with a client, can one?

But, in point of fact, one can. It happens a lot and in many forms.

Many of my clients have told me of sexual overtures from professionals — of both genders. Physicians, physical therapists, masseurs, "body workers," and others for whom the patient/client undresses partially or wholly are among the most frequent. But psychotherapists, attorneys, teachers, group leaders, clergy, and others have also been involved.

And I've been sexual with clients — not engaging in overt actions, but times when we're each aroused and recognize the other is also. When Helen detailed her weekend with her lover, I was stimulated — no denying it. And she clearly enjoyed reliving the love play with an appreciative audience. I tried to bring it out in the open, but I was clumsy and self-conscious.

Later, when Lia wore an almost transparent top with no bra under it, my eyes were continually drawn to her breasts. When her nipples grew hard, I guessed she was teasing me. It took some effort, but I was able to help her talk about her impulse to seduce me. She was ashamed to be caught, but I don't think she felt shame about the wish. I had a matching wish, and my feeling is that this can be useful, if we keep our balance.

How can it be otherwise? If men and women try to tune in deeply to their inner lives, to bring out feelings, to open up emotionally, it will inevitably bring them to the edge of acting on these feelings and impulses. Healthy erotic urges cannot be — should not be — shut off if we're to do the job we've undertaken. How well we recognize them, how carefully we monitor them, and how wisely we direct them — these are the issues. But those issues are often difficult to weigh when we're feeling strong physical and emotional promptings.

Moreover, our unreflective assumption that these impulses are always countertherapeutic is moot. I had the opportunity several years ago to administer a questionnaire to about fifty highly experienced and well-respected psychiatrists, psychologists, and social workers from all over the country. Their candid and anonymous answers were surprising:

- About three-fifths admitted that a client might be nude or nearly so during a session.
- About half could conceive a situation in which the therapist sexually stimulated the client or the reverse.
- Fully three-quarters could accept encouraging the client to role-play with them behaviors they had previously avoided, such as hostile or seductive actions.
- About two-fifths could conceive a situation in which they and a client would remove some or all of their clothing during a session.

Clearly the pendulum has swung well away from the prudery that ruled for many decades. I'll be reading a report on this study at the Western Division meeting of the American Psychiatric Association and then will publish it in the journal of the American Academy of Psychotherapy. I hope it will stir up a storm. That would be all to the good; we need to discuss these matters more openly and with greater recognition of the kind of work that makes such daring conceivable.

Jennifer. The woman's voice on the phone is tight, urgent. "Dr. Blue-men-thal, I won't keep you long. But I must see you today! It is really important. Please trust me. Please see me today."

Schedule full except for my rest period. Still, she sounds desperate, under great pressure.

"Mrs. Stoddert, I can hear how important you feel this is; so let me level with you: My schedule is completely full today, and tomorrow, too. I could see you Thursday at 4:00. . . . "

"No, please, listen. I *must* see you today."

"I gather you're in some emergency situation, and I'd like to help, but are you sure it can't wait two days? I'm sorry to put you off, but my time is very full today."

"I know, Doctor, and I would wait if I could, but I really can't. I simply must see you today. I'll come at any time you say, even midnight."

"All right, I'll make time at 2:15, which is my usual break time. If you feel it is essential that we talk today, come in then." Had to make her a bit guilty, didn't I?

"Thank you. Two-fifteen. Thank you." She's too caught up to notice my thrust. Maybe it's just as well I am seeing her.

It's always a jolt getting such a phone call. I need a minute to quiet all the questions crowding my head — Is she violent? Will I have to see her or take phone calls after hours and weekends? Will she show up? Sometimes they don't — and that can be a worry and a blessing.

Well, we'll see what we'll see at 2:15.

Jim. When I was first in practice, I made a point of assuring my clients they could and should call me whenever they needed me. I gave my card to restaurant headwaiters and theater ushers so that my exchange, always having my location, could reach me promptly. And I got lots of calls and requests for special appointments.

Time has taught me that this fire station readiness was for my benefit, not solely for my clients'. It made me feel needed and important at a time when I had misgivings about being in "private practice" (unusual for psychologists then) and about being able to handle what might come up. By being exaggeratedly prepared and responsible, I reassured my clients — and myself.

After some work with myself, I now set realistic limits on clients' demands and my needs. I'm still available to clients who are in genuine need of my attention, but calls are infrequent, and my clients are well cared for — perhaps even better.

Still, an emergency call, especially a call in the night, after we've retired, sets off alarms. I never know when it may be a true emergency or what it may be necessary to do — or even what risks may be involved. I have been fortunate.

Hal. Although Hal chose to come to me, a therapist with a view of human nature that contrasts with his own, he is far from convinced that there is much use in getting into his subjectivity.

Repeatedly he is frustrated with my calling for inner awareness. Thus is set the first task for our work: to introduce Hal to his own subjective life.

"Jim, you keep telling me to 'listen to myself,' and I keep telling you that's what I'm doing. When I tell you how mad Tim makes me, how discouraged I am with being so quick to blast him—those are the things I hear inside of myself. What is it you're looking for that I'm not giving you?"

"You're right, of course; those are some of your inner experiences. The point is, though, that when you tell me about these feelings you tell them as things you *already* know about yourself, not as discoveries in the moment, not as living experiences."

"I don't know what you mean. I sure lived the experience of being so mad. And, of course, that's something I know about myself. But anything I tell you would have to be something I knew about myself, wouldn't it?"

"Yes and no, but leave that for a bit. Right now, I hear how sincerely you're trying, Hal, and how you just don't see what I want you to get to. So let me give you a little lecture, eh?"

"Go, man. Sounds good to me."

"Okay. I tell you to 'listen' to your own experience, but there are no words to directly describe what I mean. Suppose you were blind from birth, the only way I could tell you about the sense of sight would be by unsatisfactory analogies with hearing or touch. My words would be awkward hand-me-downs from other senses. What I'm trying to tell you is that you've been blind—or maybe I should say blindfolded—since childhood. I was too, and even now I'm only partly able to get the blindfold off."

"I get what you're saying about how hard it is to explain vision to a blind person, but I'm not getting what you mean about being blindfolded."

"You were blindfolded by being taught, as most of us in our culture are, to ignore or devalue your inner experiencing. Most of us were told things like, 'You don't really feel that way' or 'That isn't what you really want, now is it?' or 'Nice people don't have feelings like that' or 'Your emotions are confusing your thinking' or even 'It doesn't matter what you want, you've

got to deal with the real world.' Again and again we were told
that what went on inside of us was irrelevant, inappropriate,
or even dangerous."

"I kind of see what you mean, but I don't think I ever
bought that completely."

"I hope not, Hal, because people who do buy it completely
are literally crippled — often for life. You see, the inner awareness I'm trying to help you recognize is really an expression of
your whole being — the same as your feelings of love, anger, or
full involvement in something you're doing. Inward vision tells
you moment by moment how well what's going on fits with your
own unique nature. In that way it's like outward vision — the
basis of your knowing where and how you are in yourself; it
gives you orientation and helps you know and take the direction you want."

"Well, then my inner sense says I don't want to get into
all this inner sense stuff," Hal grins.

"Yes, I imagine it does." I refuse his gambit and keep a
sober stance. This is not the time to treat matters lightly. "But
the point is not to follow that inner sense blindly, even though
there are people these days who preach it's the thing to do. 'Go
with the flow' can go right over the cliff. The point is to open
your inner sense and let it feed in with your other senses and
with your mind as well."

"Damn! I thought I had a way to get you off my back."

"No such bad luck." My smile is rueful. "Hal, I know you
intend to kid me, but I think you also really would like to avoid
the implications of what I'm saying."

"No, no. I like what you're telling me. It makes sense.
But so far I don't see how I'm going to be able to use it."

Jim. This existential sense, as I told Hal, is similar to sight — in
giving us an inward orientation, as vision does externally. It
is also akin to hearing — that is, it is best to use it with open
receptivity, as when we listen intently. Putting those together,
then, I think of it as a "listening eye."

On another level this inner sense is also the "listening *I*."
It is *I* who is listening, *I* who is the very process of listening

itself, and (at least implicitly) *I* who is listened to as well. These words sound strange because I'm using explicit and objective language to describe a process that is the opposite, implicit and subjective.

What is plain is that *I* am and need to be the center of my own life. "I" is a word that refers to a unique experience, unique in that as a noun (not a pronoun) "I" does not point to an object to be seen or touched but to the very *process* of seeing, touching, and being aware. Just as the eye in my head cannot see itself, so the *I* of my being cannot see itself, cannot make an object of itself.

To say the *I* needs to be the center of one's own life is the opposite of counseling selfishness. The *self* is an object, and preoccupation with enhancing the self — selfishness — prevents truly subjective centeredness.

If Hal is to fully experience his life and have more understanding of his emotions and greater charge of his actions, he must experience from his center, must be the driver — not, as he is now, the complaining backseat passenger.

All this is difficult for Hal to grasp. He is extremely bright and extensively educated, which means he's learned to look with objectifying eyes at other people, at the world, and at himself. Thus he is skillful in focusing his rational powers on the objects he encounters. For many parts of life this works well; but for self-understanding and self-direction it is self-defeating.

So is being centered the final answer to the question of how to be more alive? No. The only true answer is Gertrude Stein's: "There is no answer. There never was an answer. There never will be an answer. That's the answer."

Jennifer. Mrs. Stoddert, the insistent woman on the phone this morning, is in the waiting room at 2:00 — fifteen minutes early. I finish the hour with Hal, see him to the door, and then go to the waiting room. What sort of person will this be?

The woman standing restlessly waiting for me is slightly taller than average, has a slender figure, and is wearing brightly colored but poorly matched clothes that contrast with her gray face and disarrayed hair. She nods a quick response to my self-introduction and comes into the office with no-nonsense directness. She sits tensely forward in the big client chair and lights a cigarette in a preoccupied manner, which tells me she is bracing herself against an inner tide of emotion.

"Thank you for seeing me today. I'm sorry to have intruded on your rest time. It is important, though." Hah! She did hear me after all. But I don't know whether she really sees me now; she seems to be concentrating on an inner battle.

"I understand. Suppose you just tell me about it."

"I'll try." She pauses; then plunges ahead. "I am thirty-three years old. My husband, Bert, is thirty-nine. I have been married eight years. I . . . we have no children. My husband is an electronics engineer at Levy Company. Actually he's in charge of an engineering group. I have a master's degree in educational administration and counseling and am dean of women at Sloss College. I've been there three years. My parents are dead. My husband's parents are both living, but his father had a stroke last year and may not live much longer."

She is talking in a forced, earnest fashion, enunciating carefully, pausing often, reading a formal "case history" she's prepared.

"Yes, and what is it that particularly seems to concern you today?"

"I'll get to that in a minute, Doctor. Please bear with me. I think it would help if I gave you background first. Is that all right?"

I nod agreement. If I just listen to the content of what she's saying, I get impatient — I didn't give up my break time to get a routine case report. She could have done this at the Thursday time I offered.

Yet as I look at this troubled woman and hear the unspoken strain in her, I realize she is already communicating much that may be important if I am to help her in any way. The iron clamp she has on herself right now is fantastic. Obviously, she is bursting with some emotion; but she is not permitting it to interrupt her careful reading of her invisible data list.

"Thank you." Correct, formal. "As I said, we've been married eight years. Nearly nine. Our anniversary would be next month, the twenty-second. We have been, or at least so I thought, reasonably happy. I have tried to think about the course of our marriage, and I believe we had the most difficult times when we had been married about five or six years. At that time—when we had been married six years, that is—at that time, we seriously discussed divorce, but we decided to stay together, partly because my husband insisted. I think I was more inclined than he was to seek a divorce at that time. But I may be wrong."

"Mm-hmm."

"Yes." She pauses again. "We are not religious people. We do go to a Lutheran church on certain holidays. We are both in generally good health, at least physically, that is." She looks at me. "Are there other things you would like to know by way of background?"

"Mrs. Stoddert, there is such an abundance of information you might give me that I don't know what to ask for. Only after I have a better idea of what concerns you can I suggest what further information we ought to think about together."

She looks troubled, uncertain. The iron grip seems less. I think she's frightened right now, but it's hard to read her expression. She bites her lip, grimaces. I start to explain further, but she speaks quickly.

"Yes, yes, I understand." Impatient, but disciplining herself at once. "I'm sorry, I didn't mean to speak sharply. I'm having trouble knowing how to say what I need to say next."

"Why don't you just let it come out the way you find it inside, and then we can get more details as we go along?"

"Very well." She pauses, catches her breath, getting set. Then slowly, feeling her way, enunciating each word distinctly, she says, "All right, then. . . . I think I am going to kill my husband." She sits back breathlessly, and I feel the same way.

Calmly, softly now. "Since you're here telling me about it, you must have other thoughts about it as well." She isn't looking at me but is staring down at the floor. When she speaks, after a pause, her voice is flat, distant.

"Yes. But if I don't kill him, then I must divorce him. And if I do that, I'll kill myself." Unaccented, a statement of fact, eyes still down.

"Those are hard choices. Take it slowly now, and just tell me about it in any way that comes. Don't push yourself to cover things in any particular way." I keep my voice firm and even, letting some energy be felt.

"I'll try," her head lifts. "But I don't want to waste your time and mine. It would help if you'd ask me questions so I can more efficiently give you the information you need."

"When you say 'the information you need,' what do you have in mind? What do you want me to do?"

"Why to help me, of course" (surprised).

"To help you what?"

"So that I won't kill my husband. Oh!" Suddenly she cries in quick, convulsive sobs and crumples forward, doubling up.

I wait briefly and then say quietly, "You seem surprised to find out how much you don't want to kill him."

"Yes. Uh-huh." She pulls her body up, wraps her arms around herself, and rocks herself back and forth. She's gulping air, finds it difficult to get her breath or to speak because of the dry, choking sobs that are racking her, but she keeps trying.

"Wait a minute now. Don't talk yet. You're doing something far more important right now." She fights with herself, choking, gasping. She doesn't let go to the weeping, and it doesn't let go of her. She's having a hard time breathing, although there are hardly any tears. She is so evidently at war with herself, her body the torn battlefield.

After several minutes of this struggle, I tell her to rest while I get coffee for her. When I bring it, she is able to sip the drink slowly, and gradually the physical torment subsides. It has hardly done so when she lights a cigarette. Her first puff brings on a new siege of choking, which passes sooner — and without the cigarette being put out.

"I'm sorry. I just couldn't get my breath."

"I understand. But what you just went through is important in itself. It expressed better than any amount of words how much in conflict with yourself you are."

"I suppose so. Thank you for the coffee." She's unimpressed by the idea of her nonverbal communication. "Now tell me what would you like to know, and I'll try to keep better control of myself."

I'm tempted to try to help her see how quickly she dismisses her inner experience but decide against it now. She's still under too much emotional pressure. She needs to feel she has dealt in words with her violent impulses; only then will she feel she is regaining control.

"Tell me what happened recently to make you feel you might kill your husband." Amazing that we can say such terrible words calmly, conversationally!

"He told me Friday . . . no. . . . What day is this?"

"This is Monday, the fourteenth." Within myself, a wry smile: Today is Valentine's Day, the day for lovers.

"Thank you. He told me Saturday that he has been having an affair with a woman I thought was a friend of both of us. She and her husband have been in our house many times, and we have been to their house. Now he says they have been carrying on this affair for several months."

"Hmmm."

"He has been with her — having sexual relations with her — once a week or more for over two months. He says he cannot remember just exactly how long." She is reciting facts, reciting them intensely, but still reciting. Her emotion is unreadable — rage or panic or hatred, I can't tell. Only intensity.

"I understand the shock, Mrs. Stoddert. What I need to know more about is how you came to feel that you needed to kill him." Keep this in the past tense if possible.

"Just because the bastard deserves it!" The words come out in an abrupt torrent. Then she stops, reinstates the iron discipline. "No, I don't want to get that way now. It's just that he is so unfair. So damned unfair!" Again, she ruthlessly pushes down the surge of her feelings. "I mean, how would you feel, how would anybody feel? I'll never trust anyone again. I really feel all alone now." She pauses, swallows with difficulty. "But that's not the point. It's just that he's got to be punished. I'm embarrassed to see my friends. I wonder who knows. But it doesn't matter. I have no friends. I can't believe people can be so selfish, so unfair!" Repeatedly, her emotion breaks through briefly, is instantly suppressed, breaks out again, is again shut off. Now she puts out the stub of her cigarette and at once lights another.

"Mrs. Stoddert, I get the impression that you feel it is obvious why you should think of killing your husband — because of his affair. Candidly, it is not obvious to me, and I'd like to understand better the way you feel."

"Yes, I know I'm not thinking straight. That's why I need your help. I might have gotten by till Thursday as you suggested, but I just didn't trust myself. I mean, I felt so wild. I'm not usually that way, except sometimes, of course. I suppose I'm not making much sense." Apologetic smile.

"That's all right. Just go ahead and talk it out however it comes to you."

Toward the end of the hour, I interrupt, "Mrs. Stoddert, our time is almost up, and. . . . "

"And I've just talked in circles, and you haven't had a chance to learn enough about me! I'm sorry! But I think you must have helped some. I really don't think I will kill my husband. That sounds so silly now. I really was frightened about it, though. At least, I think I was. Maybe I was frightened that I would just give in to him. No, I'd never do that."

"Yes; well I'm also concerned about your other impulse, to kill yourself. How do you feel about that now?"

"Oh, yes. Well, I don't think I'd do that now either. I guess I might if something else happened or something. . . . I don't know. I shouldn't say that. I don't think I'd do that. Anyway, I think I feel you can help me, and so. . . . "

"I'll be glad to work with you on that feeling and any others, but I don't want to work with you or anyone under constant threat."

"No, no, I'm not threatening you. It was. . . . "

"I know, Mrs. Stoddert. I understand that you did not intend to threaten me, but nevertheless there *is* a real threat to me. If we work together, it will matter a great deal to me if you feel impelled to do something violent to yourself or to your husband."

"Oh, no, I don't think now that I would do anything violent to him."

"All right, but there is the other threat, and I don't want it hanging over our work either. That threat is the possibility of your doing harm to yourself. I am also concerned about it."

"I can't promise anything."

"Yes (firmly), *you can promise* two things: First, that you won't do anything to him or to yourself for at least a month, while we talk things over; and second, that you won't do anything violent at any time without talking to me first. Those promises are absolutely essential if we are to work together."

"Well, I. . . . "

"If you can't decide right now, you can wait until you leave and give me a call after you've thought over my requirement."

"No, no, that's all right. I can promise those things. At least I think I can."

"No, Mrs. Stoddert." I speak strongly, then pause. "I mean this very soberly, and you must hear it so. I *will not* work with you if you cannot genuinely make those promises to me. I will be glad, if you wish, to refer you to someone else who may not make this requirement, but I want a relation of trust with you. Without those assurances we would not have such a relation."

"Yes, I can see that. All right, I will promise you not to do anything violent to myself or my husband without talking to you first, and . . . oh, yes, and not to do anything for at least a month. Is that right?"

"Yes, that's right. Thank you. Now, I will open up a time for us tomorrow at 3:15. Will you come then, please?"

And so we begin our work together. With Mrs. Stoddert it is necessary and possible to insist on this formal agreement, although I now doubt she has any deep impulse to kill her husband. I am less confident about the suicidal possibility.

I arrange to see Jennifer Stoddert each day this week. Because I take any threat to kill very seriously, I want to know her a lot better, and quickly.

Jim. Why would this woman want to kill the man whom she feels is so important to her that she would kill herself if she divorced him? Is this some bizarre psychotic impulse? By no means. It's so familiar that it's a part of our case law, an accepted reaction to infidelity, and in some venues the "proper" response. Astonishing!

One would think that it'd be harder to say "kill" seriously than to say "fuck" or any of the other once-forbidden words. Not so. Killing is much more an accepted part of polite social conversation than is sexual activity!

But why is Jennifer impelled toward killing her husband or herself? How can they be alternate ways of dealing with the shock she experienced when she learned he had been having sex with another woman? Superficially, they seem opposites. Yet for her they serve a common purpose: Each seems a way of maintaining an image that she clearly deems more essential than life itself—the image of her perfect marriage. By killing him or herself, she seeks to restore the image that existed before the disclosure of the affair, a disclosure which destroyed that image.

No, it isn't logical; but the heart has a logic of its own, and wounded pride joined to blasted love disdains usual reason. We therapists learn this and the futility of attempting to argue emotionally aroused clients out of or into anything.

Yet we also learn to attend carefully to the impulses that surface at these times. People *do* kill each other and do kill themselves. When therapists are asked the sources of the greatest stress in their practice, the threat of violence (to one's self or to others) almost always ranks the highest. To misjudge the client's will at these times is to risk tragedy and with it our own emotional integrity in our profession. Whatever it may take to handle such threats is what must be done.

After Ben, my last client, leaves I plop down at my desk. Writing the date on a note, again I think wryly of Valentine's Day and of the pain and struggle into which our mythical hearts can erupt. Yet they can also produce such wonders of delight and fulfillment. Ah well, let's get done and get out of here.

Today's mail brought a long, typewritten letter. The writer, from upstate New York, has read my book and glowingly tells me how much it means to him. It's a tonic for my weariness to reread his praise.

Writing a book is sending messages in bottles out on the

tide. I wonder if there is anyone out there, anyone who will read and really hear what I've tried to say. When I first began publishing, I hadn't anticipated that men and women would write moving, personal accounts of how they had truly heard me and been affected in their lives. What gifts they give!

Fred is one of these. From a continent away he describes himself — mid-twenties, unrewarding job, lonely, hoping to grow and change, to live more in keeping with his own ideals.

Before I leave tonight, I want to send him some response. His quest for his life deserves what support I can give him. After I do that there are some notes to make before I leave. But I don't get down to work yet. Fact is, I'm pooped. I ought to make those notes, return some phone calls, answer some more mail — but I don't want to.

Right now I'd like a highball. But none is at hand, so I'll settle for another cup of coffee (how many is that today?) and ten more minutes to unwind.

Tom's latest: "Life is what happens while you're planning something else." Thinking about it, I feel I'm lucky. Most of the time I feel as though I'm having a really good life — pretty close to what I've planned in recent years. Only exception is that, in my personal life, I don't really relate to people as well as I want to. Even at home, I'm more separate than I really want to be. Why can't I feel as genuine there as I do in the office?

Still, what *does* it mean to be alive? The philosopher Ortega y Gasset wrote, "Life means the inexorable necessity of realizing [recognizing and making real] the *design* for an existence which each one of us is. . . . The sense of life . . . is nothing other than each one's acceptance of [this] inexorable circumstance and, on accepting it, converting it into [one's] own creation."

We are born into life and spend our time contending with, creating from, and realizing that fact. All else is secondary.

Too simple? Don't kid yourself. Being alive is a full-time, lifelong job for which we are all poorly prepared, about which we continually have to learn, and in which repeatedly we have to make changes as we go. It is also true, as some wag has observed, that life is a sexually transmitted disease with a prognosis of 100 percent mortality.

Three

"I Need to Get into Therapy."

Tuesday, February 22

Frank. It's time to pick up from the waiting room that angry-sounding guy who called a week or so ago . . . Frank Connelly. Let's see how he is in person.

The first impression puts me off. He's distinctly scruffy in appearance — not a word I've used much, but it surely is apt now: close to thirty, bearded, wearing hard-life jeans, a dress shirt that is never going to see a tie or jacket again, a dirty fatigue jacket, tennis shoes that have forgotten tennis courts if they ever knew one. His manner fits his clothes: a long hard stare, a resolute lack of facial expression, and an uncertain stride into my office. As he passes me I get a strong whiff of sweat and dirt. Great!

Frank accepts the chair I indicate, quickly pulls out a pack of cigarettes, offers me one (which I accept), lights his own, and puts out the match. Then he notices I'm getting a match from my desk. Embarrassed, he quickly covers it by speaking loudly.

"I need to get into therapy." He pauses, examines my face belligerently, as though he expects I may laugh or angrily reject the preposterous idea. Since I only wait quietly, he goes on. "I've thought about it for a couple of years. Read a lot of stuff. There sure are a lot of crackpots in the field, aren't there?"

Before I can answer he hurries on. "Nothing personal, you understand. I've read some of your stuff, and you sound like you're okay. I mean it's hard to tell from what some guy writes, but . . . anyway. . . . "

"Anyway, here you are."

"Yeah, that's right. So what do you want to know?"

Frank's story is as impressive as his appearance is depressive. He never knew his father, and his mother died before Frank was ten. A sister four years older seems to have taken over his care, but much of his childhood was spent on the streets and, very likely, in juvenile hall. He and his sister subsisted on minimal rations and their wits, but somehow they survived. Now, although it's unclear where, when, or why, the sister is gone.

Frank is a bellman in a second-rate hotel. He hates his job. He hates his coworkers. He hates the city. He hates most everyone with whom he has any contact. And he avoids any unnecessary contacts. When not at work, he is usually at the library or in his room, reading. He professes to have no friends but hastens to assure me that he doesn't need any anyway.

I'm impressed with Frank's story and the way he tells it forthrightly and always with a hint of a challenge, seeming continually to say, "Wanna make something of it?" He also interests me because he is so different from most of my clients, who are middle-class, well educated, and rather conventional in life-style. Frank is anything but conventional, and he makes sure to be so. He is, apparently, self-educated through his omnivorous reading, and he is street-educated in a way that I and most of my clients will never be.

Jim. Ben canceled today, so I've got time to reflect on Frank's way of relating by anti-relating. He depends on constantly being vigilant and (apparently) ready to do combat.

We human beings live right in the middle of the paradox of being always *a part of* other humans and yet always *apart from* them. Some of us emphasize the part-of half, as does Louise.

Frank depends on the apart-from. As it is, he is forced to live in the world of people, but he angrily, desperately rejects being at one with them. He clings to his separateness as a drowning man clutches a log in a rough sea. Frank fears drowning in the demands, comparisons, expectancies, and judgments of people.

To keep oneself as separate as Frank attempts to be is a full-time job. One must be ever-vigilant against the outer world, but at the same time one must ruthlessly put down inner impulses toward others. There must be no tolerance or recognition of loneliness, caring, hungering for intimacy, or of needing others. The best safeguard — and a hidden way of relating — is anger — continuous, unrelenting, easily triggered anger. Frank is, accordingly, an angry man.

At least that's how he appears on the surface.

I strongly suspect, however, that his anger is a shield rather than a deep-seated hostility. Nevertheless, I'm going to respect it and keep a careful space to protect us both. Once we develop an alliance, we may be able to explore what's under the anger. My guess is that Frank both fears closeness and yearns for it.

I feel a strange kinship with Frank. I've not been an angry person; in fact, I've too long denied my anger. I was so taught to fear my parents' anger — not so much directed toward me as toward others — that I implicitly resolved not to be angry, an impossible resolution, of course. Still, the fact is that I'm never simply angry at home. From time to time, though, I get into such a rage that my family is frightened; thus the provocation that led to the blow-up doesn't get satisfyingly dealt with, and I end up feeling guilty rather than relieved.

No, I'm not an angry person like Frank, but I'm not comfortable or skillful in "hanging out" with others either. I usually need some activity — a game, an informal debate, an opportunity to teach or to learn — to be comfortably really present. So it is that as a therapist I'm much more genuine and at ease than at other times.

Monday, February 28

Jennifer. In two weeks Jennifer Stoddert and I have nine interviews, and I'm reassured about her impulses to violence. They're not to be forgotten, but they no longer need to be at the forefront of my awareness.

Jennifer's painful way of dealing with herself has become manifest: It is not surprising she is so punitive toward her husband; she is equally unrelenting toward herself.

Today there is more color in her face. She sits in the big chair with one leg tucked under her, leaning slightly forward, accenting what she says by abruptly hunching her shoulders and thrusting her hands out and upward in movements that seem strangely more emphatic than what she is saying.

"I have so many things I need to talk to you about. I wanted to make a list of them so I wouldn't forget, but I know you don't like me to write things down and. . . . "

"Jennifer, if it helps to write things down, by all means do so. I have asked you not to rely solely on a list of things to talk about when you're here because I'd like to help you get more in touch with. . . . "

"Oh, yes, I know," she interrupts hurriedly. "I shouldn't have said. . . . I mean, I know you don't ever tell me . . . (quick breath). Well, I just was thinking that you thought it was better if I didn't have lists, sort of." Her hands move up and then drop down in frustration as she continually aborts what she is saying.

"It isn't that I'm against lists, Jennifer. I use them myself for some things, but. . . . "

"But I'm too dependent on them." Her mouth twists ruefully as she averts her eyes. "I know it (quick breath). Yes, I know that." Now she makes a fist with her left hand, extending her right hand almost beseechingly.

"That's not what I was going to say. What I wanted you to understand was. . . . " Again she cuts me off.

"I know," she says sadly. "I know. I just didn't say it right." She hurries on before I can speak again. "You don't mind my making lists, it's just that . . . that . . . uh, that you think it's not a good thing for me to do." She finishes vaguely, uncomfortable, aware that she's lost the point. She looks unhappy and in some way guilty, avoiding my eyes.

"Jennifer, it's hard for you to hear what I start to say to you because you have to know it already."

"Oh, no (urgently), I'm really glad to have you advise me, but I just didn't want to waste your — our — time."

"It seems you'd feel you had failed in some way if I told you that your understanding of what I said about writing things down was different than I intended."

"No, no, not failed, but. . . . It would be perfectly all right." She grabs a quick breath. "I mean, I'd be glad for you to show me where I misunderstood you (another breath). After all, that's why I'm here." Palms up, hands open, head cocking to one side appealingly.

I'm beginning to feel breathless myself, a pretty dependable clue to what's going on with her. "Jennifer, I want you to pause a minute now. Stop talking, stop thinking about what to say, stop trying to think what I want. Just pause; get your breath." She looks troubled, starts to speak, catches herself, reaches for a cigarette.

"Wait a minute on lighting up, okay?"

"Oh, yes, of course, I. . . . " Her busy hands come to rest in her lap.

"And wait to talk. You are still all revved up inside — and not really — with yourself." I'm talking slowly, pausing often, very deliberate in manner, trying to get our conversation into a different key. "I know it's hard to wait — when you have so much to say — but you really need — to get your breath — let yourself get collected here."

We wait, but probably Jennifer is only humoring me. She doesn't seem to know what I'm talking about. Let me try another way: "Jennifer, now I want you to listen to your breathing. Don't say anything yet. Just attend to your breath." I pause, wait. She is holding herself tightly, frowning, attentive.

"Now, feel your breath come into your nose and mouth. Feel it in the back of your throat. . . ." She starts to speak. "Wait, now, really let yourself go with my words." Now she catches herself and is apparently quieting. "Feel your breath in your throat — and then down into your chest and stomach. Then follow it back up. There, that's it. You're beginning to get it. Stay with it." It's tough for her to let go of her tension enough to use my suggestions, but the impatient strain seems a bit less. She's trying.

"Now, Jennifer, feel inside of yourself in the same way you are doing with your breath, but this time feel for the way you were talking at me and trying to hear me a few minutes ago."

"Yes." She's eager to do well. "I can see that I. . . ."

"No, wait a bit more. This is important to what we're trying to do here. So hang on a minute more."

"All right." Her hands, which had briefly come to life, return to her lap. She's the picture of the good, attentive child.

"Good. Now when we started talking about how you make lists of topics to deal with here, it felt to me that you got kind of anxious and very concerned to show that you understood what I wanted and were trying to do it. Can you feel that?"

"Yes, I think so (considering). I just didn't want you to feel I wasn't paying attention or really understanding or. . . ."

"Yes, and Jennifer, it was so important to tell me that you understood before I had to tell you again, wasn't it?"

"Well, maybe. . . . Yes, I guess so. I mean, I didn't want to. . . . I mean, I didn't mean to interrupt you or. . . ."

"But if I told you again, then I wouldn't know that you had really understood already."

"Yes!" She brightens, nods. "That's right. I didn't want you to tell me again because then you wouldn't know I'd understood before." She considers this. "That seems kind of strange now."

"But it was very important to you for me to know you'd listened to me and understood me very well."

"Oh, yes. Yes, I wouldn't want you to think I wasn't really listening and paying attention and. . . ."

"It sounds like that would be a bad thing for you to be caught at — not paying attention when I talk to you."

"Well, yes, of course." She pauses, considers. "I . . . I guess so. Well, you don't want to have to repeat and go over things all the time." She quickly catches her breath. "And . . . and I certainly should use whatever you tell me (earnestly). I mean, I think I try to. . . . " Her tempo is picking up.

"Jennifer, wait, go slow." She quiets the agitation that had started. How quickly and ruthlessly she controls her feelings! "Let me try to help you see a bit more."

"Yes, please do." Earnest, going to learn the lesson now.

"I think you could sense a bit ago that it was really something about not paying attention that felt bad to you — not just that I might have to repeat myself."

"Well, of course. You can't help me if I wander off, wool-gathering." The words sound recited.

I have a hunch, and it's time to try it. "It was like you would be bad if you didn't pay attention to what I might say."

"Mmm (pause). Yes, I think so. I mean, that doesn't make much sense, I know. But it was that way for a minute there (pause). I mean it was like you were my mother and would be mad at me if I weren't giving you good attention. That's silly, I know, and. . . . "

"It was like I was your mother — " Leaving it open, inviting her completion.

"Well, yes . . . yes." Her face falls. "Like my mother said I was always absent-minded, not paying attention."

"She scolded you for not listening, huh?"

"Oh, yes! And she would get so cold if I didn't listen."

"So cold?"

"So cold. And then she'd say that obviously I had more important things to think about so she wouldn't trouble me by talking to me. Oh, I felt so awful. Here she had been so caring toward me, and I didn't listen (eyes moistening). I've always been so distractable. I don't know what's the matter with me."

"What would happen after she said she wouldn't trouble you any more by talking to you?"

"Then she wouldn't speak to me at all." Jennifer's whole body expresses dejection; a single tear appears on her cheek.

"Not at all?"

"No. And sometimes it would go on for days. Until I

would just cry and cry and beg her to forgive me and promise not to be distracted any more and to listen very carefully."

So I get my first look at that sad, cold, distant woman who was Jennifer's mother, who always held out the promise of closeness if only Jennifer were good enough, but who never could really yield to the little girl who yearned for her. Often, in our hours together, the influence of Jennifer's mother is so strong I seem to sense her presence in the room. Jennifer has so thoroughly taken into herself her mother's critical demand-ingness that repeatedly I have the impression of hearing Jennifer begin to speak and the mother instantly start to criticize.

Late in the hour I return to Jennifer's lists of topics for our sessions. "Our time is just about gone, Jennifer, and I want to do two more things today."

"Yes, of course." She settles herself attentively.

"I want to explain about your writing lists of things to talk about here. This time, try to let yourself hear me without worrying that I might be repeating myself. I don't think I've said this before, but I may say it again several times in the future, and that will not only be all right but part of what I can do here."

"Yes. Well, all right." She is very much the bright and receptive student. Now's not the time to work with that, though.

"The most important reason I don't want you to depend only on lists about yourself is that they distract us from what is going on in you right at the moment. It's a very different thing to talk about Jennifer-on-a-list than it is to explore something that is alive in your experience right at the moment." I pause, decide to wing one: "You've had far too much of making yourself an object of rules and lists. Now we want you to discover your inner aliveness, just in each minute."

"Yes, I see. Well, I'm really glad you explained that to me." Her hands are actually folded in her lap, a clue to her state of mind, I think.

"Now, Jennifer, if I read you rightly, you kind of understand what I said, but you don't really see the point right now."

"Oh, no. I think I understand all right. It's just that I was wondering. . . . " Her hand lifts and then drops back. "Well, I suppose it doesn't matter anyway."

"Why not try it out?"

"Well, I wonder how I'll ever tell you what's happening in my life, if I only talk about what's going on inside of me when I'm here."

I pause, reflecting that her question is shared by so many new clients who have lost touch with their inner living. Jennifer assumes she cannot trust her own sense of concern but must use an external aid, the list, to remind her of what matters to her.

"Well, see what comes to mind right now as an example."

"Well, like the meeting Bert and I had with Ellen and her husband, or what Bert says he wants or. . . . Oh wait!" She suddenly smiles in delight. "I see! I *am* thinking of them right now, aren't I?"

"That's it. You see, *you* are here, and *you* are someone we can trust. *You* will be here."

"Oh, that's. . . . " Abruptly, her eyes are swimming. She looks confused but pleased. "That's so nice. I mean, to have someone say I can be trusted like that." She smiles again. For a minute she's silent, savoring the feeling. Then she calls herself to order. "Well, you said there were two things you wanted to tell me."

"The other you have already begun to answer: What would be some of the things on your list?"

"Well, like Bert and Ellen and her husband." She stops abruptly. "Oh, I get so mad when I just think of her . . . and of Bert . . . and of what they did. . . . Anyway," she pulls herself together a bit, "they're going to move to Fresno."

"Who?"

"Ellen and Dan. Good riddance, I say. She and people like her just. . . . Anyway, Bert and Ellen and Dan and I had a meeting the other day, and I told Bert to clear out and go with them. But he said he didn't want to. And Ellen and Dan said they were going to Fresno, where Dan has a new job. They are trying to work things out between them. And I hope they can make it, but a woman who'd do that. . . . And I thought she was my friend. . . . But I don't want to get into that now.

Anyway, they'll be gone in a couple of weeks. It can't be too
soon."

"And Bert?"

"I told him to move out. I couldn't stand having him
around. He's been sleeping in the guest room, but I don't even
want him in the house."

"You're still so mad."

"Well, I just don't think there's any excuse for what he
did. I suppose I should be more forgiving, but. . . . "

"But you don't feel forgiving right now."

"No, I don't. That's not the right attitude, I know. I should
be really cool and just say it doesn't matter, but it does matter.
Oh, I don't want to get into those feelings again (pause). Anyway, Bert's moved out. But he keeps saying he wants to come
back. Why does he say that? After what he's done."

So Jennifer writhes in her anger, hurt, and outrage.

Jennifer constantly resists Bert's overtures and insists on
his blameworthiness. It's unclear what she wants positively, what
she hopes for in her future. She is so caught up in her fury at
the betrayal that she looks backward only; and, looking backward, she repeatedly proclaims her innocence. She succeeds so
well at that that she can only view herself as a victim and spend
her energy on protesting, on crying that she has been fouled —
by Bert, by life. Her protests are cold comfort, and the underlying reason she comes to therapy is her feeling of powerlessness,
which takes far too much of her aliveness.

Jim. Thinking about Jennifer's blaming pattern holds up a mirror to my own frequent tendency to cover my tracks and be prepared to avoid blame for any action someone might question.
Too often I've found my thoughts composing involved explanations to account for some minor misdeed — banging the tires
into the curb when parking, being short with a caller on the
phone. As Jennifer and I work together, I am repeatedly impressed with how this preoccupation with blame creates such
a flood of self-criticism that it weakens the structure of a person's life and undermines relationships.

Thursday, March 3

Hal. Hal strides intently in from the waiting room, purpose evident on his set face. Once in his chair, he leans forward, frowning dissatisfaction. "Jim, I know I'm supposed to come into your group tonight, and that's okay if you really think it's the thing to do. But, frankly, I'm so pissed at myself for the way I am with Tim that I don't see how being with a bunch of adults will be any help to me."

"It's *you* who's pissed. It's *you* who has feelings you don't like, and it's *you* who will be in the group. We're trying to understand more of what goes on in *you*."

His intensity sags as he takes this in. "Okay, I guess so. I'll leave it to you. I just want to keep my eye on the main target."

"I know that, Hal. But I can feel your motor's racing so much right now that I don't think trying to talk about group will get very far. What's got you so wound up?"

"Well, I did it again (renewed urgency). Damnation! Can't even let the day start before I have to eat Tim out for something."

"Okay, let's use that. Now — right now — you're full of feelings. Focus on them, on what's inside of you right now."

"Well, like yesterday: I told him to get a haircut and. . . . " He's startled when I cut in abruptly.

"Not yesterday! Right now!" We've been working together three months now, and he really doesn't understand yet. It's time I put more pressure on. "I asked you to see what thoughts or feelings you had right *now* about bawling him out. Wait, wait a minute." He's starting to respond too soon.

"You're so anxious to vomit out your frustration that you're wasting it."

"Wasting what?" He verges on anger.

"Wasting the intensity of your feelings right now. They can lead us some place useful." I'm speaking with force.

"I don't know what you're talking about." But he relaxes a bit in his chair, loosens his tie, opens his collar.

"Okay, picture this morning at breakfast. Try to get the feel of that image in you now. You can't go back there in fact, but you can get in touch with how you feel *now* as you remember what happened." I pause. He's sitting forward again, but his face seems unresponsive. My guess is he's steaming about what happened this morning and can hardly hear me. Still, I must try to get through to him.

"Right now, you've got a lot going on inside you. Just get that feeling that's in you right now. Don't give me an account or explanation; just the feel." He's restless, impatient. "What is happening in you *right now?*"

"Hell, Jim, I was no perfect student in high school or even as an undergraduate. It's okay if Tim needs to sow his oats, kick over the traces a bit. I'm just scared that he'll go so far that he can't get back. I remember a guy who was on our squad when I was a freshman at Brown. Good guy, just kind of wild. . . . "

"You're throwing it away." I insert it flatly into his tirade.

"Throwing what away?" He's annoyed.

"You're still dodging your inner experience right now." My tone is flat, subtly challenging.

"Right now (hard voice), I'm remembering that I told him to get a haircut yesterday. He said he would. He took the money. He knew I wanted it shorter. I don't think I'm unreasonable. I know how the kids wear their hair."

I start to speak, but he pushes past me. "For crying out loud, I'm not that square! I've got a beard myself. I just wanted him to look less like the Wild Man from Borneo. And he walks in with it in a fright wig, an Afro, or whatever the hell you call it! Jesus Christ! He looks like the village idiot! So I let him have it. I told him I wasn't going to have a freak living in my house, and. . . . "

I've got to pause and regroup. I'll never help him if I'm knocked out. I need to find a better way of showing him how blind he is to his inner life. It's clear he still doesn't have the idea, doesn't see the whole world of difference between thinking *about* himself and being aware *in* himself. I need to help Hal move from the world in which Hal is a troubling object, a puzzle to be solved, to the world in which Hal is simply himself, doing or not doing what he wants to the extent the world around him makes possible.

"Hal, you came in here intent on working on why you

have no control when you talk with your son. But you're not working on that. Instead you've got such a head of steam up that you can't hear me or even really hear yourself. You're standing outside of yourself, waving your arms and shouting, but you don't know what's going on inside you."

"I know what's inside of me all right (angrily). I'm mad as hell at that kid. That's what inside of me (pressing on). He just seems to use every chance to bug me, and it makes me so damned mad that he knows just how to push my buttons to tee me off."

"You're right!" I come back quick and hard. "He knows how to push your buttons to make you furious, but you don't know how to push your own buttons so you'll act as you really want to. Fact is, you don't even know how to push your own buttons right here so that you can use our time for what you really want."

He starts to speak, then stops. His face changes, becomes sad. Hal is torn by his love for and his fury at his son. Tim seems to challenge Hal continually. His hair is only one issue among many. He seems to refute everything that Hal has spent his life on. Except words. Tim and Hal once were bonded by endless talking and arguing; now that bond has broken down into endless verbal combat. From this combat, Tim emerges the victor (at least he doesn't overtly show his wounds), whereas Hal's emotional agony is increasing.

As I reflect on this, Hal is sitting with pain-filled eyes, not speaking.

"You're really hurting right now, Hal."

"Yeah, yeah, I know." Head down, eyes moist. "But damn it, what gets into me?" He's dismissing his feelings as irrelevant. "What matters is I can't keep doing like I did this morning."

In some way I need to use this break in Hal's momentum. Talk slowly, forcefully, look him straight in the eye. "Hal, you *are not* in touch with yourself at all right now. Instead you're hammering at a problem named Hal Steinman and telling me not to distract you by asking about what goes on inside Hal Steinman."

He lifts his head. "Yeah, I suppose so, but I really don't

see what good it would do to go into all that psychoanalytic stuff and talk about my toilet training and so on."

Half-consciously, Hal is using sarcasm to lead me away from pressing him for subjective awareness. He has no idea how little real access he has to his inner feelings and thoughts. The "psychoanalytic" allusion is to lure me into another of our repeated debates about the unconscious roots of his conflicts. Remember, I tell myself, Hal chose to come to me for therapy even though he knew I believe in subjective influences. Now I must justify that confidence by not taking the bait for an intellectual dispute.

"No deal, Hal." Let him sense my irritation as well as my support. "You're still trying to keep us from focusing on what's going on inside of you."

"Ah, yes, Doctor Freud, it is the mysterious unconscious, is it not?" Exaggerated Germanic accent.

I snap back: "Look, do you want to play games, or do you want to work on why you pop off so quickly at Tim?"

"Okay, okay. So you're in charge. Tell me what to do, and I'll be good and do it," overly docile, mockingly acquiescent.

"Hal, for Christ's sake! You're just dodging and squirming every which way to keep from settling down to work."

"Hell, Jim, I don't know. I just feel kind of out of it. I know you're trying to help, but it seems like you want to take such a long way around, and I really don't understand what you want me to do now."

"There, that's it! That is the problem. You don't know what is going on inside of you; so you constantly find yourself acting in ways you really don't want to. You are a black box to yourself, and things you don't like keep coming out of that box. So, I'm saying, let's look into that box."

"That would make sense if I really didn't know what was going on inside. But I know. I know I want Tim to look decent, to study, to finish high school, and to try to go to college, to. . . ."

"God dammit, stop!" I practically shout it right into his face. "You're off and running, telling me all about what you want Tim to do. The only words you've said about yourself are 'I want.' We're trying to talk about what goes on *inside of you,* of Hal."

"All right (angrily). I'll tell you what goes on inside of Hal. He gets damned mad. That's what. Mad that that kid doesn't have the common courtesy to. . . . "

"Hold it!" Loud, commanding. "Hal, you know and I know that you can go on the entire hour telling me about Tim and what he does. You've done it here a half-dozen times in the past month. And what's different?"

"Not a damn thing!" He's coming back with more energy directed toward me, rather than ranting about Tim. A good sign. "So what do *you* propose?"

"I propose you really see the basic difference between focusing on Tim and what he does on one side, and getting in touch with your own inner experience on the other." I modulate my tone a bit, making it more measured and, I hope, persuasive. "Now I know you have trouble understanding that difference, but it's very important, and so far I don't think you've really tried to get with it." Pause, check his attention; he's beginning to listen. "Here's the key point. Get this in your head and get it in solidly: *This is what keeps you doing things you don't want to do.* You do them because you're out of touch with the place where your actions come from."

"Still not doing it, eh?"

"Still not. And some part of you knows it damn well."

"Now why would I want to do that? I just think I. . . . "

"Hal, shut up! (voice rising) You're about to go off on another of your wasteful sidetracks. It's obvious that it's as frightening as all hell to you to be told—and to half believe—that there's something you don't know how to do. You're just running in every direction to keep from facing how cut off you are from really listening to yourself—or to me."

He catches his breath, angry, challenged. "All right! What do you want me to do?"

"Let's start with you using the couch!" He catches his breath, opens his mouth to protest. "Wait! I can see you getting wound up to give me a speech about psychoanalysis and God knows what else. Skip it! I don't want to hear it. I want you to be in an unfamiliar situation, and I hope to help you get in touch with yourself in unfamiliar ways. So, *use — the — couch!*"

"I thought you guys only used these things with good-looking females. I don't know whether I can trust you." Grumbling, getting up, lying down stiffly, not liking it.

"That's okay. You're not my type."

"Okay, so here I am on your damn couch. Now can we get on to this thing about my blowing my top at Tim, and. . . . "

"No! First off, when you use the couch, it's usually well to shut up. I command that to you right now. *Shut up!*" I pause and wait until he seems to be settled down.

"Now listen, Hal, and really try to hear me. We've been bantering with each other, and that's okay. But now I want to be very serious with you, and I want you to open yourself up as much as possible to understand not just my words but the intentions behind them. Okay?"

"Yeah." He squirms, uncomfortable in his jacket, getting better settled, but there is a change; he's really going to try. "Yeah, sure, I just like to give you a hard time."

"Hal, I know that mostly you feel you're being kind of playfully troublesome with me, and I certainly enter into that. We both enjoy it as a kind of game between us. But, Hal, there's something more going on. You really don't know much about your inner experiencing, and that troubles you. You don't feel as much in control as you'd like to be, as you absolutely need to be. So you make it seem a game, and tell yourself and me that you actually are in control and could stop the game if you really wanted to. Hal, here's the point: *You can't stop the game.*"

"Oh, come on. I don't have to joke it up all the time."

"No, that's true. But the game is not the joking."

"What is it, then?"

"The game you have to play is that *you* are in charge of your life and of what you do. Thus you must act as if it's only a minor exception that you have trouble being as you would like to be with Tim or that you can't really get with what I'm asking you to do here."

He's silent briefly, chewing on it. "Well, maybe so. I kind of see what. . . . " He trails off, still musing.

"Hal, look, we need to work together very seriously right now. I'm going to give you a fresh picture of what you need to do. Then, your job is to try it, to *really* try it. I don't want to test you, but I do want to challenge you to give yourself the best possible chance to get more deeply in touch. Okay?"

"Okay." Voice sunken. His restlessness lessens.

"Good. Now here's the idea: Most of the time we're dealing with things, people, situations outside of ourselves. When we come to think about ourselves, we tend to do it the same way — objectively — as though we were objects to be dealt with. For many situations that works well enough. But it doesn't work worth a damn when we're trying to understand why we feel or do as we do or when we're trying to change our feelings and the actions that flow from them." I pause, watching him. He seems to be taking in what I'm saying, face intent, eyes shut.

"Like you trying to understand why you have such a short fuse with Tim," I continue. "If you came up with the right explanation — whatever that might mean — it still wouldn't help you change unless you got in touch inside of yourself." He's more relaxed now. Finally I may be reaching him; got to get the message over now.

"So we need a different way of thinking than the objective. That different way is when we *listen to* or *in* ourselves, instead of *figuring out things about* ourselves. Hal, you really don't know much about listening to yourself. And, at some level, you sense that and are threatened by it. You like to be competent. More than that — you absolutely need to be competent. And you are, most of the time. But this is one place you're not. And you don't like that, and you don't like to know it."

I'm talking too long, trying to say too much. Stop, give him a chance to digest this and react to it. But first I need to say, "Now, I'm going to stop talking in a couple of seconds, and you just lie there silently and let my words and your own thoughts sort of mix together. Don't try to report on them. Don't try to solve anything. Don't try to reply to me directly. And, as much as possible, don't *try* to do anything. Just lie there. And then, when you feel ready, tell me whatever is going on inside you of its own accord. Remember: *inside* of you. Okay, now I'll stop talking."

I sit back, take a deep breath, wait silently, expectantly. Wow, I sure gave him a lecture! Didn't mean to go on so long. Just kept thinking of things to add in. Still do. Wish I'd suggested he start with body awareness. Think he'd find that easier. He's being very quiet. I think he's really listening for the first time. Wonder if he's threatened by the apparent passivity of what I'm urging him to do. Could have said that.

He's certainly taking long enough to start talking. Did I make him think he couldn't talk until he said something new?

Wait! Could he be asleep? Oh, no! He couldn't do that! He could and is!

Jim. After Hal leaves I reflect on our work today. His going to sleep expresses in yet another way his resistance to getting into an area of inner experience that he has long avoided and denied. In this denial, Hal is like a great many people in our educated, middle-class society. We have been taught to disbelieve in our whole inner world of intentions, emotions, imagination, and wantings. Incredibly, we have come to think of these inner feelings as ephemeral and inconsequential. We have come to believe that these — the very stuff of our living, immediate being — are not as significant as what is external and public.

What Hal doesn't recognize yet, and what is strange to many people unfamiliar with this kind of therapeutic work, is the strength of our need to protect our ways of seeing ourselves and of having power. Hal rightly sees himself as generally able to do most things, especially in his chosen field of psychology. Now I'm telling him he doesn't know a very important part of himself, and he unconsciously fights against hearing that. Hal's apparently random jumping around from argument, to joking, to protest, to confusion, and finally to sleep — all of these are occurring despite his very real intention to use our time to gain control of himself. These are diversionary efforts to keep himself — even more than me — from confronting how little he knows of his inner impulses. They demonstrate that very point as well.

Hal, who invests so much in being competent and knowledgeable, senses that he would be lost and wandering if he once entered into that unfamiliar inner world that is his own being.

Thinking about today's session I can see how once again I got caught up trying to reason Hal into being more inwardly aware, and how — as usual — it didn't work. My clients have tried to teach me this lesson again and again, but still I often and unthinkingly act as though all they lack is my teaching and then they'll do what they need to do. Frieda Fromm-Reichmann, one of the great psychotherapists, is reported to have said, "The patient needs an experience, not an explanation." I agree, but I keep forgetting. Clearly, I've got some resistance here also. My reasoning is one of my much-relied-on ways of handling life; I use it even when it's unreasonable to do so.

What Hal needed was the experience of frustration with his own dependence on rationality, with my insistence that he was not doing what he needed to and that he didn't really know how to do that. And he needed this while he was really invested emotionally. Only as we began shouting at each other, as we both were angry with the frustration that each typified for the other — only then were we able to penetrate his detachment.

Later after Kitty leaves, and before I see Ben, my lunch comes. Today all my office mates have other break times or are out of the suite. At my request, Phyl picks up a roast beef with mustard and onion and some cherry pie from the deli, and I settle in to enjoy solitude and thought.

First, a letter from Fred, the young man in upstate New York who is so positive about my book. He's excited, has arranged to come out to California on his vacation in May, wants an interview. Of course. It will be interesting to see this enthusiastic fellow who gives me such great feedback.

Next, I've time to speculate some more about what's going on with my clients. There are changes that I've only incompletely recognized, but that I want to grasp better. Sipping an after-lunch coffee, I lean back in the chair and speculate about those changes. What's the common thread? I think it's that we're working deeper these days.

Deeper. That's the key word. We're exploring subjective issues that were beyond our reach a few years ago. Recognizing this brings back images of Helen, Laura, and others who finished up with me several years ago. We couldn't do what my current clients and I are doing. They had the potential, but I lacked the skill. I suppose every therapist who works to grow at his art must know such regret. It keeps us humble.

Why this evolution? As simply as I can put it, it's because my clients are teaching me we need to do something quite different than what I used to think of as psychotherapy or what most people—both in and out of the profession—see it to be.

What we need to do, one client after another implicitly insists, is to reexamine the way each is alive. Saying it out that way seems presumptuous. Perhaps it is, but that's precisely what I mean: Depth psychotherapy is, and needs to be, the careful and detailed review of how one carries out the task the universe has given each of us: to create our own unique pattern for being alive.

Musing, I stand, stretch. Get the kinks out of arms and back. Bathroom pit stop. All the time my thoughts go on.

Back at my desk, loosening my tie, pursuing the trail of thoughts. When I see the outcomes of therapeutic work—my own and others', so often those results are disappointing: some gains made, some improvements in emotions and relationships reported; but, all too often, the basic problems and emotional distress persist. Nor is this unsatisfactory record just my own ineptitude—of which there has certainly been a considerable, but now diminishing, portion—or that of the other therapists.

What explains this sad product of so much devoted effort? My search for an answer brings me to question the root assumptions of our work: What is the nature of psychological distress? What can bring about the desired changes? What is the healing/growth agency and where is it?

I believe that the answers to these questions point to the need for a revolution in our thinking about the nature of the processes we call "psychotherapy."

I believe that psychological distress arises from the way we—all of us—are in our lives. Simply put, the life design we have adopted is not working well. I do not believe that we "cure" or "heal" anything or anybody. I do believe that the power to make the changes that are needed resides in the client, not the therapist. Trying to "cure" with "insight," usually insight offered by therapist interpretation, does little to change or relieve the problems or distress.

Time to check the clock. Oh yes, Ben isn't coming in today. I still have time to think some more. Good.

For some time now I've been learning how faulty is the notion that the concerns that bring us to psychotherapy parallel those we take to our physicians. This analogy is accurate for one-fifth or less of the reasons for which people come to psychotherapy — phobias, some learning difficulties, addictions. But those are a minority of presenting issues.

What we most often hear from new clients are such troubles as repeated poor relations with the other sex; angry complaining patterns extending back to childhood; longstanding feelings of worthlessness, depression, shame, guilt; continual inability to know and express one's own feelings and needs; recurrent failures in undertakings; and relentless loneliness and isolation.

These are not diseases or injuries. To treat them as such is to perpetuate a fiction — and a misleading fiction at that.

Our present concept of human nature fails to confront that the pains and unhappinesses for which people come to therapy are, at base, brought on by poor understanding and management of life in our continually changing world. The forces therapy must combat are deeply entrenched, and the work of disentangling lifelong patterns so as to win through to new perspectives is more demanding than we are usually prepared to accept.

There it is. That's what I've been working toward. *I tip up the cup and find the coffee's all gone, debate going for another cup, and decide not to use up the little time left.*

For this reality to be accepted would mean discarding the medical model and developing a more realistic educative conception of what we now call "psychotherapy."

Now there's a simple sentence and a simple idea!

It might also be nice if we'd ask all people who have more than $100 million to turn the excess over to those with incomes of less than $1,000 a year. Or what about having highly trained individual tutors for any students having difficulty in school? Or wouldn't it be good if all public transportation were free?

And what about. . . . Ah well, these are all simple sentences and simple ideas; so what's the problem?

A good idea isn't enough. That's not news.

Come on, come on. The buzzer will sound shortly. I want to get just a little farther now. Take the recognition that many of the reasons people seek psychotherapy are rooted in their having lived certain patterns most of their lives. Changing these patterns is time-consuming and highly demanding for these people and their helpers; thus we should prepare those helpers differently. A simple idea; though not so simple a sentence this time.

To put this recognition into general effect, however, would upset a variety of governmental agencies concerned with professional standards, with the provision of "health" and similar services, and with many other matters. It would disrupt the insurance industry and its programs for health care. It would confuse the professional associations and their various boards, committees, and other instrumentalities that regulate standards of preparation and conduct. The universities and professional schools would have their curricula and degree sequences questioned. Other perturbations would occur, of course, and we still haven't come to the tremendous task of educating the public to the meanings of this shift in understanding.

In short it would be widely unsettling to recognize this simple idea. Powerful forces would resist its acceptance. The odds are against its being generally adopted.

Hold on! All this is familiar: This is exactly what happens with our clients. They come to be "fixed" or "cured." Gradually they move toward recognizing that they've undertaken a different task, that they must change long-established patterns of life if they are to have the outcomes they want. Then, consciously and unconsciously, they push that recognition away.

Another simple idea that is resisted because it upsets the way we do things.

This parallel is no coincidence, I realize. It is precisely the same process and conflict, whether we look at the broad society or the particular individual. This is the *resistance* that is familiar in all depth psychotherapy.

Yet people and societies do change. That's the miracle

of human life. Despite all the forces arrayed against it, a new idea may gradually win acceptance, and ultimately the world is a different place or an individual life is freed to attain greater fullness.

Or, face it, a great new idea may die unrecognized.

As I reflect on all this, I feel uneasy. Our field is not ready to recognize the need for—let alone attempt—such a total redirection as I believe to be needed. Key people and organizations have investments in denying this proposition; winning them over will be a slow and difficult task. Change is needed, but I'm skeptical that it will occur any time soon. I am hopeful that in the long run it will occur.

The buzzer tells me Kate is here. Put away the notes I've been making, straighten my tie, go to work.

Group Psychotherapy. Experience has taught me that a thoroughgoing course of psychotherapy usually requires some time in a therapy group to complement the individual work. To be alone with an intimate evokes very different inner experiences and outer actions than those usual when we are with a group. Therapists discover this truth when they introduce into groups clients whom they know very well in the one-to-one setting. Those familiar clients may startlingly reveal heretofore undisclosed patterns of emotions and relating. Of course, this is the value of the group medium.

I have an ongoing therapy group available for my individual clients. Currently, it is down to five clients, and two of those, Kitty and Bob, will be leaving soon. Kitty is a mid-thirties homemaker, part-time secretary, every-time flirt, and would-be mother. She will leave therapy in early summer, when her husband completes graduate study and they move to Colorado. Bob is a fellow psychologist teaching in a junior college, currently trying to turn out research papers in the hope of an appointment at a larger institution.

The other three current group members are Dave, Billie, and Ben. Dave is a physician who came following a miserable divorce. He is very caught up in his therapy and assures me he will be with me until I retire. His discovery of his inner life has been a continuing source of amazement and excitement to him. Billie, sixtyish and grandmotherly, is an omnivorous reader who resists and yet depends on being everyone's grandmother. Ben, a tall, leathery, counterculture writer, is inclined to be provocative.

It is into this group that I've encouraged big Hal and ultrafemale Louise to come tonight.

Louise arrives before the others. She is sitting demurely to one side of the group room when I enter with Dave and Billie. As is my custom, I let group members handle introductions. Dave takes the lead with Louise, and I can see he's pleased with her. Billie is her usual warm but slightly vague self. Louise, predictably gracious in her responses, shows none of the anxiety I suspect is under this good front.

Ben and Kitty enter laughing. Ben is perennially coming on to her. He pretends it's kidding because he's pretty sure it's a hopeless suit. Kitty encourages him up to a point but so far has maintained a firm line.

Bob and Hal come in together, having met in the hall. It turns out they know each other casually, and, though they are talking cordially, each seems a little hesitant in the other's presence. This may account for Hal's entering the group somewhat diffidently. He's more shy than I would have expected.

The group members give their first names and express pleasure that Hal and Louise are joining them. Hal smiles, says only "Hal," and lapses into silence. Louise takes a more active part in the exchanges. She manages to say something pleasing to each person within the first half hour, and yet she isn't gushy, just a bit overly sweet for my taste. Manifestly, she needs to gain each person's good will as quickly as possible — and she succeeds.

The group talks about the impending changes as Bob's and Kitty's plans are known to them. Quietly, Hal asks to be filled in, and the two comply. This calls out of Louise an expression of regret that she won't get to know them more. I'm struck again by how subdued and formal Hal tends to be. I hadn't expected that.

As the two-hour session goes on, Hal slowly emerges, commenting occasionally on what is said but somehow avoiding the center of attention himself. He is friendly, occasionally slightly humorous, concerned to understand what is said, and subtly apart from the others. Of course, I remind myself, this is only his first session; but still I'm intrigued by the contrast to the more outgoing man I'm now so familiar with in our work together.

I'm not surprised that Louise receives a lot of attention and support from the group. She is, by contrast with Hal, much more outgoing. While it is clear that the men are attracted to her, it is soon evident that she finds ways to include the other women so that — with the possible exception of Kitty — everyone is charmed by her. Kitty is a trifle put off by having this other powerful female presence on the scene.

The session ends without incident. Everyone is congenial, and the feeling is not unlike that of a social event. I have a hunch this won't last — even if I have to see to it that it doesn't.

Four

"Blame Is All I Have Left."

Thursday, March 24

Kate. In the two months we have been working together, Kate, so emotionally detached when she first came, is learning to postpone demands for immediate changes and to trust—very limitedly—the value of talking to me about parts of her life other than those explicitly linked to her work. This is a big step for her, and one about which she is still uneasy. Yet the relentless therapist must pursue further into the guarded realm of her emotions and even risk bringing her to cross the frontiers of her consciousness and begin to explore what she has up to now kept hidden from herself.

As I try to help her recognize and loosen the tight constraint she has on her inner life, I need to be sensitive to the amount of discomfort and threat she can tolerate. Thus my approach is best made through the medium with which she feels most comfortable and capable, her excellent reasoning capacity. That path, however, takes us perilously close to the seduction of cognitive speculations as a substitute for living experience—a lure to which we both are vulnerable.

"Dr. Bugental, I find it very unsettling that I am having more rather than less instances of emotional reaction since I've been talking to you."

"You don't like that; yet it seems to happen anyway, huh?"

"Yes, of course (nettled); that's what I said. Anyway, I'm troubled that I have reactions to circumstances and people, reactions that, on reflection, seem quite groundless. Just today, when one of our staff was describing his study of a group of senile patients, I quite lost track of what he was saying."

"What was that like for you?"

"It was annoying."

"As you recall it now, what went on — or is going on — inside your thoughts?"

"Oh, I dislike these questions about things inside of me!"

"What do you think about this dislike you're experiencing right now?"

"Well, it seems so intrusive of you to ask such questions. I suppose you think it's necessary, but I still don't like it."

"So, though your reason says it's okay to inquire into your inner experience, your emotions don't coincide with your reason."

"Well, (pause) yes, I suppose you could say that."

"Why 'suppose,' Kate?"

"Oh, I don't know (annoyed). What does it matter? It's just a figure of speech."

"But you're annoyed about my asking about that also. And again your reason doesn't support your feelings."

"You do seem to be pressing the point. Why is that?"

"Kate, again today you're telling me how baffled you are that you have feelings and sometimes do things for reasons you can't make out."

"Yes, of course. That is why I have consulted you."

"Well, then, you surely recognize that the roots of your difficulties must lie in your unobserved thoughts and feelings."

She pauses, not liking the implications of what I'm showing her, but her reason concedes the point. "Yes, I suppose that must be so."

"It is indeed so, Kate. The implication is just as evident: You cannot decide *consciously* what is the best way for you to talk to get at what is *unconscious*."

"I understand. But since you seem unwilling to direct the topics with which we deal, that seems to leave us at a dead end." There is more than a hint of asperity to her manner.

"By no means. At another level, you do know what to

talk about." She starts to protest, but I move on quickly. "No, wait. We've already agreed you don't consciously know. But if you can let yourself talk about things that have mattered to you over the years — have mattered emotionally — you will lead us where we need to go."

She is silent, digesting this. It is apparent she feels reluctant to accept the conclusion her reason endorses. Finally, she looks up. "Yes," she purses her lips, considering. "Well, let me think."

Again she is quiet; but it is soon evident that she is thinking up explanations involving past emotions for her work difficulties. "Perhaps I am angry at our director as I was at times with my parents. Or it could be that I am too much of a perfectionist." Again she pauses. I have gained some ground, but I must go slowly, avoid pushing her too fast. Too much too soon yields more blockage. Still, I must make some effort.

"Kate," I interrupt her, "you have an excellent mind, and mine is pretty good too. Between us we can conjure up at least a thousand possible explanations. But rather than helping us, they'd leave us more confused than ever."

She looks startled and distinctly annoyed. Her face is quickly masked again. She adjusts her skirt and wiggles slightly to bring her posture more erect. "Well, then, Dr. Bugental, just how do you propose that we should find those mysterious roots in my unconscious? You seem so convinced that they are there; surely you must know how to discover them." Her voice is careful, precise, and more openly angry.

"It annoys you when I show you that you can't use your usual ways of thinking, doesn't it, Kate?" She has understood far too superficially; I need to help her again. This time I'm trying to phrase things as sensitively as possible. If I am too blunt about her feeling, she'll withdraw even further. Yet she needs to begin seeing how suppressed are her emotions.

"Well, I wouldn't say 'annoys,'" she frowns. "I find it . . . unsettling. I really don't see how we can proceed if you are correct in your objections to using reason." Her mouth purses slightly as she stops.

"Kate, we *must* use reason. What I'm trying to help you

see is that your familiar ways of obtaining material to which you can apply your reason — these familiar ways are part of why the sources are hard to discover. That very familiarity tells us that if that route would work, you'd have already arrived at the understanding you want on your own. Can you see? . . ."

"Yes, yes (impatiently). I do see what you mean. Thank you for explaining it. But we are still at the same place, aren't we? How can we proceed now, given the unsuitability of my usual ways of approaching issues?" Kate's precisely phrased question is sensible, but there is a growing undercurrent of distress. Her good mind is beginning to anticipate where this line of thinking will lead. She is starting to be frightened, and is trying to hide her fright from herself with controlled anger. I decide not to bring this out now. Her question is valid, and I don't want negative feelings to be tied up with the process she needs now to learn.

"What we need at this stage of our work is for you to tell me about your life, what sorts of experiences you can recall as having aroused your emotions — what caused you to feel happy or sad, guilty or proud, misunderstood or appreciated."

"I'm afraid that mine has been a very ordinary life," she answers, too promptly. "You're not likely to find any deep traumatic events in my story." Her tone is final; the implicit message is, "Try something else, Bud."

"No, Kate, you're answering too quickly and with almost no reflection or genuine exploration of your memories. We all have times of strong emotion. I'm sure that when you're ready to really look within yourself, you too will recall such times."

Kate takes my mild rebuke with no apparent upset, and reflects briefly. Then she tells me very skeletally of two incidents in her childhood, the loss of a pet and a disappointment at missing a family picnic when she had measles. I observe that her manner is detached; she is simply reporting facts. She grants the accuracy of my observation but makes no effort to seek any further for emotions. Okay, enough for today.

Jim. Kate, in common with Hal and so many of us, thinks of her emotions as the adversary of her reason. What a sad, self-defeating way of seeing ourselves that is! And how widespread! In fact, our reason is apt to be impotent or distorted without the support of our feelings; while feelings unguided by reason can be dangerous and destructive.

When Kate first came to our sessions she assumed that information about herself would be exchanged so that she could then live more as she wished; thus her feelings would be finessed and made to fall in line behind her rational intent. Even now she does not expect — and would positively reject — the idea of being openly emotional right here in this room.

New clients frequently hold this aseptic expectation. It is parallel to a custom of some centuries ago in which "ladies of quality" would never permit their physician to see their bodies. Instead a servant was brought in, and the troubling areas of the lady's body were pointed out on the servant's body. Kate, and many others, would prefer some such means of indicating, but never showing, the troubling subjective feelings and thoughts.

It is not surprising — nor is it without sober significance for psychotherapy — that the healing efforts of this procedure were often futile, even disastrous.

The point is that the client in life-changing therapy needs to be as wholly present as possible. And that means that all aspects of the inner life must be exposed, including reason and emotion. This is not a need solely for the therapeutic hours; truly vital living requires the same fullness of being, though not the same outward manifestation. Here is the startling and crucially important significance of this recognition:

> *What keeps us from being fully*
> *present in the therapy hour is the*
> *same pattern that cripples our living*
> *fully in our lives outside of therapy.*

This principle dictates that the therapist must continually monitor how fully present the client is and deal with the ways that presence is lessened. The chief instrument for tracking this crucial state is the therapist's own presence — a reality often overlooked by whodunit therapists.

Kate is not the only one who hesitates to be fully present. Hal, who is in such pain and confusion, wants to solve himself like a puzzle — and he doesn't want to be fully here either. Indeed, this is true for all my clients — for Ben, Frank, Jennifer, Louise, and. . . . Oh, oh, something just tried to slide by: "and for me?" I almost thought. Well, now I'm thinking it.

Once, when I asked George, my analyst, to show me my "resistances" the way my analytic supervisor was teaching me to do, he answered, "That's like asking a man in the middle of the Rocky Mountains to show you a stone!" Umph! Clearly, I wasn't present either.

It adds up to this: Often — and not just in the therapeutic hours — we are only partially in our lives. What different lives those would be were we more often really present in them! What a different world it would be!

Group Psychotherapy. Hal and Louise have been in three previous sessions and are pretty much part of the group now. But though they both enter in, the difference between them that was evident at their first session is even more pronounced. Louise frequently interacts with the others; Hal is more peripheral.

Tonight I will help the group to be aware that they are not really seeing Hal, and at the same time I want to confront Hal with the fact that he's not using the group for himself. An opportunity comes as Hal is talking with Ben and Dave.

Hal: "So the way I see it, Dave, you and Ben are really saying the same thing, but you're saying it in two different ways. Dave, you talk about the principles, and Ben — well, old Ben's the practical type — so he's talking about particular applications. I don't know. Maybe I'm wrong, but it seems that way to me."

Dave (considering): "Well, yes, I . . . I suppose you're right, Hal, but. . . . "

Ben: "Of course, he's right. You just hate to admit it because you always want to have the answers yourself."

Kitty: "Oh, Ben, you're such a meany!(laughing)."

Ben (pleased): "Just wait till I catch you sometime!"

Dave: "No, no. I was just thinking it over. Yes, I'm sure you're on target there. Appreciate your pointing it out."

Louise: "Hal's our group Solomon." She smiles at him, and he grins back.

Jim: "Solomon or not, Hal has a different role in our group. For example, he's just resolved the argument Ben and Dave were having. Great! He's been useful to your ideas, but aside from that, how do you feel right now about Hal, himself?"

Ben: "Oh, he's all right. I'm glad he's pointed it out. Now maybe Dave will quit having all the answers all the time."

Billie: "Hal is trying to keep you two from your usual macho-nonsense quarrel. I'm glad he did it."

Kitty: "Ben wouldn't be happy if he didn't argue with somebody — would you, Tiger?"

Ben: (Turning and making a ferocious face) "Grrr!"

Dave: (Picking up Jim's question) "Well, Hal made a very interesting point, and it really seems to have unwound the confusion Ben and I were into."

Louise (looking to me): "What did you have in mind, Jim? I think we're missing the point."

Jim: "None of you are really reacting to Hal. You're thinking about what he said and about each other. That seems to be the role Hal is taking in the group. He says helpful things and then rides away — 'Hi-ho Silver!' — before anybody gets around to thinking about that person who is Hal."

Ben: "Hey, yeah! That's right. I don't have much of any idea about him." (Turning to Hal) "How's about it, big man? What gives with you?"

Kitty: "Hey, Hal, can I be Tonto?"

Hal (slightly flustered): "No fooling, I don't know what you mean, Jim. I just got interested in what Dave and Ben were kicking around, and suddenly it hit me that they were kind of missing each other, and so. . . . "

Billie: "You know, that's right. Hal's hardly ever said anything about himself."

Dave: "Or about how he feels about what's going on."

Bob: "You're sliding away, fellah."

Ben: "Yeah, he's kind of a shy guy, I guess. Come on out and jump in, Hal."

Louise: "He was just being helpful. Why pick on him?"

Hal: "I can see I'm not doing what you all want me to do, but darned if I know what that is."

The group is going gently with Hal, unlike how they might deal with someone else. I think his size combined with his very apparent confusion makes it more appealing to support than to confront him. They're going to need my help to get him more involved.

Monday, May 16

Jennifer. Though the threat of violence is now past, Jennifer is still unrelenting in her insistence on Bert's blameworthiness, and she is as self-critical as ever. It's time for me to begin pressing her for recognition of this crippling pattern.

Today she is on the couch, a working place to which I introduced her toward the end of our first month together. She has found it helpful, but, as today, she often only half-reclines on it rather than lying prone.

"I talked with Bert again yesterday. I don't know why I do; it's just so frustrating. I ended up with another of my headaches."

"Frustrating?"

"He says such contradictory things. How can I trust him?"

"How do you mean?"

"He has such a sad face and says he really is sorry for how much he hurt me, and I think he means it. I mean, for a minute I think he means it. Well, I don't suppose I'm really convinced, but he seems so sincere. Maybe I just want to believe it. But I can't see why I'd ever want to believe anything he says again. Anyway, he looks. . . . But it's so hard to read looks."

"Jennifer, your mother has butted into what you're saying so much I've lost track of what you're telling me. You're such a good daughter to allow her to use up your time—and your life this way."

"What? My mother? Oh!" She stops, startled, not knowing whether to be angry. I wait silently.

"I know," she continues, "but I can't help it. Well, maybe I just don't really try. I really hadn't known how much I did it until you began pointing it out." She pauses, digesting the way she has just been speaking.

"You can't trust yourself, obviously."

"Yes, I . . . I mean, no, I guess I think I can't. It's hard to know. It was so nice when you said one time that I could be trusted. But . . . but I really wanted to tell you about Bert's lying to me." How she cuts herself up! It must be a subtle agony for her.

I think of renewing the labeling of her self-interruptions; but since this is the first time, I don't want to do it so much that she'll be unconsciously impelled to wall off the impact.

"Tell me."

"Well, he says he's sorry that I was so hurt by his affair with Ellen, and then he turns right around and says he can't really feel sorry for having had that affair! How can I ever believe someone who is as two-faced as that? How can I ever believe anyone again?" I note to myself that she didn't break up her account this time.

"It's hard for you to see how he could feel positive about his experience with Ellen and still feel badly hurt about its effect on you; is that it?"

"Yes, of course." (Angry, excited.) "What hurt me? His caring more for screwing Ellen than for my feelings! It still makes me so mad. And then he says he cares about my feelings! It's obvious he doesn't care a damn. Why does he lie to me?"

"You need to insist that Bert is lying to you, I see."

"What! Why do you say that? I 'need to insist'? That's what he's doing, isn't it?"

"No."

"No?" Rising tone. She sits up straight, stares at me in confusion and anger. "What do you mean? Are you trying to excuse him? Isn't it his fault that I got hurt?"

"You really get angry when I don't agree at once with the way you see things."

"What do you mean?" Voice becoming shrill; face flushed. "I just don't understand you. I know you're not trying to make me angry, but it seems that you're telling me he's not to blame for hurting me."

"I didn't say that. I didn't say anything about blame. You are so concerned about blame, though, that you have to limit your ability to hear what he does say to you."

"I can hear what he says, all right. He's just trying to have his cake and eat it too. He's trying to say it was all right to go to bed with Ellen because he's sorry I got hurt. Well, I just won't buy that!" She sits up, feet on the floor now, glaring at me. "And you, you seem to say he's not to blame for it either. Well, who is to blame, if he's not? Am I? I suppose I'm to blame that Bert and Ellen went to bed together. Is that what you're trying to tell me?"

"You really are mad because I don't agree with you."

"Well, I wouldn't say 'mad' — more disappointed. It's just unfair. Not that you're unfair. Well, it was sort of like you might be, but . . . I know you're trying to help me, but. . . . " She trails off, considers, then I can feel the tempo pick up again. "But what I really want to know is, are you saying I'm to blame for Bert's going to bed with Ellen?" Angry again, challenging.

To answer directly now would be to lose an opening that is bringing Jennifer more into this present moment — at last. It's time to bite the bullet, Bugental.

"Well, are you?" Challenging, intent, voice demanding.

"No!" Practically a scream. "No, of course not! What a terrible thing to say! Why should I. . . . "

"Who said it?" Pressing, harsh.

"You did. And don't play any of your tricky games with me. I heard you." She's frantic, lashing out wildly.

"Wow! You're really mad. You want to fight me or anyone who crosses you right now." I speak with energy but try to avoid sounding either aggravating or mollifying.

"I'm what?" She's not about to meet me.

"Right now you are frantically shoving me away, pushing past what we were doing, ready to fight."

"I'm doing what?" (shrill, furious) "You're the one to blame for our confusion. You blamed me for Bert going to bed with Ellen. Why do you blame me? . . . " Voice trails off in a wail.

"Blame, blame, blame! That's all that seems to matter to you: keeping score. Who's to blame is the only thing you seem to think about. It's more important than what's happening to your life, to your marriage, to your therapy. 'Let's just get the blame score right in that big scorebook in the sky.' What about something besides blame?" Hard, demanding.

"Now *you're* blaming me! It's so unfair! You're so unfair! You are to blame because we're all mixed up now. Well, I hope you're satisfied!" Her voice has a tremble.

Time to pause, let things simmer in her. Suddenly, I see it; can I help her to see it also? "You sound just like you were accusing Bert."

"But you . . . you. . . . " Her mind is working rapidly; her mouth moves, aborting response several times, then, "That's right! I am just like I was . . . am with Bert!" She's taken an amazing and important step — and one that requires real guts.

"Who is to blame is so important to you." Kindly now; the sudden insight is painful and very fragile.

"It's the only thing I have left." Eyes flowing. "He took everything else." And the tears cascade.

Jim. Alone in my office after Jennifer leaves, I am emotionally drained. I didn't handle this very well, got too caught in her content. Yet it worked out. She needed to get into her blaming right here with me, and I kept enough distance not to have to overwhelm her. That's why she could risk letting that awareness come through. For her, it truly feels as though her only remaining validity is in being the unfairly mistreated victim. What a miserable consolation!

How regularly the person caught up in blaming settles for that paltry role, thereby giving up having power in life. Just as it is for Jennifer, the victim's only possibilities seem to be total responsibility or total blame. Of course, she didn't cause Bert and Ellen to choose infidelity; but if Jennifer can find some ways that she contributed to making her relation with Bert such that he was open to an affair, she (Jennifer) will begin to feel some power. Then she can give up the futile preoccupation with the bookkeeping of blame.

Her collapse of control as she became emotionally dis-
traught let through an astonishing clue as to what is going on
beneath her consciousness. It came out as a projection onto me,
but it hints at what she is not yet ready to examine: what part
she might have had in setting the stage for his infidelity. This
she must shout down both outwardly and inwardly. Yet it's a
good sign and it encourages patience with her need to go slow.
(There is a danger in this thought: If I become too convinced
that such a thought is in her unconscious, I may blind myself
to other possibilities.)

Jim. "Why did you do that?" Mother asks, seldom really asking for reasons. So we learned early that that question really
means, "You've done something wrong again!" Thus we learn
to avoid blame and responsibility. Yet there is a measure of "why"
in that pseudo-question if only we are quick to use it: "The rules
said I should," or some other answer that points away from ourselves, may let us escape.

A couple of answers that are sure losers are, "Because I
wanted to" and "I was just acting on impulse." Those just ask
for trouble. Nothing that assigns the reason to something inside ourselves will help in this situation. Something external,
something public — even better, something official; that's the winner. Of course, authority is always out there, never in here, never
in us or our feelings. So we learn that responsibility is apt to
be an unwelcome burden. The idea that the word *responsibility*
might signal an opportunity — for anything except trouble —
only occurs to us much later.

To clarify my thinking about all this, I've found it helpful to assign distinct meanings to two words that are often used
as though they were synonyms: "blame" and "guilt." This is only
my own usage, but it has proven to be helpful clinically and
personally.

For me these two point in opposite directions psycholog-
ically. The need to escape responsibility comes about because
we have it all entangled with blame. *Blame* is a denial of one's
subjective power ("It's your fault that I . . . "). Even when I
blame myself ("I'm selfish to have forgotten about . . . "), I'm

really assigning the cause to some supposed attribute (my "selfishness") rather than truly accepting responsibility.

On the other hand, *guilt* accepts at least some responsibility and stays focused on the act and its outcome ("Yes, I really did do that. I'm sorry you feel badly as a result. How can we work together to make it better for you?"). Thus guilt and responsibility are forward-looking, saying that we still have the power within us to act further and produce better outcomes. In this sense, opportunity is the other face of responsibility.

When we are chiefly concerned with blame, as Jennifer is, we lose our inner sense. When we claim responsibility, we claim a vital role in our own experience. Jennifer and other clients are teaching me that if I am to be fully alive and know my own potency in my own life, then I must accept that I always have at least some responsibility for whatever I do.

Avoiding responsibility, I end up impotent and angry. Rules, laws, traditions, others' views, or anything else can help me make choices; but *only I* can actually choose for me.

Louise. It is striking how Louise's manner of focusing with unusual directness and intensity on my face and words can be at once disturbing, intriguing, helpful to the work, and yet ultimately an obstacle to her progress. If we are to do our job, she must be able to attend more to her own inner living. She is still far from being able to do that.

"You're watching me like a hawk, Louise."

"Again?" She's flustered. "Yes, I suppose so. I just do it without thinking. I'm sorry." She's sitting on the couch in an attentive posture, face tilted slightly upward. Her dress is summery, light.

"Are you apologizing to me?"

"No" (miffed). Pause. "Yes, I guess I was. Well, it must be a nuisance the way I keep doing it, despite all we've tried to do here."

"If it's a nuisance to me, then you'll try to stop doing it. Is that it?"

"Oh, that isn't what I mean." She's confused, and I'm moving too fast. She needs to experience the loss brought about by this displacement of her center onto others. All I'll accomplish this way is that she'll learn to word things differently, but it will still be a way of pleasing the other person. Why do I push Louise more than others? Reluctantly, I know the answer: It's a disguised erotic contact. Okay, so that's not why we're here; keep it in check.

Louise is becoming aware of how much she lacks genuine inner vision and the sense of identity it evokes. That much is good. Clearly, I need to be learning that too.

She sighs, kicks off her shoes, and lies back on the couch. This serves to make it difficult for her to watch me. It also serves to make me more aware of her body. Got to think about this more — and soon.

"I don't really know who I am. I almost would say, I don't know *if* I am. I mean, I am only sure I exist when I'm with someone, especially someone who needs me."

"But for yourself?"

"For myself, I really don't know. Lately, since we've been talking, I find myself wondering: If nobody needed me, would I just disappear?"

Later, Louise brings up the last group session. "I get so confused about who I am in the group. I know that people seem to like me, and I like that. But I'm not sure who it is that they like. Am I just a warming machine who pleases them, or am I a real person?"

"That question haunts you, doesn't it?"

"Yes (eyes moist), yes. I really feel so unsure inside that . . . that I don't know what or how I should be. I watch Hal, and he is so quietly solid. I don't think he'd ever have any question about who he is. Maybe I should be like that. But then you were pointing out that he was really not there, only helping others. That astonished me. Maybe Hal's like I am. But that just doesn't seem possible."

"Hal couldn't feel as lost inside as you do."

"Well, maybe (pause). But that's hard to imagine. But anyway, pretty soon I'm watching Kitty, who is so playful and . . . flirting with the men. That looks like fun. I wish I could do that, but . . . but I think I'd look silly or wrong and people wouldn't like that or it might make Billie feel left out."

Jim. Louise is typical of so many "good" people in our culture, concerned with what others think and want, ready to put themselves aside, and finding only emptiness when they look within. I know this from my own life as well as from the teachings with which my clients repeatedly present me. Yet I feel that I am gaining in experiencing my "I-ness."

So, what is "I-ness," with quotes around it? That's one of those subjective states that's miserably difficult to put into explicit words. When I attempt it, the result usually is a shopping list of good things that sounds so idealistic that it turns even me off. Once more, here's a stab at it:

I get a sense of vital involvement when I let myself experience my own emotions and wantings; when I let ideas flow out of me without trying to preshrink them for any reason; when I am spontaneously in my body; when I am really open with another person who is with me in the same way; or when I explore deeply within myself in solitary inner exploration or in the process we call depth psychotherapy.

So said, this sounds like an impossibly demanding prescription. It is only so when spelled out in this fashion, adding one dimension to another, rather than — as is actually the case — expressing a unity.

These descriptions of being fully present sound as though I sought to be the sole determiner of my life and actions. That would be both naive and impossible. Among the many aspects of myself that I seek to bring into each moment are my concern for others, for my moral and ethical values, for the future, and for my own limitedness in the midst of unlimitedness.

Human beings are capable of assimilating enormous amounts of material from diverse sources and subtly, unselfconsciously unifying them in potent ways. The failure of our species to recognize and value that unity is one important root of many tragedies we bring on ourselves. Too often, we choose sides — spirit vesus senses, behavior versus experience, intellect versus emotions, considered versus spontaneous — rather than claim the wholeness that is our potential.

Well! I have gotten far from what I meant to confront in this time between clients: the impact of Louise's erotic appeal on me and our work together. It's time to deal with this more.

I love the erotic, the sexual, the sensual. Always have. I've always been plagued and blessed with a lively interest in such matters. My memory has many snapshots of delight, guilt, shame, ecstasy, adventure, ambivalence. These days I seem to have fewer such times. I miss them.

The old memories and their attendant shame come back when I think about my response to Louise's sexual attractiveness. So many hours I've been the one on the couch working with these feelings. And, of course, the feelings and thoughts are not gone — never will be. But at least they're more conscious now and not operating behind the scenes. I hope this greater consciousness means less is hidden in me and from myself. It's going to be important to keep bringing out into awareness whatever is stirred up in me with Louise.

Only a brief interview and I'm sitting here stunned. I'd love to have a cigarette or a highball right now. I'm feeling knocked out. Glad I don't have a client for at least an hour. Better check to be sure that's so. Yes, nothing till 2:00.

Let's run it all over again. Just now Fred, the young man from upstate New York who liked my book and my views so much, was in to see me. He was a bespectacled, earnest student sort of person, who swamped me at once with his appreciation for what I had said in the book he clutched in his hand. Then he wanted my autograph on the flyleaf. What a fulfillment!

As we settle back, he announced that he was thinking of giving up his job so that he could move to Los Angeles and come into therapy with me. He was eager, and he clearly wanted me to join in his enthusiasm.

Somehow, the more he went on, the more I lost my own center. I was stiff, uncomfortable. When I tried to respond, I sounded awkward and forced to my own ears. I worried that he was disrupting his life in the belief that everything would be magically different here — because of me. I tried to express my misgivings, but they sounded formal, artificial.

Then, scarcely a quarter-hour into our conversation, Fred was weeping! I couldn't believe it. I tried to express concern, but he withdrew emotionally as much as he'd been forthcoming just a few minutes before.

He said bitterly, "You're so phony. You're not like your book at all. Why can't you just be like you write about being?" I don't remember what I replied.

It was such a letdown. I don't know what I really expected. It was clear I wasn't what he expected. He was so disappointed in me, in me *as a person!*

Tumbling from the heights of his appreciation, I fell into the depths of his disillusionment. I encouraged him to be candid; he told me how he found me so much less authentic, so much less the embodiment of what he had expected from what I had written, what he had hoped for in planning a major life change.

He was right, of course.

I have wept myself, more than once, about this same sad, persistent discrepancy within myself. My own vision for my life shines such a bright contrast to the ordinariness, the compromises, and the subtle and half-conscious deceptions that I practice still. There's some comfort in the real gains I've made over the years; yet I know so well how partial they are.

Of course, there is another side to the story too: That unsettlingly perceptive young man was weeping for himself also — however unknowingly. In our brief meeting, we did not have sufficient relation so that I could help him see that. I wish we might talk again. He would still find me less than his ideal, but he might come to some terms with his own incompleteness and thus be ready to accept my limitations as well.

Sinking back in my chair, closing my eyes, I remind myself that the vision I hold for myself — and that I hold for those with whom I work — is still valid, is still inspiriting, is still loved by me. This vision grows from a deeper, ultimately inexpressible intuition I have about what it means and what it can mean to be human.

But finally, when all the thinking *about* it is done, I'm really sad that Fred's bright hope and the bright hope he raised in me came to such miserable ends.

Five

"And No One Came. No One."

Thursday, May 19

Hal. It's cold for mid-May in Southern California, but the weather shows no respect for the Chamber of Commerce. As I come in, I am glad for the warmth in the office, but the office reeks of tobacco; so I have to open up the air-conditioning at least briefly. Hal notices it the minute he comes in, of course.

"Christ, Jim, you ought to pay your rent so they wouldn't shut off your heat this way."

"I wouldn't have thought a beefy guy like you would even notice a little coolness."

He grins and plops into the big chair. This kind of playful skirmish is our familiar opening gambit. Still, I make a mental note that it may be becoming ritualized; if so, it could obscure what needs attention.

Having thought about Hal's therapy before, I now have my mind made up. Thus, after we're settled in our chairs, I'm the one to begin our work—not my usual pattern.

"Hal, we've been working together a half-year now, and we ought to look at how our work is going. What's your take on it?"

"Yeah, that's a good idea, Jim. Let me think a minute, okay?"

I nod, and we're briefly silent. I am inwardly marshaling arguments for what I want to propose and thinking of counters to what he may respond. This is no good; it's getting me tensed up. I take a quiet, slow, full breath and let it out, willing some of the tightness to exhale with it.

"Well, Jim, I think we're making progress, but, to be frank, not nearly fast enough to suit me. I worry that I'm going to really estrange Tim from me." He pauses, and his eyes moisten. "And that is just more than I can handle."

"It's miserable caring so much for him and yet finding you can't stop blasting him."

"God damn it, yes!" He slams his hand down on the chair arm. "Yes, it is goddam miserable. I've absolutely got to get hold of myself." He pauses, turns to me, face strained. "Can't you help me get there any faster, Jim?" He slumps back in the chair, head slightly bowed.

"I really want to, Hal." My voice is firm, caring.

"I know it. I know it, Jim. It's not fair to put it on you that way, but I'm really scared. I don't know what to do."

"Hal, I've been thinking about that too, and I want to propose something."

He raises his head to look at me steadily.

"We had a session nearly a week ago, and by the end of it you seemed to be closer to getting into yourself. Remember?"

"Yeah, I guess so." Listlessly, discouraged.

"Now we've waited nearly a week. We'll make a bit of progress today; then we'll have another session in a couple days and push a bit further. Then we wait nearly a week again, and — well, you know the rest."

"Yeah, I know, but I can't really see that it would make that much difference if I came three or four times instead of twice a week."

"It's as though we went to the beach together and dug in the sand for an hour. Then we go home for four or five days before we come back to dig in the same place again. When we come back, we have to dig mostly the same sand all over again."

"You're saying I really need to come in more often."

"What do you think?"

"It would help, I guess. But I'm so damned busy, Jim. I've got the class at the college on top of some extra work at the Institute, and I want to get my paper done for Western. . . . Well, you know how it is."

"I know and you know; so what?"

"So I just don't see how I can take any more time now. Maybe in a couple months — No, that's crap! You and I know that in a couple months I'll be right in the middle of a pile of stuff just the same way."

"And will you and Tim be in the same place?"

"Umph! You know where to hit, don't you?"

"You didn't answer the question."

"No, Tim and I won't be in the same place. I just hope we're still in the same house."

"Hal, take a look at how things have gone in the six months we've been working together. You've just said you want to make more progress. Now I urge you strongly to increase our working pace. You know that you're having trouble getting with your subjectivity, even though it's essential to our work. It's time to face the question squarely. Can you afford to wait five days to follow up on what we do today, or most days here?"

"Well, it's not as bad as it was. I'm in group tonight and every week now."

"Hal, you're making it a bargaining session between us. I'm not playing. You bargain with yourself. What do you need?"

"It'll raise hell with my schedule."

"I would think so."

"But Tim's more important. Okay, let's find another time for next week."

"Tim's important, but so is Hal. If your decision is just for Tim. . . . " I let it hang in the air.

"You don't stop do you?"

"Not if it matters."

"It matters. Got a time open tomorrow?"

Group Psychotherapy. I'm going to gamble and put Kate, who is finally learning that reason and emotions can be allies, in the therapy group now. In many ways, she's not ready for it; but it's my hunch that there is a genuine yearning for companionship under that icy exterior. The group is not highly confrontational at this point, and they're mature enough not to victimize her. If I'm wrong, I can always intervene.

Kate arrives promptly, as always, but stands at the door in uncharacteristic hesitation. I've been watching for her so that I can walk in the room with her. Ben, Billie, Dave, and Louise are already seated. They look up and smile at us, greeting me; and then they turn toward Kate, who stands uncertainly beside me.

Billie: "Hello there, I'm Billie." She offers her hand. Kate takes it a bit slowly, but quickly recovers. She really looks Billie in the face and smiles a little smile.

Kate: "I'm Kate. Shall I sit any particular place?" The question is directed toward Billie and toward me, as I've taken a chair already.

Billie: "Sit here by me, Kate. It makes it easier at the start to be with someone friendly, rather than with those ogres." She grins teasingly at the men, while Louise comes over to Kate.

Louise: "Hello, Kate, I'm Louise. And these 'ogres' (gesturing) are Dave and Ben, and here comes Hal. Actually, Kate, they're not such ogres as they pretend."

Kate has been slow to realize the teasing, but now she does. When she tries to follow suit, it comes out rather stiffly. "Well, I am glad to hear that."

The session starts slowly. Billie takes Kate under her wing, explaining things to her. She's unaware that she's actually annoying Kate, who would much prefer to remain silent and unnoticed.

The discussion circles around Dave's news. He's received an unusually attractive invitation to go to another state and take a residency in psychiatry. I've known about his big secret for a while — he has been debating whether to make this change in his practice and whether to leave therapy. The group is divided on whether he should accept the offer, and Dave acknowledges that he is ambivalent also.

Dave says that since he is approaching fifty, he feels that

he must take this opportunity now. If he ever is going to make the major life change he says he wants to, there won't be many more chances. This brings up the topic of aging, and everyone gives his or her age. Ben and Dave are both forty-seven, Louise is thirty-seven, Hal is forty-six, Billie is sixty-two, and Kate, the last to respond, is thirty-nine.

Ben asks Billie how she feels about being the eldest in the group. A bit hesitantly, she admits to feeling like an outsider in this regard. She says she regrets that so much of her life she has been so concerned to be proper that she missed out on a great deal; and that she longs for a life companion, but has largely given up hope for one now.

I'm astonished to hear Kate volunteer, "I know what you mean, Billie. I have no companion either, and more and more I find I'm wanting to have someone." Then she falls silent, embarrassed by her disclosure, eyes swimming.

Hal tells Kate how appreciative he is of her willingness to share this, and several others add their support. Kate has pulled back into herself, though, and I'm not sure how much their messages get through to her.

The discussion of aging segues into personal disclosures about feelings regarding changes. Louise tells of her concern that she may miss having children, saying that when her period is irregular, she feels the shadow of menopause. Dave reassures her that this is premature; but, as Ben points out to Dave, it is clear that Louise's anxiety is not really alleviated.

Toward the end of the session, Louise takes the lead in asking Kate about herself. Kate responds carefully to factual questions but volunteers little, except to express her discomfort with being the focus of attention.

Monday, May 23

Kate. Over and over again I show Kate her compulsion to deny her emotions, even though she now, reluctantly, concedes their importance. This process is slowly but discernibly helping her to end the exile of her feelings. Cautiously, she admits to awareness of inner thoughts and promptings she had once strictly banished. But the work must be carefully paced, and her determined restraint melts slowly indeed.

Kate's face is clouded and her body seems rigid as she enters the consultation room and sits tensely on — not in — the big chair. She is holding herself tightly, whether against me or against something within herself isn't apparent. She barely acknowledges my greeting with a nod and then sits silently, squeezing her hands tightly on her purse.

"You're in a tough place, Kate." Careful tone. Don't crowd her. She's miserable, that's clear enough.

"The group. . . . " She chokes on tears and looks up at me with pain-filled eyes. I'm startled. Nothing in the group session that I was aware of could have been so hurtful to her.

"The group? . . . "

"Louise talking about her menstruation . . . and Billie's feelings. . . . " Her sob bursts through her determination to stifle it. "I don't know . . . I didn't know . . . that it would be like this. Oh!" Her pain is so manifest.

"Try to tell me, Kate. It'll help."

"I have had a memory come back." Her voice is almost a croak; her throat is so constricted. She isn't looking at me.

"Mm-hmm." Just barely a sound. She needs no pressure from me right now.

"I imagine this is what we've been looking for. But I didn't know it could feel like this." She rouses herself a bit, looks briefly into my eyes, catches her breath, drops her eyes. Abruptly, she pushes her purse away from her lap to the side of the chair cushion. It is as though she resolved to stop defending herself with it.

"The spring I had my eleventh birthday, I. . . . " She stops to catch a breath. "The spring I was eleven, something happened (pause). I had my . . . my menarche. My menstrual periods began (another pause). I wasn't prepared for it. I mean, I didn't know. Didn't know it would happen." She lapses into silence, exhausted. I'll just be quiet, give her space.

She breathes a little more easily, but she is still very tense. Now she gathers herself and continues. "I remember that I woke up a little later than usual because it wasn't a school day. A Saturday. I woke up feeling strange, sort of relaxed and something else. The being more relaxed was nice because I knew I had been tense and irritable lately. Yet I was uneasy. Then I . . . I suddenly knew something was wrong. . . . "

"Something was wrong."

"Yes, I felt wet . . . wet down there . . . between my legs . . . and . . . when I looked, it was blood. I was so scared. I didn't know what was happening. I wondered if I was dying. I felt guilty too, but I didn't know why. It was as though there was something I should do or should know, but I couldn't think what it was (pause). I don't know how long I lay there, afraid to move or to even make a sound, even to cry.

"Finally I heard someone in the hall outside my room. I was afraid it was my brother or my father. I couldn't stand the thought it might be either of them. But then it sounded more like my mother; so I sort of whispered as loud as I could for her. But I guess she didn't hear me. So I just lay there. Oh, I was so scared." She is slightly rocking her body, arms folded.

"How miserable for the little girl!"

"Yes," Kate starts to weep. "Yes, it was. I was so frightened." We are silent for several minutes. "After a long time, I heard my father working out in back in the garden, and I thought my brother must surely have gone off to his friends. He never liked to be around the house much, because either my father or my mother would give him chores (pause). I thought only Mother would be in the house; so I got up as carefully as I could and put on my robe and went down to the kitchen. Mother was there doing the dishes."

This brings a fresh burst of tears and, for the first time, Kate actually sobs. She gives way to her feelings only briefly, and then pulls herself back to the task at hand. I think of interrupting to counsel more space and acceptance of her present misery, but her manner says she needs to go ahead with this account.

"Mother looked up as I came into the kitchen and started to say something, but I guess she saw something in my face. Instead she stopped suddenly and asked me what was the matter.

I was afraid to tell her, but I knew I had to. She seemed surprised, but then the most wonderful thing happened: She stroked my cheek, told me I'd be all right, and she got tears in her eyes. She actually got tears in her eyes!"

Once more the wave of misery comes over Kate. She gives in briefly. "So Mother took me into the bathroom and gave me a sanitary pad and a belt and showed me how to put them on. Then she brought a clean towel and put it over the soiled sheet and told me to get back in bed." Kate is now sobbing openly. "She was so gentle, so gentle. In that moment I loved her so.

"You see, I don't know whether I'd ever seen Mother cry except when she and Daddy were fighting, and that was a very different kind of crying." After a pause, Kate continues. "Pretty soon, Mother came with a tray, and she had orange juice and an egg and some toast and jelly. I'd never had breakfast in bed before, except when I had the measles; so I wondered again if I was very sick, but Mother said no, everything was all right.

"Then she said I could stay in bed today and that I could pick out a game I'd like to play and pretty soon she'd come back and play it with me." This brings a storm of tears and, it seems to me, there is a different quality to them now; although I can't identify the difference.

"Mother never played games with me. I liked games very much, and my brother and father often played them with me, but Mother always said they were dumb. So I was . . . was thrilled, I guess you'd say." I hear anger in Kate's voice now, though it is very restrained.

"I loved to play Monopoly, so I got out the board and all the pieces, the money, the hotels, all those things, and I fixed up a card table beside the bed so it would be very nice when she came back. I thought of going to get tea for her, but she'd said to stay here; so I got back in bed and waited. I waited quite a while and thought of reading in my book—I always had books out of the library—but I didn't want not to be ready as soon as Mother came, so I just put the book aside."

Kate's voice is steadier now, but she is clearly under great emotional pressure. Again I debate whether to press her to express those feelings directly. I'll make an opening and see whether she can use it. "Kate, I can see what a lot of emotion there is in you right now. I wonder if it wouldn't be useful to stop and just let that come out. Then you can return to what you're telling me later — or even next time."

"No!" Her firm tone seems to startle her as it does me. Then she speaks more softly, urgently. "No, please. Please I must tell this all right now, or I can't . . . can't hold on . . . to it."

"It's all right, Kate. Go on."

"It was a long time before Mother did come back. I would forget and start to play with the Monopoly pieces, but then I heard footsteps, and I put everything back as quickly as I could. Mother stuck her head in the door and said she had to go across the street to Mrs. Gantly's for a few minutes, and she'd be right back so we could play. I think she'd been crying some more.

"The time just dragged along. I was restless and thought I'd get up and try to get dressed, but then I thought maybe she wouldn't like that. So I decided I could start looking at my book if I was ready to put it down as soon as I heard her coming. But then I couldn't seem to understand what the book was saying."

"You were all tensed up, waiting, and. . . . "

"Yes, so tense. I know now that I was afraid to think about why Mother was taking so long. And I got to worrying again about the blood. Maybe something really was very wrong with me, and Mother hadn't wanted me to know. When Grandma had cancer, everyone tried to hide it from her. I began to cry a little, I think, but I didn't want to be crying when Mother came back; so I forced myself to stop."

Kate has stopped crying now; instead there is a stern determination in her manner. "I kept thinking about the blood and everything, and I got so scared I didn't think I could breathe. Then I went out in the hall to the telephone and called over to Mrs. Gantly's. When Mother came on the line, her voice was funny, but she said she'd be home in just a couple of minutes and for me to get everything ready for our game.

"I'd planned to ask Mother some more about the blood, but then I didn't want to after all. So I just went back to my room and fixed everything up again and waited. I waited a long time. This time I really cried quite a lot, and I thought of calling my Daddy, but I knew I'd never be able to tell him about the blood. I guess I dozed off after a while, for it was around two o'clock when I looked. I felt kind of hungry.

"I took my breakfast things down to the kitchen and looked in the refrigerator for something to eat, but nothing looked good, and I decided I really didn't want to eat after all. Instead I went back to the phone and called Mother again. This time her voice was so different I had to let myself know it was because she had been drinking. You see, sometimes Mother drank too much. Once when she got really drunk, Daddy yelled at her, and they were so mad at each other, and Daddy hit her. When I remembered all of that I began crying on the phone and begging Mother to come home.

"She said she'd be home right away, but somehow I didn't think she would. I sort of half-fixed up the game, but I didn't much want to play it any more. After a while there was a noise that I thought was the front door; so I quickly got up, turned on the light, and fixed the game up again. But no one came. I guess it was the paper boy.

"And no one came. No one." She's crying again. "I called once or twice more, but I didn't really think it would help. I remember crying and telling Mother how much I loved her and how much I wanted her to come. She kept saying she was coming right away, but she never did."

"So you were miserably alone all day."

"Yes, all day. A long time later I heard Mother and Daddy yelling at each other; so I knew she had come home, and then I heard their bedroom door slam. Daddy came by and looked in at me and asked me if I was all right, and I said I was. He asked me if I needed anything, and I said no, I was fine."

Kate cries quietly for some time, and I sit silently with her, reflecting that in the more than twenty-five years since that sad Saturday, Kate has done everything in her power to be sure she never needs anyone again.

Jim. Pain such as Kate is experiencing is more intense because it is internal and because it derives from the recognition of what can never be changed. Kate mourns the fright and abandonment she knew a quarter-century ago, but the pain is not only the recollected pain. The pain is importantly today's pain also.

The pain of now is compounded of grief for the lost years, the years in which she withheld from fully living in order to avoid another betrayal, and of recognizing the inexorability of today's reality. She doesn't have, has never had, the good mother she yearned for (and briefly, on that Saturday, thought she did have). She will never be a young woman having close friends and romances, and she does not have them today. She knows, at some level—not altogether consciously yet—the impoverishment of her present life as this memory spotlights it.

Would it have been better to have spared her this agony, not to recover this memory? Absolutely not! Only through the cleansing catharsis can she recover access to her inner living. This single episode will not yield that outcome, but it significantly furthers the thawing of the frozen emotions, thus adding to her potential to relate with others. She needs to actualize that capacity if she is to take her life in new directions.

The sense of our lives, the existential sense—this is the only route to truly claiming choice and power in life. When that sense has been muffled as long as it has been for Kate, slow, careful unearthing of the buried treasure of true vital awareness is required. Then it is possible, patiently, to help life flow back into the nearly atrophied veins of her emotions.

Kate's session today was massively emotional for her and for me. And it was important in another way. I really felt Kate here with me as I never have before. What she experienced as a child struck resonant chords in me. I wept with her—although I don't know that she knew that—because she brought back memories of times when my father failed me and our family because he was drinking. There was a big difference though. I knew he loved me, and many other times he was very much there for me.

So many people use alcohol to suppress feelings that they don't know how else to handle. Dad was cursed with coming to his mature years of responsibility at a time when he was con-

tinually frustrated in his efforts to fulfill that responsibility—
the Great Depression. I've often thought how much luckier than
him I have been: My coming into maturity occurred at a time
of expanding opportunities. No merit of mine made the difference. It was what Rollo May calls "destiny," the time and circumstances into which our birth casts us.

Thinking of Dad and myself, I feel lucky that psychotherapy is now an increasingly accepted and—in my portion of the
world—approved avenue for dealing with our life issues. Dad
would have done great with a good therapist. He unfailingly
returned to optimism after each disappointment, repeatedly
came up with fresh ideas and schemes for repairing our family's
finances (and making us the millionaires that he dreamed for us).

I'm sure Kate's mother's story is one that we could sympathize with if we knew it. But we don't. The hard truth is that
understanding and sympathy don't correct the hurt.

My work brings me many stories of pain and disappointment. Lia's father was killed in an accident just when she needed
a male guide to help her deal with her emerging adolescent sexuality. She mourned her loss, and she sought male supports so
many places and so unwisely. Bob's mother died of cancer when
he was twelve, and he resolved never again to let himself need
someone as much. Trying to protect himself from hurt, he con-
demned himself to a succession of failed relationships. There
are many other stories like these.

But the work also gives me the joy and encouragement
of seeing people claim their lives against what seem like almost
impossible odds. Timothy, one of the two black men with whom
I worked deeply, came out of a ghetto that bred many addicts,
criminals, and failures. Somehow Timothy fought his way through
school, into a profession, and over the prejudices of employers
to a position of evident achievement. Leslie was crippled when
she was a small child, but she was not crippled emotionally, and
she is now one of those people who bring courage and example
to others who are handicapped.

People ask me, "How can you stand to listen to so much pain
and sadness?" I usually answer, "It's a price worth paying for hearing so much courage, determination, and joyful realization."

Monday, May 30

Kate. It's 9:00 and no Kate. She is always on time, always. What can be going on with her? When she comes, she's nearly ten minutes late. No comment on the time, no acknowledging my greeting. Her face is tight in a way it hasn't been for a month or more. Indeed, after the breakthrough last week, when she recovered the memory of her first menstrual period, I hadn't expected to see her this barricaded again. In her other two sessions, later in the week, she seemed quietly present, more open, but cautious about getting into so much emotion again — an expectable pattern as she digests the recognitions of her lost years and, unconsciously, prepares for whatever she needs to deal with next.

Yet here she is, much as she was a month or more ago, sitting stiffly in the big client's chair, body resisting the chair's invitation to relax. Something is really troubling her.

"You look very forbidding, Kate."

She frowns slightly, says nothing. I wait; we wait. Several minutes of silence. Then she stirs a little, takes in a quick breath, tightens her hold on the purse in her lap, and speaks in a flat voice.

"I have nothing to say."

"Take your time. When you can, tell me about what's going on in you right now."

"Nothing."

"That's hard to believe. Your body, your face, your posture — all are shouting that something powerful is at work so that you need to shut down."

"If that is so, I am unaware of it. You seem to read all manner of things into what I do without knowing it. Suppose you tell me what it is that's going on in me" (challenging).

"I don't know. I can only tell you what you're showing without words. My hunch would be that you're very angry or very frightened."

"Since I have nothing to say," ignoring my reply, "it's obvious there's no point in my being here." Abruptly, I realize she's preparing to leave, though she hasn't changed her posture.

I say flatly, "There is much reason to be here, Kate."

She holds herself even more tightly. "You either can't or won't do anything to help me, and I have nothing more to tell you." She starts to rise. "So it is only sensible to conclude this futile. . . . "

"Sit down, Kate" (insistent tone). I lean toward her slightly. "I think you'd like to anger me. Then you could tell yourself you left because of my anger."

"I really have no desire to anger you, Doctor Bugental." She uses my name as if she is holding a stranger at arm's length. "I simply want to know whether you will do anything to help me."

"I want to help you, but right now, you seem determined to ward off anything I might say."

"I will listen carefully to any suggestions you may choose to make. I can do no more than that." Voice even, enunciation precise.

"You can do a great deal other and more than that, Kate." I'm speaking forcefully. "But right now you fear being open, and I understand that. Still, I want to help you free yourself, at least a bit. Try a small step: You are evidently in the grip of strong feelings. When did that begin?"

"I don't know what you mean. I really don't experience these strong feelings you seem to think I have. Could you be mistaken?" Her irony breaks through the veil of politeness.

"Yes, I could be. I have been many times. Right now, however, I am not. But right now I do believe that you are not conscious of those feelings." There is concern in my voice.

"I feel like granite or ice inside; nothing else." She seems to hold herself even more tightly as my feeling becomes evident.

"I believe you." I keep my voice neutral, deliberate. "Yet you haven't been feeling this way as much lately. We need to know about changes in your emotional states. Please tell me about your morning so far today." I purposely adopt a detached tone.

"I really don't see the point of doing so. I had a quite ordinary morning." She pauses; I wait. "I woke, breakfasted, took care of some correspondence, and came here. There was nothing out of the ordinary."

"How did you feel when you woke up?"

"Oh, this seems so pointless." She stops. "Well, actually, now that I think of it, I felt rather well (pause). But let's not waste time on these trivialities. I need to know whether you can help me."

"I want to very much, Kate, but you must cooperate with me, if I am to do so. You felt rather well on awakening; how about at breakfast?"

"I don't remember (impatiently). Should I keep a record of my feelings?"

"What were your thoughts at breakfast? Come on, Kate, work with me." She's loosening a bit; got to keep her talking — about almost anything, if possible her feelings and thoughts.

"Oh, I can't. . . . Well, I started to read the paper, and then — " She pauses, a brief look of recognition flashes.

"Yes? Kate?" Softly, insistently. Excitement awakening.

"I thought about coming here this morning and about my brother's saying Mother may need an operation." She trails off; there is pain or some distress leaking into her face.

"Your mother is ill?"

"Yes, Terry says it's her back. I think she had a fall last year. Yes, that's right. In November." The trail is cold; she's slipping away.

"And, Kate, what were your thoughts about coming here this morning?"

"Oh, I thought of some other things about my childhood that I might tell you, and I. . . . " She stops abruptly. Once again, I feel anticipation.

"Yes, Kate?"

"Well, really, it's very simple." Her tone is icy again. Her hands grip her purse so tightly her fingers whiten. "I discovered that I was having certain feelings that would interfere with our work. 'Transference,' I believe you people call such emotions." Her face is stern.

Of course! I should have anticipated this. She's been shut off from feelings and from emotional involvement with other people for so many years; it's inevitable that the group experience and then the outpouring of feelings last week would seem to her to be the breakdown of protection she erected so long

ago. Finding more emotionally loaded memories coming up
would confirm her fear that the dike is really broken and that
she is about to lose all control. No wonder she's replaced the
granite wall. I must give her support and try to keep the opening from being closed off again.

"Of course, Kate. It's frightening to find these feelings you
didn't expect coming up."

"I have taken care of those feelings, and now I wish you
would tell me just how is the work we're doing supposed to be
of assistance to me?"

"I will try to answer that, but now is not the time. We
need to work at once on what affected you so strongly this morning. That is manifestly something powerful in you."

"I don't know what you mean, but I will make certain
that our work is not disturbed by those inappropriate emotions."

"Tell me what you can of these feelings."

"Well, I realized I was looking forward to coming here
and to telling you more about my life. Of course, that is not
the point of our work. I am not here to get cheap gratification
from a listener paid to hear my story." The thrust calculated
to push me away is too obvious.

"What is it about those feelings that makes you so anxious?"

"It is not important. I have taken care of them. They are
unnecessary and inappropriate."

Got to respond quickly and sharply. "It is quite appropriate and completely necessary to our work that you let your life
matter to you!" It's important to break through her rejection
of her emotions. Otherwise, she'll soon abort therapy, as involvement with the process and with me panics her.

Kate's face is fluid as she takes in the sharpness of my
response. Then, hesitantly, "I hadn't thought of these feelings
as concern for my life, as you put it."

"I imagine there are various aspects to them, but for our
purposes the truly important part is that you are beginning
to get in touch with your own motivation for your life and
its activities."

As she considers this, I ask myself whether I'm misleading her by directing attention away from the relation with

me. That's the underlying threat, and we'll have to deal with it sooner or later. She can't handle that now, and we must keep going on or she'll never get any further. These feelings are what have been lacking from our work and from her life. For over half her life, she's avoided such investments. Of course she frightened.

She stirs slightly, and her face is less stern. "Very well, I suppose that is so. However, I will try to keep my feelings from intruding on our work. Now, about those childhood events. . . . " I interrupt her; she mustn't suppress the feelings so quickly.

"Wait, Kate, look at the matter this way." Slowly, Jim, keep it impersonal and even academic. "It's our task to try to recover the emotional sources of the interferences with your work and other aspects of your life. Right?" She nods uneasily.

"But we won't be able to do that job if you are pushing down those very feelings that it is our task to bring to the surface. You can have more direction of those feelings only when you are aware of them."

This is the crucial point. Can I give her enough understanding to get her to work with me for emotional exploration? She does not want to do that, for she senses it will carry her out of her isolation, and her isolation has been her refuge.

"I do not understand you. It seems as though you intentionally try to confuse me." Stiffly, distantly again, but with a difference; tears are near; anger is only on the surface.

"You're angry, and I'd guess you're angry partly because you are beginning to understand."

"You do seem to insist on being mysterious and making me guess your meanings. Is that necessary, or is it a personal idiosyncracy of yours?"

"Probably both, Kate; although I certainly don't wish to confuse you." I'm sounding as formal as she does.

"I'm pleased to hear that, but the fact is you do confuse me (pause). How is all this supposed to help me?" She is crying.

"Kate, I am really sorry about your unhappiness. I am trying to help you understand about feelings in you that are not readily put into explicit language and that affect your life in ways that our ordinary ways of talking don't express well."

"Do you mean that you're trying to engage in some sort of telepathic communication with me?" Oh, wow! She's reaching for almost anything to hold off the dreaded emotions.

"Oh, Kate, no." I am amused and chagrined. "Really, I feel as though I lose a yard for every foot I gain in trying to help you see what's going on." Uh-oh, I'm stung. I can hear my anger coming out. Remember, Bugental, this woman is fighting off a terror she believes can literally destroy her.

"I don't understand that either, Dr. Bugental." She has regained overt composure and is once again distant, as I inwardly squirm, feel like a ham-handed bungler, and wonder what happened to all my practiced therapeutic technique.

"Kate, let me tell you something I have just found in myself. When I said that about losing ground, I now realize I was subtly trying to make you feel guilty. I don't approve of that, Kate, and I hope you did not feel so. But, Kate, that's the kind of openness we need to have here for our work. Can you see that?"

"I'm sure that if I've done anything to upset you it was unintentional, Dr. Bugental, but I can't really make that my concern, can I?" She is regal and stilted as she blocks my effort to flank her guard. Now she stands, and I realize our time was up nearly five minutes ago. In honesty, I'm relieved.

Kate draws herself together, gathers her things, nods stiffly, and departs without another word. I sink back in my chair, knee-deep in invisible debris of words, intentions, observations, half-phrased ideas, and aborted interventions. I need a drink or a brisk walk or ten minutes at a defenseless punching bag.

Kate's fear has held its ground on the surface, but it is already being subverted as she is beginning to recognize that she is looking forward to our talks, thinking of things to say — not simply to fit missing pieces into an intellectual puzzle, but as a participant in a shared venture.

Jim. Today's session is so important, and it called for such delicate handling! I sure wasn't as delicate as I needed to be, but once again the client's inner strength and determination made up for my lapses.

Unknowingly, Kate is turning a crucially important corner in her inner life: She is beginning to feel emotionally and to recognize it. Further, this is leading to an investment that involves — even depends on — another person. This is the basic terror.

When she began telling her memories, it probably seemed to her to be equivalent to reading a book she already knew thoroughly. Surely, she did not anticipate that her life would escape the pages of memory, would prove to be not just past and inert facts. Thus she is surprised to look forward to telling of her experiences — surprised and frightened. Frightened because talking to an open, responsive listener is very different from solitary remembrance, and that difference is evoking present emotion.

While most of us learn to be both appreciative and cautious of our own and others' emotions, Kate has been essentially phobic about them. The trauma at her first menstruation was not by any means the first emotional blow of her childhood, and it was not just that her mother failed her and Kate was left alone with her fears. Her mother's unexpected (and unprecedented) tenderness and solicitude led Kate to let go of her usual fears and guardedness only to have her vulnerability result in a massive betrayal.

Today Kate is moving toward being vulnerable once again, and her alarm signals are screeching. It is essential that I be steadfast, receptive, and yet avoid too overt a sympathetic or emotional response. She feels as though she is struggling to maintain control of her feelings; too much evident emotional response from me will look to her as though it could overbalance her ability to keep from being swept away.

She must come out of her retreat under the impetus of her own need and her awakening emotionality, not because I pull her. I need repeatedly to help her recognize her impulse to draw back while being urged forward from within.

She needs plenty of time to test the water, to find out that she can have her emotions and not drown in them or be hurt because of them. At this stage, her fear is less of me than of herself; but in the wings is the threat that will come as she finds herself caring about me personally. I must be gentle but still persistent.

Although she has never said so directly, it is likely that
Kate's notion of what happens in psychotherapy is taken from
the popular media. Many people expect that the work is similar to that of detective in a TV series: looking for clues, developing a theory of who (or what) was the culprit (cause of
distress), and then revealing this in a dramatic denouement,
after which the problem ceases. This is the superficial notion
of "insight" — which, sadly, even some would-be therapists also
hold. Such a whodunit view of psychotherapy reduces human
experience to objective terms and diminishes the immensity of
human subjectivity.

To make a crude analogy, the nature of our subjectivity
is similar to an entire Sunday *New York Times*. The therapist
who tries to give a client insight offers the front-page headlines
and expects this will convey the entire edition. Such second-
hand insight is more likely to confuse than to enlighten. It certainly will not produce the desired changes. The "well-analyzed"
but fundamentally unchanged client who has had seven, ten,
or more years of depth therapy and knows a lot of information
about herself is the product of this kind of work.

There will be no sudden, dramatic breakthrough in which
Kate comes to accept her emotionality without anxiety. The day
after day after day business of life-changing psychotherapy is
repetitious, low-key — would be boring for an uninvolved observer. Even for the two participants, it often has a wearying
quality of sameness.

A realistic view of psychotherapy sees it as an expedition
into a great continent where only the coastline and a few coastal
valleys have been charted.

Friday, June 3

Frank. Sooner or later, I'm going to have to do something that
I dread doing. One of these days I'll get my courage up and
ask Frank about his bathing habits. Boy, will the stuff hit the
fan when I do that! Yet it is really more than a nuisance. Frank's
odor of sweat not only distracts me while he's here, but often

lingers — seeming to cling to the big chair or the whole room — after he leaves. I've taken to scheduling him so that I have my break right after he's here and I can turn up the air-conditioning. Phooey on buildings with no windows you can open! And deodorant sprays leave a scent that's almost as bad as the one they try to cover.

As he comes in, I get a whiff that tells me I'll need more of an airing today than usual. Bill, whose office is on the same air circuit as mine, is going to get a chill.

"Yeah, hi!" Frank slumps in the big chair, returning my greeting at an angle. It seems as though he needs to avoid face-on contact except when he's challenging. Have to watch for a chance to bring this out with him.

"How's it going?"

"Same old shit," he growls, but his face is working in a way that I haven't seen before.

"Nothing you want to work on here?"

"I didn't say that. I just got to think what I want to talk about."

"Okay, take your time."

He's briefly silent; then he bursts out in a protest.

"You always make such a fuckin' big deal out of everything that it gets me all confused."

"Are you confused right now?"

"No (pause). Well, yes. Shit! I don't know. What do you think I should talk about? You're the doctor."

"Seems to me you've got something on your mind but hesitate to talk about it."

"Hell, I'm not hesitating. I just don't want to waste our time with a lot of crap."

"Yet this crap, as you call it, is keeping you so busy you don't seem to get to anything else for us to work on."

"I just came from the hotel, you know." Inwardly, I sigh. Frank has spent a lot of time just complaining about the hotel and its — in his view — terrible management and guests.

"So?"

"Funny thing happened today. I mean, I don't want to waste a lot of time telling you about it, but, like you say, it's best to get things said so we can go on to what is more important."

"Okay; so what's the story?"

"It's not a story. It's just a dumb thing that I was kind of thinking about."

"Okay. So what about it?"

"Well, there's this guy in 411, paunchy dude who comes in about every four to six weeks. Think he's a salesman for an auto parts company. Anyway, he usually has some girl—you know, some whore—come up to keep him company."

"So?"

"I wish you'd stop with the 'so's' all the time."

"Shall we interrupt this story that you say is crap to have an argument about how I say 'so'?" I can hear the sarcasm and weariness in my voice already. Come on, Bugental, give the man a chance. Just because he literally stinks doesn't make him a fair target for your impatience.

"Damn! You're in a great mood, aren't you?"

I'm very tempted to say "So?" but I curb it. "You're right, Frank, that was uncalled for. Would you like to go ahead with what you were saying?" Almost said, "your story." I get his gambits mixed in with my own so easily.

"So what's the matter with you today? You got some kind of beef with me?"

"No." That's not so, but now's not the time. "What about the salesman and his woman?"

"Well, anyway, they been up there an hour or so, probably humping their stupid heads off. Then he calls the desk and says to send someone up, and I'm the someone. When I get up there, the dude is wearing nothing but a pair of pants, and the broad is mother-naked except for a pair of shoes. She gives me a big smile like she's hoping for more customers. They're both pretty blotto on the Jack Daniels I brought up earlier, or on some kind of dope. I don't know or care. So the guy gives me a bill and tells me to get some Luckys for them and keep the change. Big spender type, hah!"

"What is it that makes this whole thing stick in your mind, Frank?" I don't know much about Frank's sexual life, if any, and wonder if that's why this incident is important to him.

"The bill the schmuck gave me is a twenty, not a one, as I bet he thought it was."

"So—I mean, what did you do?"

"What'd I do? I covered it with my hand right away and went off and got his lousy butts for him and kept the change, just like he said."

Frank settles himself more comfortably in the chair and pauses. He is waiting for me to react to his latest fling at petty larceny. I keep quiet—partly, I suppose, out of simple contrariness. The set-up has been too obvious.

"Hell, why not? (suddenly) The creep was asking for it." So Frank is going to argue with me, whether I give him anything to argue with or not.

"What do you want, Frank?" My tone is weary, I know. Perhaps I'm punishing him—he gets to me more than I realize.

"I don't want anything." His tone is angry, but it usually is. "I just am telling you everything I'm thinking about, like you said I should." To my knowledge, I've never told Frank to tell me everything he's thinking about, but that's not important either.

"You sound angry."

"I'm not angry. You guys always want people to be crying or angry or something. I'm just trying to tell you about my crummy job, and the freaks I have to deal with. Like this old character—Gandowsky, his name is—who lives at the hotel all the time. He's really not too bad . . . threatened to have me fired if I give him any more lip. I can't figure what I said that got him so hot, but he was ranting and raving at me and. . . ."

"Frank, I'm getting tired of the *Adventures of Frank Connelly, Boy Bellhop.*"

"What, what do you want me to do? You tell me to talk to you about whatever's on my mind, and when I do, you tell me you're tired of what I'm saying."

"Look, Frank, I suppose I am riding you a bit. You ask for it in some way, and. . . ."

"How do I ask for it? Christ, I don't want your trip. I don't ask for anything like that."

"Okay, okay. I don't want to get into that now."

"So you just lay it on me and then say, 'Forget it.' I don't get you."

"You're right, Frank. I can't just drop it like that." Wearily. "Okay, you always seem to be looking to be mistreated. I feel as though I have to watch everything I say doubly, or you'll find something in it that you can bitch about — like right now."

"What kind of thing is that? You tell me I'm right and turn around and tell me I make you up-tight because I'm wrong."

"Frank . . . (half-laughing, half-annoyed) you're doing it right now. In terms of the words said, you're right again. But always being right that way is a pretty lonely business. It's playing for peanuts because you're only in touch with me at the most superficial level."

"Every time you agree with me, you take it back right away. I just don't know what you expect. I feel it's like you said, that you enjoy riding me."

"I never said that I enjoy it! Oh, skip it."

So Frank wins another round, but Frank is losing too. Wherever he is, whatever the circumstances, whomever he is with, Frank has to play out being the mistreated, angry, disappointed butt. And it's a self-fulfilling system. Pretty soon, whoever's with Frank finds himself fitting in — nagging, needling, and nitpicking.

After Frank leaves, I have a break in my schedule. I get a cup of coffee and some cookies and sit in my office thinking about our conversation. Frank is a challenge to me. He is so different from most of the people I see, and I have a real desire to make contact with him in a way we haven't managed yet. But boy, can he be a pain in the neck! Ruefully, I recognize how often he catches me off base. And yet he never seems to gloat in catching me. It's just the only way he knows to relate.

Six

"If I Ever Gave Up My Misery . . . "

Monday, June 13

Frank. To estimate movement that is largely implicit requires intuition more than observation. Yet that is the job. My hunch is that some change is occurring in Frank's determined quarrelsomeness. Like the first hint of green in tree limbs after the long winter, I think it's there but I can't be sure it's not just my hope that paints the tips of the branches.

Today is story time again. "I was at the library, you know, and this character—kind of a fatso business type—comes up to me and says, 'Why don't you take a bath, you bum?' So I told him to go fuck himself, and he gets all red in the face and says he'll have me arrested. Arrested! Can you believe it?"

"So what did you do?" Damn! I didn't mean to get caught.

"What could I do? He headed for the phone. The creep was really going to do it! So I high-tailed it outta there."

"So? . . . "

"Christ! What creeps there are everywhere. Who asked him to stick his nose into whether or not I take a bath?" Frank glowers, and I swallow my laugh at his unconscious humor: I'd bet it was the "creep's" nose that alerted him to Frank's need to bathe. I wonder whether I can hitchhike on this incident to risk suggesting Frank wash more. He's fragrant again today. But now's not the time (will it ever be?), and I don't want to be classed with the creep.

"So what's the point of all this?"

"What point? (angry). They ought to lock those nuts up and not let them run around loose."

"Yeah, I know, but what about it for you?"

"What do you mean, what about it for me? I told you, the guy's off his rocker."

"So he's off his rocker; so what?"

"So he's a menace."

"Okay, so he's a menace. So what? Who cares?"

"I sure as hell don't."

"You sure as hell must. You've just used up ten minutes telling me about this guy you say you don't care about."

"I'm just doing what you told me to."

"What's that?"

"Tell you whatever comes into my mind. Now when I do it, you gripe at me. Honestly. . . . "

"Frank! For crying out loud, let's get this straight. I don't want you to tell me everything that comes into your mind. There's far too much for you to be able to do that in the first place, and in the second, a lot of it may be trivial. It is for most of us. Instead, find out what you're really concerned with right now, and tell me about that. Then when you're talking about what really matters to you, tell me about whatever else comes into your thoughts."

"First time you ever said that" (aggrieved).

"Okay, okay, so now it's said. So what matters to you right now?"

"So how come you always sound like you're just barely able to put up with me?"

Whammo! I deserve it too. But also, great! He's bringing his way of being and its effect right out in the open. Gutsy!

"Frank, you got me. I do sound that way. And it's important that we take a look together at how that happens. Do you have any notion about it?"

"How come when I ask you about what you do, you turn it back and ask me to explain it?"

"Okay, it's happening, right now. Some way I feel invited to argue with you more than to join you in thinking about this pattern of your repeatedly getting people angry with you."

"So who said people are all the time getting mad at me?"

"Well, is it so or not?"

"There are a lot of nuts around, like this guy at the library, if that's what you mean."

"I'm not a nut, and I feel you jabbing me pretty often."

"Oh, hell, I don't mean to lay a heavy trip on you. I just feel so lousy most of the time, and I have to work at this shitty job, and pretty soon I get all fucked up in my skull; so I figure, what the hell, I'll do it to them before they do it to me."

"So you find yourself just doing it to people because it feels so lousy inside, huh?"

"There's plenty of crumbs out there that'll stick it to you if you're not quicker'n they are."

"So you have to be ready for whatever might come at you."

"Yeah, it's not personal to you, you know."

"Sounds like it's just part of how miserable you feel."

"If you had to eat as much shit as I do at that lousy hotel and go around saying 'yes sir' and 'no ma'am' to as many assholes as come in there, you'd be fed up too." His tone is flat, uninflected, making a familiar complaint.

"Frank, there's something about the way you say all this that sounds as though you've said it a lot. Is that so?"

"What's that supposed to mean?" His voice rises, complaining. "Because I tell you about my life, and what a batch of shit it is, and the creeps that I have to deal with, you tell me it's just the same old stuff. What do you want? You said to tell you what was the matter. Now I'm doing it and you're beefing at me." He's incensed, but it sounds like it's all on the surface. I think he opened up more than he was really ready for, and he's got to get the protective wall back up.

"You sound as though I've accused you some way."

"Well, it sounded that way to me." And he's right; I can still sense the element of blame in my tone. Damn! I played into his familiar routine.

"I'm accusing you" — I say it levelly and with a bit of apprehension that I'm pushing too fast — "of needing your unhappiness, of holding on to your misery."

"Now, why would I do that? I don't like being unhappy. It isn't any fun seeing other people having all the jollies while

I'm all alone and just going around the same shitty treadmill all the time."

"Take a minute, Frank, and try something difficult but important."

"Now what are you. . . . "

"No, wait a minute. This is really worth an effort. You're doing important things today. Try one more."

"What 'important things'?" I don't answer, and after a minute he makes some inner decision. "Okay, okay. So I'll try whatever it is."

"See whether you can feel what it would be like not to feel miserable."

"It would be a great relief." Quickly, flatly.

"No, Frank. That was too fast. You didn't really try it on inside." I slow my own speech and make it very sober and deliberate. "Give yourself a better chance now. Go slow, and feel deep into it this time, what would it be like not to have that unhappy, lonely feeling?"

He starts to speak, then stops. He is giving it a real try. It is almost a full minute — a long time in the circumstances — before he looks up suddenly, with his face intense. Then he bursts out, angrily, "If I ever gave up my misery, I'd never be happy again!"

Jim. After Frank leaves I sit at my desk, still sort of stunned by the remarkable and only partly conscious insight and power of Frank's statement. That's it. That's the whole thing, right there. Without doubt, this is one of the half-dozen most significant things a client has ever said to me in thousands of hours of listening to people.

How clearly he reveals that the way he has learned to cope with life is essential for him. It is not a source of "happiness" really, and Frank's misery is very real. But to give up his main way of being in the world would be so terrifying that his present misery would seem happiness by contrast.

The story of Karl Wallenda is a vivid illustration of this point: He was the patriarch of the "Flying Wallendas," one of the most remarkable high-wire teams in circus history. Their culminating act consisted of a three-tier, seven-person pyramid in which the whole group moved on wires stretched high above the floor and running the length of the big tent. Working, as they always did, without a safety net, the act was truly death-defying.

One evening Dieter Schepp, a nephew, joined the act. Some distance out on the wire, he lost his footing and the whole pyramid came apart in mid-air. Dieter and another man died on the concrete floor; another became paraplegic. The "Flying Wallendas" were no more.

After a time, Karl Wallenda resumed performing, despite the pleas of his family and others. When pressed, he replied, in effect, "This is who I am."

Many years later, Karl was the star of a carnival in San Juan, Puerto Rico. There he was to walk three hundred feet on a wire ten stories high. He started out confidently, holding in his hands the sixteen-foot-long balancing pole on which high-wire artists count for balance. When he had gone about half-way, a gust of wind hit him. He fell forward to grab the back-up cable that ran parallel to the wire on which he walked, but he could not get a firm grip on it. He couldn't grab it *because he still had the balancing pole in his hands.* That pole, which had so often saved his life, now killed him. He fell to the street to die of massive injuries — holding the pole the whole terrible way down.

Frank's pole is his misery, his continual complaining, his aggravating way of relating. Not good? Of course not, but better than going out on the high wire of life without even that.

Pictures of starving people sorting through rubbish and garbage for something to eat or something that may bring a few pennies portray this same insistence on doing whatever is needed to have our lives.

What we need to be in our lives is not always pleasant or satisfying or even very effective, but if it's all we have. . . . Psychologies like behaviorism, which cast everything in terms of rewards and punishments, are much too simplistic to truly account for the complexities and subtleties of human life.

Tuesday, June 21

Hal. The pace of our work is picking up. More frequent working sessions means less draining away of what we've gained,
and Hal is really aware of his subjectivity now, although his
access to it and use of it is still erratic. We spend less time in
visiting and discussing; more in being engaged with Hal's struggle with his longstanding pattern of operating without real inner awareness.

Today when I see Hal in the waiting room, he's frowning;
but he returns my greeting warmly. He's wearing an old sweater
that still has letterman's stripes and jeans that have clearly had
a long history, not all of it immaculate.

We're barely seated when he launches into his exasperation. "I did it again! Things have been better with Tim for a
while now, and then this morning I'm damned if I didn't go
right back into my old tantrum at him."

"Discouraging, huh?"

"You know it. I was trying to pay attention inside myself, like we've been working on. When Tim and I started talking about his schoolwork, I said to myself, 'Take it easy. You
won't get anyplace by shouting at him. Pretend he's someone
else's kid.' And then he made one slur about how dumb school
is, and I started shouting, threatening him! I don't know what
the hell gets into me."

"That is disappointing, I know, Hal, but look, you tried
to handle the situation by telling yourself two lies."

"What 'two lies'? I didn't lie" (aggrieved).

"First, you told yourself to treat Tim as if he weren't your
son."

"Oh, come on, Jim. You know what. . . . "

"I know what you were trying to do, but how come you
have to trick yourself in order to get yourself to do what you
want?"

"Yeah, but I've tried and tried and—. What's the other
'lie'?"

"Talking to yourself as though you were another person.
If the only way you can run your life is lying to yourself or trick-
ing yourself, it says you're not really in the driver's seat."

"I can see it when you put it that way, but it's part of how I've really been trying to be inside myself. Sometimes I think I'm getting it; but now you're saying I'm just fooling myself." He sounds disheartened.

"I know you're trying, but you overlooked that you're basically a unity. When you divided yourself up in your thinking, you lose control. The point of what we're trying to do is to get you back in your center and where you can steer the way you want to go."

"I'm for that, but I don't seem to be able to do it. I thought I'd gotten more into my inner stuff, like we've been talking about, but. . . . "

He's so earnest, and yet I wonder whether he is really in touch inwardly. "Hal, I want you to try someting so I can see what happens when you try to use your inner self more."

"Okay, what do I do?" He brightens, expectant.

"Just try, as best you can, to think out loud about how come you keep popping off at Tim when you really don't want to."

"Damned if I know. I've told you everything I can."

"I know, but you know more than you've let into your conscious mind; so give it a try again, and maybe I can help you see what goes wrong."

"Want me to try the couch again?" Half-grin, serious too.

"Sounds like a good idea."

He peels off his coat, gets settled on the couch readily. He told me recently that he thinks he heard all I said to him the day he fell asleep, and that it was only during the silence when I stopped talking that he dozed off.

"Now, ask me again." Good enough! He's recognizing the difference between the abstract idea and the immediate experience.

"What comes to your mind spontaneously when you think about yourself and your getting so mad at Tim?"

"Hmm. Wait a minute. Well I just think to myself what might be the reason and. . . . "

"No, wait. Don't tell me about it. Just do it now."

"Well, I wonder if we've got some kind of Oedipal thing going and maybe I resent Tim as another male in the house, but frankly that seems nonsense to me. Then I . . . uh . . . I think probably I never had a chance to go through my adolescent rebellion because of the war and all; but if so, I don't get any flash or ringing bells." He pauses, shifts his position. "Then I think I ought to go read some Erikson and see if I can get a better idea."

"Listening to those thoughts, I could imagine you were thinking about John Smith and his son, not about you and Tim. You're just thinking up theories about these strangers."

"Yeah. I guess that's right. Well, sometimes I get mad and wonder what the hell's the matter with me. If I keep on blasting Tim, I'll drive him utterly away or cause one or both of us to do something really damaging. It makes me so mad, I'd like to kick my own ass for. . . . "

"Hal," (interrupting, urgently), "when you're not treating yourself like a puzzle to figure out, you act like a tough drill sergeant cussing out a dumb recruit. Don't you ever think your own thoughts for yourself on your own side?"

"Well, yes, I guess so." He's really troubled now, sensing his difficulty more than ever. "I sometimes feel really sad and kind of sorry for myself, but I try not to dwell on that. It doesn't do any good, and I don't want to waste the time."

"Wow! If you're not a dumb recruit to be cussed out, you're a poor inept slob to be pitied. You really don't have much chance just to be Hal, the person in the midst of his own life, trying to work things out as best he can, and feeling a lot about the people in his family and their lives. No wonder it's so hard for you to change things the way you want!"

"Ugh! I don't like that. I mean, I think I really understood you this time, but I sure don't like you pitying me."

"Pitying you!" Anger a little exaggerated to drive the point home. "You dumb jock, I'm not pitying you, but I sure do feel a lot of fellow feeling for you. That's a damned hard place you're in, whether you know it or like it or not. I know it because I've been there a number of times myself."

He's silent at least a minute digesting this and what we've been doing. Then his voice is subdued. "I hear you. And thanks."

Jim. When I was first in graduate school, before we entered World War II — in other words, shortly after the Ark found dry land—the prevailing approach in counseling ("psychotherapy" was not a word in our vocabularies) was that of collecting as much information as possible about the client, the client's life, and his external situation, then we'd work out an explanation and a set of recommendations. In many ways, the process paralleled what Hal was doing with himself today. And usually it was no more productive.

Hal mistakes being aware of these various speculations *about* himself for being truly present to his innerness, open to what may come up, and exercising concern. How is it different from what I've been saying one needs to do?

The key difference is that Hal is split into the observer and the observed, the problem solver and the problem—or, in more formal terms, the subject and the object. The difference is the most crucial of all. So long as he stands outside of himself and his concern, he has no real power to do anything about it.

Monday, June 13

Jim. It's been an intense day. Frank and Kate especially need me to be acutely there for them right now. Both are demonstrating such courage and determination. When that happens they push back their own boundaries, and the call is on me to met them at a deeper level—which can push my own boundaries. It's stimulating, rewarding—tiring.

Still I'm exhilarated seeing them risk fresh territory. It challenges me to understand better just what we're doing and what brings clients to mobilize themselves, to confront their demons, and thus to make these gains. Often they, themselves, can't verbalize what they're doing; so it's my job to keep grounded and aware of where we are.

I keep saying psychotherapy is not repair work, is not a medical process, is something other. What? Sometimes I use "educative" and that serves as well as any. The point is this: My clients keep teaching me that in each of us there is the capacity to cope with our life issues more effectively, more satisfyingly. They also teach me how difficult it is to learn to really use those capacities.

Why? Because that vital capacity — learning — has become a captive of objectification. We expect everything we need to know to be point-at-able and explicit. Unfortunately for us, however, the crucial recognition we need to achieve if we are to have better life governance is neither. My clients want me to tell them how to do the job, and that's impossible.

Kate asked me just how what I told her to do was supposed to help her work better. Hal protests that he can't see what getting in touch with his subjectivity has to do with his blowups at his son. Frank argues that my telling him to attend to what is within him won't help him deal with the creeps he has to work with. Louise wants to change her dependence on others, but can't find anything but hollowness when I tell her she needs to be in touch within herself. And Jennifer is looking for a rule book that will get her right with the ways she should be. They are each seeking something different, and yet to each I say essentially the same thing: Get into yourself, regain your lost sense of your own life. Am I stuck in a rut, or is there a common path for all these people — and for myself?

How different each person is; yet how much we all need to better use our capacities if we are to have our lives more as we sense they could be. There are common steps we need to take to have that greater access to what is possible for us. I want to try to spell them out now so that I can think them through further.

What I'm trying to get all these people to do is to get more into their own centers, to regain (or gain, since most have never really possessed) dependable use of their inner (existential) sense, to open themselves to their own healing/growth powers. Each of these phrases points to the same potential, one which all of us have.

My work continually seeks to help the client *be* in the hour in a crucially important way. My work calls for me to be persistent in challenging evasions from that way of being here.

Some evasions are so superficial they're easy to spot and address. When Ben first came, he tended to be flip about his life and to dismiss his feelings as "stupid." I refused to go along, and I insisted he had to take his life seriously if he was to make the changes he wanted — chiefly, freeing up his writing talent. Kitty played the happy child and pouted when I wanted her to face what she was doing with her marriage. She seemed to want only to complain about her husband, while pulling back from candidly weighing the implications for herself if she brought about a divorce. I denied Kitty's child self my paternal sympathy and challenged the underlying adult to take hold.

Other ways we avoid being really in the therapeutic work are less easy to spot and more difficult to bring to the clients' attention so that they are moved to try to change them. Hal's rational coping is his effort to grapple with his concern, but it is also a way to keep a distance from it. Kate's stiff formality and Jennifer's self-critical confusion serve the same purpose.

So what is this way of being that I'm trying to help my clients achieve? As I see it now, it has three main aspects: presence, openness, and concern. Here's what those words mean to me:

First, we need to be *present* in the immediate moment. Uh-oh, trouble already. What does that mean? Well, look at Frank for the most obvious example. He isn't truly letting go to joining me in the effort. He is restive, disputative, evasive about letting himself be really reached during the hour. Kate, so different in other respects, is the same way. She wants to have her personality cleaned and pressed while she keeps her distance from the whole operation.

Louise gives us another perspective on being present. She is so concerned with what I — or others — want from or think of her that she literally draws a blank when she looks within. But who is it that brings Louise to the hours? Who is it that is distressed that she is "hollow"?

Second (I know I've not made "first" completely clear yet, but maybe getting on a bit will help clarify it), we need to *open* to life as it is going on right now. Being present is the foundation step for trying to reduce inner chatter and be open to experience our living *right at this moment*. This is not an inventory of plusses and minuses; it is a organismic sensing of the general state of our being. Specifics may be present, but it's the overall assessment that is the center. When Frank recognized how much he depends on his misery, he was getting an opening to his life. It was more precise and heavily emotionally loaded than usual, but it was the kind of global recognition we need to continually seek.

Now, what I've just said makes it clear that we don't just turn a switch and become open to our lives. It is always a partial condition. Those who spend years in meditational practice probably are those who most attain this state. But any of us, if we will only put aside to some extent the endless businesses of operating in the world and the equally endless internal chatter, can make material gains in this important step.

Third, as we are present and open in our lives and in this very minute, we are likely to find that one or more *concerns* press for our attention. A "concern" is some life matter about which we feel a combination of worry, anticipation or apprehension, and recognition that we may have some role in affecting the outcomes of the matter. It is this constellation of subjective feelings which brings forward in consciousness life issues needing our attention and which, if effectively worked out, will result in significant life changes. Hal is concerned about his relation to his son and, having exhausted his own repertoire of ways of working out this concern, he seeks my help. Jennifer is concerned that her rage at her husband for his affair may lead her to violent action, and she turns to me. Frank is concerned that his life is on a futile treadmill, and he asks for help in finding new directions. Concern brings people to therapy, powers their work in therapy, and guides that work when all goes well.

Tuesday, June 21

Kate. A surprise: Kate's dress is light colored — a first, as best I can remember. She even greets me with a brief smile — and pleasure? She is less tightly held as she takes the chair and looks at me with a certain openness of expression.

"I think the group is helpful to me, Dr. Bugental. Oh, I . . . I . . . I don't know what to say." She is self-conscious.

"What is it you want to say, Kate?"

"Well, really, it's not important, but . . . but I notice everyone in the group uses your first name, and. . . . "

"And you hesitate to?"

"Well, yes. I don't want to be too personal, and probably you've known them much longer, and. . . . "

"I'd be pleased were you to call me 'Jim,' Kate."

Very gravely she nods. "Yes, well, thank you . . . uh . . . Jim." The word is almost whispered.

"You're welcome, Kate, and thank you also." We still are so careful, relying on formality to keep boundaries.

Yet, slowly, she is risking stepping short distances outside her granite fortress. As today, some days we feel the promise that she may truly reclaim her life; then last week and other days all progress we thought we'd made seems illusory, and we're disheartened. But we persevere — through deadness, sameness, seeming lack of significance, through recoveries of lost ground, through the endless details of living a life.

I continue to insist that Kate's emotional responses to our work are absolutely essential. She needs to recognize and accept her fear of those responses rather than try to deny or suppress them. I insist also that having emotions is not the same as being dominated by them, and sometimes — in carefully measured doses — I model this by disclosing my own feelings.

She is beginning to risk timid and minimal disclosures of feelings about events that she relates. Since these are about emotions actually experienced even as she tells of them, this is a major step. Heretofore, she has spoken only of past feelings.

Although there is implicit personal feeling in her asking to use my first name, she has yet to speak of any feelings about me. She tries to cling to the fiction that we are two objective technicians at work on an intellectual task.

Not too long ago, Kate said she was granite inside. She was attempting to become a thing sculpted out of cold, unchanging stone rather than a creature of soft, so-vulnerable, continually changing flesh. Fearing to know her changefulness, she ruthlessly tried to negate it by avoiding emotional entanglements with other people, accurately sensing they would lead inexorably to change. Among the most powerful influences that can move a person is a caring relation with another person. Asking to use "Jim" was a daring step toward letting that influence reach her.

Hal. After Kate leaves, I feel tuned up, mellow. That's just as well. Hal will be here in a few minutes, and while our work is better since he's coming more frequently, he needs me to press him more.

With Hal I easily slip into companionable dialogues. He's bright, interesting, shares many of my concerns. We collude, at times to *talk about* matters rather than getting into his immediate experiencing. If I can, I'm going to use the energy carried over from Kate to really engage Hal.

The subject of all this looks somber and abstracted as we exchange greetings, and he drops into the big chair with a sigh.

"A heavy sigh, Hal. What's going on?"

"Oh, yeah (pause). You know, Jim, I've been wondering if I can really do this subjective stuff you keep talking about. I know you think it's important, but. . . . "

"But? . . . "

"But it may be that I'm just not the right type for it. You know, like the Jungian types and all that."

"Maybe, just by your very nature, you can't be in touch with your inner life, huh?"

"Well, I don't like the sound of it when you put it that way. Let's just say it's kind of a different way of thinking that I have ever done, and so maybe I'm too old a dog to learn these new tricks."

"Say the last sentence again, Hal."

He's a little startled, but shrugs and frowning tries to comply. "Uh, let's see. I'm wondering whether I'm too old to get the hang of a different way of thinking. I think that's pretty much it. Why?"

"That's the gist of the meaning all right, but it's not the last sentence you said."

"No. Of course, it's not word-for-word the same. So what?"

"Why did it change?"

"Oh, I don't know. It just sort of came out different, you know."

"What does that mean — 'it just sort of came out different'?"

"Well, I don't know. The idea was the same . . . pretty much, and some way I used different words. What are you getting at? I don't understand."

"Hal, do something right here, will you?"

"Uh, yeah, I guess so."

"Tell me again the idea you say was pretty much the same."

A brief pause, considering, then: "Well, you know, you were saying something about my not wanting to get in touch with what was going on inside of me, and I didn't like the sound of that so . . . I mean, I thought . . . that is, I said something about maybe my earlier experiences had messed me up so I couldn't learn to do what you thought I need to do. Well, that's sort of like it; isn't it?"

"'Sort of like it' is fair enough, but, as you are recognizing, what you're saying has changed again — and even more this time. Are you game to tell me the same idea once again?" Important to keep the motivation his own as much as possible.

"Sure." He's starting to get interested. "I'll try to just let it come out quick-like: Okay, I'm saying it's been hard for me to get into this inner stuff because for so long I've been working mostly in the real world, the outer world. So I'm getting kind of scared I may never be able to get into myself the way you want . . . think I should." He stops. "I can hear it, Jim, it's really getting different, isn't it (excited)? Let me do it again: My inner life has got to be important to me, hasn't it? Of course, but I'll be damned if I can get to it — except right now I feel like I may be doing it at least a bit! And so. . . . Damn! Where was I? I've lost the thought."

"What's going on inside right now, Hal?" I'm excited too. Can he take the next step? I want to push him; it's so good to see him really getting the idea at last. Take it easy, Jim.

"Uh, still got kind of a stirred-up feeling, but also it's fading fast, and I'm getting scared I'll lose the whole thing."

"Go slow. Just stay with what's there. Don't try to grab it back. Stay with being scared, if that's what's there."

"I had a sense of it, but it's gone now. No, not all gone."

"It's never all gone, Hal, and it's never just the same. You did get a glimpse of the inner life that goes on in you all the time but is unfamiliar, so you felt the need to pull back and think about it. When you did that you made it something you were looking at and thinking about in your more familiar mode."

"Yeah, I can see that, but I can't see how you can avoid that whenever we talk about it."

"You can't, of course. Talking about the subjective makes it objective, the object of our talk, sure. But it's when you have only the objective that you're in trouble in running your own show. You need both."

"Yeah, I see." But Hal's voice makes it evident that he only partially grasps what this means.

"You 'see' objectively right now, but your tone of voice says you're not so sure you 'see it as meaningful' subjectively."

His mood picks up a bit. "Yeah. You're right about that. Though, right now, it feels better too."

"Okay, good. You got an important opening, a realization of how there is constant flow within you and how that flow has a lot to do with what you feel and do on the outside."

"Yeah, yeah. I did. What can we do with it?"

I quickly consider and decide it'd be best to ease off now. He's always impelled to objectify in words what goes on. I'll be better able to help him get past that if we take it slowly.

"Don't push it for now, Hal. We'll try to carry it further next time." He nods, and I feel confirmed in my decision. We've already gotten pretty much detached after what was a brief dip into living experience. That gives us a benchmark to which we can return later.

Jim. Back at my desk, I look at a manuscript I've been working over for ten thousand times (probably more realistically five or six). I suddenly recognize the same thing happens in my writing that Hal and I have just experienced. Each review of what I write opens further possibilities, better ways of putting things, deeper meanings; and so I rewrite it again.

When two graduates of first-rate psychology doctoral programs — Hal and I — only learn about such a pervasive and important human process years later, something's very wrong.

I had a professor in graduate school who had been working most of his life on a theory that was quite original. He taught
us some of it, and he was writing the definitive book on the subject. I heard from others that he'd been working on this book,
writing and rewriting it for at least twenty years. He kept trying to make the final statement, and it kept luring him on. He
died last year, and the book was never published.

Thursday, July 7

Jennifer. The holiday has come and gone leaving scarcely any
trace. When I was young the evidences of celebration festooned
streets and yards for a week at least. Burnt-out sparklers, exhausted Roman candles, crumpled gaudy red wrapping paper,
briefly sky-probing cans slumped in return to trash heaps, the
excremental remains of fire snakes — these memorialized the
past memorial.

Today the only reminders are storefronts being undeco-
rated so that summer specials of swimsuits, picnic equipment,
and snorkels can make their last appeals before the early fall
sweaters, football helmets, and pom-poms take their places.

Jennifer, half-reclining, is grappling with a recurrent issue:
how to be a fair, yet firm dean of women. In these days of student unrest and even outright rebellion, the president of her
college insists on more rather than less discipline. Now the summer students are outdoing regular session in troublesomeness.

After she's described her ambivalence about enforcing this
policy, she pauses, giving me an opportunity to move her in
what I hope is a more productive direction. "Jennifer, tell me
again the last thing you said to that student you just described."

"Well, it was something like, 'I'm glad you told me why
you needed to do what you did, but really I have no choice.
The rules are clear.' That's about what I said. Why?" She's restless, defensive, expecting criticism — from me (her mother).

"What's the basic message? Say it in just a few words."

"Oh, it's . . . it's. . . . Wait, let me think. I guess it's basically, 'It's tough, kid, but the rules don't say anything about

reasons of any kind. They just say, "You do so-and-so and then such-and-such happens to you." I try to let her know it's nothing personal."

"Did you hear how hard your voice got when you said 'You do so-and-so and then such-and-such happens to you'?"

"I didn't notice, but I'm not surprised. I hate coming down on people who really didn't mean to cause trouble."

"Then why do you?"

"Oh, come on!" She sits up on the couch and stares at me. "Don't *you* give me a hard time. You know it's not because I want to. The rules are very explicit and so is our president."

"So you're really superfluous."

"What! What do you mean?" Voice rising, angry protest.

"You're only needed until a computer will apply the rules without your being there at all. The rules judge the student and assign her punishment; you're just a pipeline."

She frowns mightily, and I see her begin to try to work this all out, to make it an intellectual puzzle, which she doesn't need.

"Look, Jennifer, I'm not judging you or telling you that you did it wrong." She looks up, her face clearing partially, but still cautious.

"Well, what should I have done?"

"Frankly, I don't know. I very likely would have done the same thing. The point now is what you find yourself having to do and what it does to you."

"It's a pain in the neck."

"I imagine so. Still, I want you to hang in on this a bit more. Can you do that?"

"Yes, I suppose so, but I sure don't like it."

"I know that, but let's follow it out. You were trying to be considerate, but what you had to say amounted to something like, 'My understanding — human understanding — of what you did and why you did it is not really significant. If it were, my understanding would help you now. Instead the rules are stronger than we are.' That's rough, I know, but isn't that pretty much it?"

She's silent, staring at me, her face verging on anger. A long breath, then, "I suppose so. I don't see what you think I could have said instead."

"I don't either; but right now let's stay with the message you did give her. I think we're getting to where your headaches are coming from and what makes you tired and angry so often."

"I do feel kind of angry now, but I'm not sure why."

"You must feel pretty much as that student did. Although my logic seems accurate, you don't think the result is fair."

"That's right. I don't like what you're saying, and I feel judged without being able to show you that it's not right. What can I do, just ignore the rules? You know what would happen if I set them aside for Fran, for the student?"

"That's pretty much what you said to her, isn't it?"

"Sure. So I make an exception for her because of her good reason, then I have to make exceptions for all the others with good reasons. Pretty soon the rules would be meaningless."

"What do you think about that?"

"It's just the way things are. I can't play favorites."

"Who's your favorite?"

"Oh, I don't mean that way. I mean I can't administer the rules one way one time and a different way another time."

"Why not?"

"What would be the point of having rules then?"

"So you're saying the point of having rules is to avoid having human beings make judgments."

"No! Well, maybe . . . sort of. We have to be consistent, you know."

"Consistency is more important than human understanding, is that it? If you made a choice to set the rule aside, then you'd lose the power to make decisions in the future. Precedent would replace you."

"Oh, I don't like this! I don't like it at all." She pauses, face working, considering. "I don't think what you're saying is true, but . . . but I guess it is . . . in a way. I feel angry at you and at myself and at the whole damn system. Maybe I shouldn't be a dean. Maybe I should. . . . "

"Wait, Jennifer, you don't like what you've been trained to think about people and rules. Just pulling out of the job won't make it easier, because every place has its rules and its reasons for wanting exceptions."

"Well, I don't like what you're saying. I don't feel helped.

Instead, I think you're making it worse. Now I'll be more confused than ever when I have a disciplinary problem."

"I know it's rough, but let yourself just kind of simmer
in all these thoughts. You're not really up against anything new
now; we're just bringing out in the open what you have to deal
with in your job all the time."

"That's right! And that's why I have so much tension. That
makes me think of one more thing I told Fran. I told her she
was restricted to campus for two weeks, and she started crying
because she had a big date next week. So I told her I didn't like
punishing her, but we were both parts of a system and had to
fit in."

"Had to fit in to the system."

"I hear it. I hear it. You know, that's it! That's it exactly.
I was telling her, 'Tough stuff, kid, but we're both parts of the
big machine, and we can't go trying to remake the machine because it's bigger than we are.' Ugh! But it's true!"

"How does it taste?"

"Awful! Lousy!" She curls her legs up under her, trying
to make herself into a tight little ball. Tension, still working at
it. "I don't know what I can do about it. My neck hurts; my
head aches, and I'm tight all over."

"Sounds like the headaches and tension you've been having lately."

"Yes, it does. It is. What the dickens am I supposed to
do now? Look, Bert . . . I mean, Jim! Did you hear that? I just
called you 'Bert.'"

"He broke the rules too."

"Yes, he sure did. And just about broke me."

"And you wanted to throw the book at him."

"What do you mean?"

"To kill him."

"Oh, not really (pause). Well, yes, I guess I did. But he
had it coming. Screwing that woman! And he lied to me. There
ought to be some justice somewhere. It just isn't fair." Her voice
is losing power fast. "Oh, hell, I don't know what I mean."

"It's hard to know about justice and fairness."

"Yes, yes, it really is." She weeps quietly, energy drained.

What a big step Jennifer has taken today! She's ventured out without the seeming protection of being the victim, of projecting all responsibility on others. She's let me lead her into considering the ambiguities of rules, the contradictions between absolute rules and relative human needs.

And as she risks thinking about the meanings she ascribes to rules, she has taken an even greater step — one that bespeaks her deep courage: She has tolerated my applying these recognitions to her traumatized relation to Bert! So easily might she have dropped back into her familiar angry insistence on his blamefulness. But she did not.

Jennifer is low and sad as she leaves today, but there is great promise in her inward turning.

Jim. What should Jennifer do when the needs of an individual conflict with the needs of a group of some kind? What should any of us do? These are the questions that have confronted our species from prehistory. These are questions that we still cannot answer satisfactorily.

Consistency is important, but how important? Human concern is important, but what are its limits? Lovers, families, organizations, nations, our world — all humans and human institutions struggle with these issues still and probably always will.

Louise. Coming from working with Jennifer to Louise's hour certainly provides interesting similarities and contrasts. Both women are beginning to attend more to their inner sense; but, not surprisingly, this means each is finding herself in conflict with outer authority. For Jennifer that authority is objective rules and codes of conduct; for Louise it is the wishes or needs of other people.

Today the changes in Louise are evident in several ways. She's still impelled to be agreeable and "nice," but there's a difference. I can see it in the way she carries herself and talks with other people — not just with me, but in the group also. She enters into the give and take with less constant alertness for the approval of every one in the room. The way she is dressed is another evidence of her emergence; light, backless summer dress and bare legs—more youthful and flirtatious than she used to risk.

But it is her frown that draws my attention; so I wait.

"I do a lot of counseling with our trainees, you know."

"That makes you frown?" Too surfacey; time to use my doodles to let my consciousness drift.

"Well, I'm feeling pulled by their needs when I have so many other responsibilities."

"Um-hmm."

"They're typical college girls—seem like children—and they find it hard working with people who have lives that are so different from their own. They want to talk to someone about how it upsets them, and I'm the someone they choose."

"Does that surprise you?"

"Well, yes and no. I have sympathy for them, and I expect they sense that, even though I'm their supervisor and have to evaluate them. Still, quite a few ask to talk to me personally."

"Mmmm. So what does this mean for you emotionally?"

"Well, I like it that they trust me, and I guess I find their stories interesting and touching."

"You 'guess,' why is that?"

"Well, I don't really 'guess' that. It's that I'm uncertain whether I should be doing personal counseling. Our director insists we have to protect our time because the agency waiting list is so long. I think there might be some criticism if it were known how much time I spend counseling the trainees."

"Uh-huh."

"I probably should get the director's approval or stop spending so much time with the students, but I—"

"You sound unsure about it."

"Oh, I just don't like to be caught in the middle this way and not know what to do" (aggravated).

"You don't like being in between so that you won't be able to please both the director and the students. Isn't that it?"

"Of course not." She pauses, and then continues reluctantly. "Yes, I know. I can see it's my same old problem, but it really is a problem just the same."

Jim. Louise is experiencing the necessary "working through," which for any of us takes many sessions. We have to see our patterns acted out again and again, and we have to weigh what they cost us against what they gain. There's no changing room where we can go strip naked of our way of being in the world and try on new ways until we find one that fits better. Typically, then, we work out realistic compromises in which we reduce the losses and increase the gains.

This whole process is not neat or once-for-all. The revisions we make in our way of being are always incomplete. What is limiting us is not a separate piece of our lives, like an inflamed appendix or a dirty spark plug; it's integrated with much else in our lives, usually with other aspects that are important and that may be working very well. Becoming aware of how our way of defining who we are and what our world is, of how this works well and how it cramps us — this is an ongoing, lifelong process. Its name is living.

That's what the working-through process teaches us: Most life situations are ambiguous; most life choices are incomplete; most life paths yield ambivalent results. That's not just the bad news; it's also the good. We can always make things better if we muster our courage and our intention to do so.

Seven

"I'm Nothing but a Warming Machine."

Tuesday, August 23

Frank. I think Frank is bathing more — or maybe I'm just getting used to his aroma. Anyway, his is not so pervasive a presence, and he's starting to risk talking about things that matter to him.

"I was reading this guy Shardine — or however the hell you pronounce it — and I think he's full of crap." Frank is annoyed — as usual. He glares at me as though I'd challenged him, and I recognize that he feels personally vulnerable to almost anyone he meets. Gradually, so gradually, I'm using that recognition to get myself to quit replying in kind.

"I'm not sure who you mean, Frank."

"Aw, that French priest, you know. He wrote *The Phenomenon of Man.*"

I'll be damned! "You mean Teilhard de Chardin?"

"Yeah, that's the one. Lousy French names. Anyway, I was reading his stuff on how he thinks a new man is going to develop, and — you know his theory?"

I'm stunned. I know Frank reads a lot, but somehow I didn't realize that he reads profound things like this. "Yes, in a general way, Frank. I haven't read much of Teilhard, though." Had to show off that I knew the author is usually called by his given name, didn't I? I think I'm miffed that Frank, who got his high school diploma while he was in the army, seems to have read more than I of this author whom I value.

"Well, anyway, I think he's full of crap. I mean it's a real pretty picture that man is evolving — you know, that evolution is working toward making a better species. But I just don't buy it. I think most people stink, and as far as I can see they're getting worse — not better. I suppose, being a priest and all, he's supposed to think God is making things better, but it sure don't look that way to me. Besides that, though, I really dig his ideas about 'convergence' and 'divergence.' I mean, as I look at it, that's really the way things happen. Take the whole reactionary rap that's going on in this country right now. . . . "

And so Frank spins on. I don't know whether to stop him and get him back on himself more explicitly, or not. I think he's implicitly saying much more than he realizes about his hunger for ideas, for sharing thoughts, for wanting to know, and for wanting my approval. He's such a completely lonely guy that he probably has no one else he can talk with this way, and besides, I'm pretty sure this is a kind of peace offering, a demonstration that he can do something besides gripe and that he can deal with the kinds of ideas he thinks I am interested in. I'll ride along with it for a bit. He really has understood what he has read; in fact, he makes me resolve to do some more reading in Teilhard myself.

After awhile, Frank pauses. He has gotten caught up in his talk, and now he is suddenly self-conscious about his involvement. "Oh shit, I don't know why I'm wasting my time on this crap anyway. It's just intellectual jacking off. I just don't see anybody but creeps who think *Captain Marvel* is the highest form of literature."

"I really was interested in what you were saying, Frank."

"Yeah, great, but I don't come here and pay you to be interested in my blatting about a lot of stuff that doesn't make any difference in my life anyway."

"I don't think that's so."

"What do you mean? What the hell difference does it make on my lousy job whether I dig this screwy French priest's ideas about the future of human beings?"

"I think it would make a big difference in your life if you never read any such stuff."

"Yeah? I dunno. I might be better off if I just threw it all in the can and flushed it."

"You want to fight me now because you're uncomfortable about getting wound up in those ideas."

"What's wrong with getting wound up in them?"

"You really need to kick up a dust now, eh?"

"I don't know what you mean by 'kick up a dust.' How come you're always telling me I'm doing something wrong?"

"Frank, I just don't want to get caught up in one of your — our — merry-go-rounds. I think at some level you know damn well you're just trying to divert our attention, and I also think we need to get beyond that crap."

"I don't know what all this 'at some level' stuff is, where I'm supposed to know that you're always right and I'm always wrong."

"You don't stop, do you?"

"Stop what?"

And so it goes. He won't concede anything right now.

I won't press him. Today he's come out of his hermit's cave a long way. He's risked showing me something that really matters to him. He's risked being ridiculed or patronized as he ventures into a realm more within my competence than his. He's ventured to relate to me in other than an angry, defensive way. Of course, he needs to move slowly, cautiously, and to pull back in after a time.

Hal. Our stepped-up pace is beginning to pay off. Hal is no longer compelled to fight off my insistence that his subjective experience is important. Concurrently the relation with Tim is slowly mending; yet we both know that this is more due to his being able to exert greater self-control rather than to a more basic change.

His interest in his subjectivity is growing; yet he still tries to grasp it with objective hands.

"Jim, I think I have a better idea nowadays about this being in myself, but I can't seem to hang onto it."

"'Hang on to it,' you say—like hanging on to a thing, an object. That's part of the problem, I think."

"Yeah, well hang on to my . . . to the idea . . . to my being inside myself. I just don't know how to say it."

"Changing your way of talking will only make a cosmetic difference; it won't open your inner awareness or give you greater choice about your life."

"Yeah, I can see that. Still, I don't know how to get into myself so that I will not be looking for 'its' and things like that. Can you help me?"

"I'll try. Let's start with the key concept that makes all the difference." I pause, make certain he's hearing how crucial this is. "Now take this slow, Hal. It's powerful, but it's extremely subtle. It is one simple truth: *In our subjectivity, there is no 'how to.'*"

"There is no 'how-to'?" He looks puzzled, unimpressed.

"That's difficult to understand, I know, and it doesn't seem like much for all the build-up I gave it."

"I hear you, and I'd like to understand something that you say is so important, but I'm sorry, I don't. Can you spell it out more? To me it seems simple logic: You can't do anything without knowing how to do it."

"I told you it was difficult. I should have also told you that you already know that key and use it all the time. When you talk. . . . "

"I do what? (astonished) How can I do something without knowing how to do it—and do it all the time?"

"You just did it. Did you have to *know how* to ask me that question just now?"

"What do you mean? Wait." He pauses to reflect. Then, his tone rising, says, "Wait. Hey! I think I see what you mean!"

I'm astonished. I knew Hal was bright, but I've never had anyone catch on so quickly. "Tell me, Hal."

"Yeah, well . . . wait. I got to go slow here." He pauses, thinking intensely. "Yeah, yeah. Well, I told you something . . . can't even remember what it was now; doesn't matter. Anyway, I told you something, and I didn't have to know how to tell you." He pauses, very intense, listening inside. "It's happening right now. No, not 'it.' *I'm* happening right now."

Suddenly he throws his head back and roars with a great

laugh. "I'm happening right now. Got it, Jim? I'm happening. Goddamn it! I got it. No, I *am* it. No, again, *I am it!*"

I'm laughing with him. "You sure are. 'And Yahweh said, "I am that I am."'"

"Hey, that's right! I never got it before." His tone changes subtly as he reflects briefly. "That reminds me of something, but it got away too fast." Again he pauses, then shakes his head and looks up smiling.

"So, no *how-to's,* huh? You're damn right, no *how-to's.* I don't know how we do it, but by God we do it, don't we?" He's excited, delighted again.

"We sure do."

"It's a funny feeling. I'm sort of watching myself and discovering what I want to say as I say it, except it's not quite that way either. I kind of know what I want to say and then it comes out in words. How do you figure it works, Jim?"

"I only know a bit about it. The principal thing is your intention. When you know your intention and you're really with yourself, then there's no *how to,* it just comes out. Of course, sometimes you need to stop and think how you want it to come out for certain people you're talking to or when the idea's difficult to put over."

"Yeah, yeah. I can see that."

"But even then, the idea you want to express comes right out of your intention, and the considerations that affect the way you phrase it also come from your intention."

"Not so fast." He pauses, pondering.

Hold on, I tell myself. I've been carried away by my delight in his reaction. Don't dump the whole load on him at once, or you'll smother what he's achieved.

"One question, Jim: Why didn't you tell me all this sooner?"

"Hal, it's basically the same proposition. To say something, you've got to be really in your intention to put it out. To hear something, your intention must be tuned to take it in. You've been going through a lot of stuff to get to the point you are in today where you can really hear this."

"Yes, yes." Head down, still working at it, keyed up but more contemplative now.

"Take your time."

"Yeah, I need time. There's so much in this, and I feel as though I'm just beginning to see into it." He pauses again; I wait, then he looks up. "But I want to see whether I can put it to work on my stupid anger at Tim."

"Hal, go slow. You're treating this recognition as though it were a single thing, a magic incantation or something that you've just gotten hold of. It's not that way. This is only one window into an immense network of meanings in and about your subjectivity."

"Yeah, I guess so. But I want to look through that window and save my relation with Tim."

"I know, and if you keep on as you have been, you'll probably do just that. Nevertheless, give yourself time to let your awareness open more about this recognition and all it will lead you to."

"Yeah, sure, Jim." He agrees, but I wonder whether he has any notion what I mean. Well, our time's up today. As always, there's plenty of work yet to do.

Jim. If there is a single central key to having more sense of power in the conduct of our lives, this is it. Yet it seems so simple, almost trivial. Many who hear it nod, "Uh-huh, so what else?" and miss the subtle but decisive significance that could make profound differences in their lives.

We are so used to the objective way of thinking that it seems nonsense to say there is no how-to in any aspect of living. "How can I get myself to work harder? How can I make myself give up drinking so much? How do I get in touch with my inner sense, which you keep saying is so important? How can I understand it when you say there is no 'how to'?" The questions flood through our offices. The answer is the same: "It's not a matter of how you can do it; it's whether you fully *intend* doing it."

Of course, there are many things we can do to clear the way for our intention to have this power. Much of what I do as a therapist has exactly that purpose. I point out how clients are not truly in touch with their innerness, the seat of intention.

I reflect their ambivalences, their conflicting intentions. I high-
light the threats that keep them from recognizing and acting
on their intentions. In these ways, it is often possible to free
up the natural power each of us has. But we cannot — we do
not need to — direct the actual process of subjective workings.

When we try to do that — and both the uninitiated and
those supposedly knowledgeable about psychology are inclined
to do so — we objectify what is most deeply subjective. The result
is mechanical conformity, not wholehearted action.

Hal's new recognition about the role of intention and its
significance for self-direction is one of the most important we
can get in learning about our lives. It is a key to living more
the way we really want. It helps us in dealing both with inward
issues and outward situations.

Just as Hal has only begun to see all the implications of
this perspective, so have I — even though I've been peering into
this realm longer.

Thursday, August 25

Louise. Occasionally, I have images of attractive Louise as, in
fact, crippled. Because she is so exceptionally appealing, her
handicap of not having a true centered sense of identity stands
out starkly. I continue to confront her with how her compulsion to win approval from nearly everyone robs her of knowing
her own needs, decisions, and opinions. At times she responds
with annoyance, at other times with sadness. And I must continually monitor my own motivation, for being toughly confronting can get an added — and inappropriate — boost from my sensual response to her.

Today she lies on the couch, arm thrown over her eyes,
one hand in a tight fist. She is angry as she reflects on her dependence on others: "I'm just a hollow shell. My only meaning
is what others want or expect. It makes me so damned mad."

"It's still so important to give to other people what they
need. So important that you lose touch with yourself."

"Right! I'm nothing but a warming machine. I'm only

valuable when I give myself over to others. In myself I am nothing. Nothing at all!" The last is a cry through tears.

Jim. There is such pain in coming to realize how we have robbed ourselves of our lives. Yet there is much hope in it also.

Hal. I'm looking forward to today's session with Hal. His delight and excitement last time infected me so that I anticipate we'll go further today. But when I go to the waiting room and see Hal sitting slumped, clearly dejected, I'm surprised — and disappointed.

He comes in, gives me a wan smile, and plops in the big chair. "Shit, Jim, I'm down, as I'm sure you can tell."

"Uh-huh. Want to fill me in?"

"Yeah, sure. I went home Tuesday higher than a kite. Thought I had the key to the universe or something. Tried to tell Greta about it, but she just didn't get it. Tim came in while we were talking and asked what we were discussing, and so I tried to tell him. He kind of laughed at it, made some remark about 'head-tripping psychologists,' and left."

"Disappointing."

"Believe me, yes! I should have remembered what you told me about our needing to be in the right place in our intentions in order to hear, but I couldn't see why they couldn't at least get the general idea."

"You wanted to share it so much. I can understand that."

"Yeah, but I haven't told you the worst yet. I went off by myself and tried to find out what I felt or intended about the whole thing and then about Tim and my temper. Zilch! Absolutely nothing. I was watching myself so hard to see what I thought that I couldn't think anything."

"The old habit of making yourself an object was back in place, huh?"

"Yeah, I guess so. Didn't think of it that way, but I guess that's it. Anyway, I really feel down just when I thought we'd finally gotten someplace. Can you see what we need, Jim?"

"Well, I can give you a little encouragement and then we'll see what's possible, but don't expect we're going to make it all work out all at once."

"Yeah, I guess I was pretty dumb to expect so much. It just seemed like such a great idea . . . or way of doing things . . . or whatever. What's the encouragement? I sure could use some today."

"The encouragement may not seem like much. That's the way with the subjective: When you bring things out into objective light, they often seem deceptively small."

"Uh-huh, just like the 'key' you gave me Tuesday. Then all of a sudden it seemed huge. Well, let's see this one."

"The encouragement is that you're still here, that the intention in you that you need is still here, that you've only been set back from a too-quick high, not from a mistaken perception of what was possible."

"Whoa. Go slow. I think I'm getting it, but I'm not sure. Do it again, will you?"

"Better yet, you do it and let me listen."

"You're saying that the important stuff is in me, it's not lost. Right?" His mood is brightening.

"Right."

"It makes sense, but my next thought is, 'Be careful, don't lose it now.' And right with that I think, 'Come on, where are your guts? Let's go to work on my feelings about Tim.'"

"Hal, you're really tuning in now. That's the sort of inner awareness you need to be in touch with." I'm more excited than he is—this is a more basic opening than he knows.

"Yeah, great. But I really am kinda scared to try it."

"Of course, You would have done it a long time ago if there wasn't something threatening about it for you."

"Yes, I guess so." He's not convinced, but he's impatient. We've a job to do. "How do I get started?"

"You're already started. Your intention is coming into play. That's the key step, remember."

Hal is silent, thinking this over, getting set. He sits rather tensely, body not really relaxed into the big chair, his good-looking features drawn into a funny, squinty expression as he tries to reach down inside himself. His voice is lower, slightly husky, when he looks at me.

"I don't know, but I want to find out. I intend to find out.

But there is so much going on inside of me. All sorts of ideas and feelings buzzing around. Maybe I ought to use the couch." He gets up, takes off his jacket, loosens his tie and collar, and then lies down.

He is wound up and continues talking as he stretches out. "I feel impatient with how long it's taking me to get into myself and to make a real change in my way of being with Tim. I want to grab the problem and. . . . "

"Whoa, Hal. You're not really lying down yet. You're pushing yourself to produce right away, and that's making you into an object again. Intention is not the same as commanding yourself; in fact commanding takes the place of really *being* your own intention. Just shut up inside and outside, and listen to yourself. Don't try to do anything; just really listen."

"Okay, but that's hard for me." He shuts his eyes, gives off a huge sigh, and abruptly begins to weep. I'm astonished, and I'll bet he is too. The tears just well out of him. It moves me to see this huge man lying there, crying so silently and yet with so much manifest pain. He doesn't fight it; just lies there and weeps. Watching him, my eyes fill also.

After several minutes, Hal sighs heavily again, turns on the couch, and reaches for the tissues I've put beside him. "I don't think I've cried in years. Fact is, I can't ever remember crying like I was — am." The tears return. "And I don't even know what I'm crying about." He gives in to the weeping, and we are silent again for a time.

As he again wipes his eyes, he says, "It feels good to cry, like these tears have been stored up a long time. Yet it feels so very sad too. Really sad, and still I don't know what is so sad."

"Just stay with yourself."

"Yes. I know what you mean now, Jim. I start to think of possible explanations — giving myself a multiple-choice test, you called it one time." His voice changes, slows, deepens. "But I don't want to. I don't want to figure it out. I'm tired. Tired of figuring things out. I just feel sad . . . and bad. That's all I know right now." Again tears and a brief silence.

"I keep seeing Tim's face. A younger Tim. Probably fourteen or fifteen — no, younger, eleven or twelve. He was such a wonderful kid. We had such great times camping and fishing together. Oh, God damn it." The weeping returns more strongly.

As he slacks off, I say softly, "Such a wonderful kid."

"You can say that again! You should have known him, Jim. He was a really great little guy. Lots of courage and smarts, but he was caring, too. I had such dreams of how we'd be together as he got older." He pauses, obviously linking this thought to his current relation to Tim. I say nothing; he's doing his work.

"You know, I never had a buddy when I was a young kid. After I got to college and became a big jock, sure. Lots of friends. Some really close. But not when I was eight, nine, ten. My family moved too much, I guess. Also I was such a big, clumsy kid. Tim would have laughed if he could have seen what an oaf his old man was then. No, I guess he wouldn't have either. He was always so considerate for a kid. Like one time. . . . "

So Hal comes home to his own center, his own life. He begins to know his own hopes and disappointments, his own needs and frustrations. It's only a beginning, but such an important beginning.

Jim. Being in one's center seems such a simple thing. Aren't all of us? Except for some people who are screwed up emotionally or in their heads. The answer, flatly, is *No.*

Most people in our culture have only limited access to their own centers. They think about themselves, direct and reprimand themselves, encourage and reward themselves, but they know true inward awareness only in all too rare moments of reflection — before going to sleep, when convalescing, after some major trauma, or perhaps in the mountains, the desert, or at the shore.

Hal worked hard to get where he is, and it's not the end of the road yet. He is, however and at last, on the road. He knows this, but I fear he thinks it will all be simple now.

The truth is, life is always simple, but living life is never simple.

Jim. A hot August day. Can't believe summer's nearly over. Our two weeks' vacation in July went by far too fast; so I'm looking forward to two more in September. I'm lucky to be able to work out my schedule this way, and to take so much time. (I must be a bit guilty about this privilege, for my next thought sounds defensive: "Not as much as traditional analysts who take—or used to take—most of the summer.") Sometimes I muse how wonderful it would be to retire, to have no responsibilities or regular schedule. But, realistically, I think I'd go up the wall without my work—at least some of it. Am I depending too much on it? Does it fill gaps in other more personal parts of my life?

These questions bring me back to thinking about how my way of working with clients is evolving, about the kinds of issues we get into nowadays, and especially the way we get emotionally involved with the work—and with each other.

What happened to "therapeutic detachment"? My clients and I get caught up in what's going on within ourselves right now in this room. It used to be just the client who recovered old emotions. Today both of us are involved in many dimensions: I am caught up in ways that carry me beyond my depth in relating, in attempting to be open and genuine, in trying to bring new vistas to others; in seeking to be more of a healer than one person can—or should—be for another; and (hidden in the background) in trying to mend the split within myself (by mending those I find in my clients?).

That theme again. I didn't plan to look into myself right now. How typical of the way this process works: I can't think about my clients as apart from myself. Thinking about their issues and the struggles they have brings me to thinking about my own issues and struggles.

That's a core part of what's different: We who attempt to help other people make significant life changes cannot stand coolly separate, pretending to be aseptic, hoping to be emotionally detached, acting as though we are only dealing with client issues. This work pulls us in as whole persons.

While the traditional differences between "doctor" and "patient" lessen, some differences are more important than ever. Three of the foremost: the obligation and incentive continually to monitor our own emotional lives; the commitment to put the client's long-term interests before our own; and the dedication to the ancient maxim, "Above all, do no harm."

Truly life-changing psychotherapy is — and needs to be — a live engagement between two people struggling with each other and with the forces in both that deny life, restrict awareness, and limit growth. It is messy, its borders are unclear and often shifting, and its processes are continually evolving.

Clients bring into the therapeutic relation their own ways of dealing with life and with other people; these are only partially conscious, and they often seek to elicit inappropriate responses from the therapist. These promptings from the client are met by similarly mixed impulses from the therapist — again only partially conscious and often seeking toward inappropriate responses from the client.

Thus Jennifer accuses me of causing her distress, and I find myself blaming her for being rule-bound; Frank continually complains about how I criticize him, and I get defensive and counterpunch; Louise seeks to please me by acting as she thinks I want, and I fantasize making love to her while challenging her prematurely; Hal questions my psychological perspective, and I leap into debate; and Kate insists on being formal and impersonal, and I demonstrate my academic correctness.

And in all these instances *nothing has gone wrong*.

These are, first and foremost, lives being lived. They are, second, engagements in which both participants struggle to increase their validity, fullness, and power. Third, to achieve these purposes, they have only their own beingness — and it is that which is put on the line continually and necessarily.

In brief, this is a quintessentially human enterprise. When it's going on and when these multidimensional, only partially conscious, often threatening, and frequently confused interactions are occurring, then the therapist has the maximum opportunity to disclose his own and the client's distortions of their relationship and its true function. Out of such disclosures — made in the living moment — true life changes can emerge.

Group Psychotherapy. The group is in a summer slump. This often happens, but still the low-key, sluggish quality pulls on me to get things going. Generally, I don't use exercises to rescue individuals or groups from their inertia. They need to take that responsibility themselves and to confront the despair and need to relinquish that underlie inertia. Tonight, however, a combination of factors — people on vacation, new people entering, and some moving toward leaving — make it suitable.

There is some semisocializing going on, which is really a "You-go-first" hesitation to get into anything significant. Just as well to interrupt this. "Okay, people, let's try something here." They look at me expectantly. That's what I wanted to avoid: Daddy's come to fix things. Too late now.

"Each of you reach down inside and find one word to represent where you are right now. Just one word; no speeches or explanations. Take the first word that's probably already come to mind. Ben?"

Ben: "Stupid." I nod and look at Billie who is sitting next to Ben.

Billie: "Sad."

Louise: "Angry, uh, confused."

Ben: "Hey, teacher, she took two, and I only got one."

Louise: "I'm sorry, I. . . . "

Hal: "Listening. No, make that learning."

Bob: "Regretful."

Kate: "Interested."

Jim: "Waiting."

The group pauses briefly, looking around, checking that everyone has given a word. Then several start to speak at the same time, but Hal gains the floor.

Hal: "Why 'sad,' Billie?"

Billie: "This is my last time here (her eyes fill), and I was just thinking how much I've come to care for all of you."

This brings a clamor of responses asking for more about Billie's plans, expressing regret she's leaving, and hoping she'll change her mind. She looks at me with brimming eyes, for we have talked in her individual session about it's being time for her to leave and how the group will feel about it. She was sure they'd hardly notice, and I insisted she should see for herself.

It is only when things have quieted a bit that Bob makes his announcement. "I'm here for the last time too, Billie. I just

got word this afternoon that I've been accepted for post-doc training at a clinic in the San Francisco area. And since it's an unexpected opening, I have to be there almost at once." He turns
to me. "I tried to call you when I got the letter so you'd know
in advance, but I couldn't get through. Sorry."

Jim: "It's okay. I knew you were hoping for it, and now
the good news is you've got it. Congratulations!"

The group now talks about the changes that are occurring and the feeling that they're losing something. When they
ask, I tell them there will be a new man entering soon, but I
don't give any other information, believing that is the right of
the person entering.

As I listen, I reflect that my exercise made very little difference. The impact of the two announcements of people leaving
has certainly enlivened the group, but the level is more social
than therapeutic — at least until close to the end when, with some
prodding from me, they express personal feelings about Billie
and Bob and reactions about their own work in therapy. It still
feels more shallow than I would like.

Jim. The group's farewell to Billie and Bob is touching, but it
reminds me of a similar situation that went amazingly differently in a group a friend of mine runs in his practice. When
one of the women members left, the whole group stripped, and
nude, embraced her to say good-bye. He said it was a very moving ceremony with nearly everyone in tears.

That group's working pattern must be very different than
mine! I can see some value in it, but I'd be hesitant to encourage
such an event. Fact is, I'd probably forestall it. Reason? I'm
always concerned about what therapy teaches about contraven-
ing the folkways of our culture. I don't think such rules are
graven in marble; sometimes it's important to override them.
But I don't feel I can monitor all the meanings a group would
attribute to that kind of collective rejection of what is regarded
as moral. And I'd feel I should monitor it. My friend feels that's
my overprotectiveness. I dunno.

Group nudity at Esalen, or other places where the setting has no compulsory quality (as I think a therapy group has),
would be — is — delightful, refreshing, and still a bit on my edge.

Well, the sixties are helping all of us push back our edges a bit. That's all to the good — if the pace is respectful of individual differences.

Monday, October 3

Frank. Rain is early this year. Gray, overcast days often nudge patients toward blue moods. We're spoiled here in Southern California by the continual sunshine, but we're paying for it more each year by the unbeautiful smog we endure.

Frank comes in carrying a dripping GI raincoat, and looks around for a spot to drop it. I point to the hooks in the hall just outside my door, and note to myself that he's more able to risk being considerate of others than he used to be. Changes — subtle, seemingly small but cumulatively significant — are occurring. As he sits down, he is intense, but less angry than usual.

Story time.

In the past I've frequently interrupted Frank's stories; but now I've come to realize that this is his safest way of expressing what is important emotionally. By setting it in a supposedly neutral account of an event away from the office, he gives an implicit portrayal of what matters to him. I'd prefer working with immediate experience and preferably with the struggles going on within Frank himself. He can't do that, and I have to respect the vehicle he has found.

"I'm working the shit shift now. Go on at 11:00 P.M. and off at 7:00 A.M. Most of the time there's just me and the night clerk and the night engineer. Boy, do we get the weirdos! Like last night. About 11:30 this old bag — and I mean she was plenty hard up — came in to where I was sitting at the bell captain's desk, reading. She says, 'Could I sit down in one of those chairs for a little while, sir?' She calls me *sir,* for crying out loud! So I don't pay too much attention because I'm reading, and I just say sure, be my guest.

"First thing I know, old shit-head Berman, the night clerk, dings his goddamn bell. I put my book down and go see what's eating him. 'Who's the old woman?' he says. 'Beats me,' I say.

'She's dirty, and her clothes are all wet, and she'll get the furniture messed up,' he says. 'Go find out if she's connected with anyone in the hotel,' and of course, she isn't. 'So tell her she'll have to go,' he says out of his big heart. 'Christ's sake,' I say, 'it's raining like crazy outside.' He says to get her a cab if she wants one. Of all the dumb-ass suggestions! It's clear she hasn't got any dough. So I tell her I'm sorry, but the boss says she can't stay. She says that's okay, and thanks me. She thanks me! Can you believe it?"

"What'd you think about the whole thing?"

"Oh, hell, it's no skin off my nose. Anyway, after a while, maybe about 12:30, 1:00, I'm all alone in the lobby while Berman goes for a break to jerk off or whatever he does, and suddenly I see this face at one of the windows. Damned if it isn't the old dame again. I watch, and she goes around the corner toward the side entrance. I figure, 'What the hell?' and beat it over to the side door and catch her as she's going by. I take her down to the furnace room and tell old Foley, the night engineer, to let her dry out and rest awhile. He says sure, and gives her a cup of his awful coffee.

"Then I high-tail it back upstairs, and of course his majesty is there and mouths off about one of us always has to be in the lobby and where was I. I tell him I had to take a crap. He says he didn't see me in the employees' john, and I say I went downstairs. So then he gives me a lecture about using the guest restrooms. Anyway, I guess Foley got the old dame out all right, because I didn't see her again."

"What a tough life."

"You know it."

"What does it stir up in your thoughts?" I have a hunch he makes some identification with the woman from his own early years, when he must have known something at least a bit similar.

"What do you mean 'stir up'?"

"Come on, Frank, let's use this and not play our sparring game this time."

"What 'sparring game'? I don't know what you mean."

"God damn it, Frank." Really mad and not caring if he knows it. Think it got to me that he could act so generously and then slide right back into his adversarial position. "You're so stupid-ass set on not meeting me that you keep throwing away opportunities to work on the very things that brought you here."

"I don't see why you're so mad at me when I can't understand what you say."

"Wait, now. Let's both make an effort to understand each other. I know I jumped you, but can you risk admitting that you need to dodge away from understanding me too?" Urgently, firmly, cautious with closeness. As much as I think he hungers for relation, he's terrified of getting caught in it.

"I don't want to misunderstand you. I'd be a damned fool to. . . . " He pauses, uncertain, entering new territory.

"No, Frank, I believe you don't consciously want to misunderstand me, but I do think you always feel a need to keep a distance between us and when I appeal to you to work with me, it makes you edgy." He's not fighting me as hard as usual. Come on, Jim, recognize he's trying.

"How do you mean 'edgy'? I mean I kind of get your idea, but I'm not quite sure how you mean."

A big step! He started to quibble about words, as so often, but then he diluted it. I want to try to meet him. "Well, maybe that's not the right word. It seems as though when I try to be with you, it makes you uneasy, and then you feel the need to pull away a bit."

"Yeah, maybe so. I don't know. Anyway, what did you mean when you said I was throwing away opportunities?"

He's really trying to meet me now. Go easy, go easy. "I felt that you'd stuck your neck out for a total stranger last night and that perhaps it would help us understand some of your concerns better if we could talk it over more. When we bicker with each other, we lose such chances."

"Yeah, I can see that. But last night wasn't really anything much. We ought to find something better than that."

He's conceding a lot. Of course he has to object some. Which way to go? I'd like to stay with his just-emerging recognition of his need to hold me off, but I don't want him to feel cornered or that I'm using his concessions "against" him.

"We can deal with something else, if you like, but I'm

impressed with your courage in doing something last night which might get you in trouble and for which there was no pay-off."

"Oh, shit! You make such a big melodrama out of everything that I want to just dump it."

"Something about what I said made you need to push us apart again. What was that?"

"It's just you making a big deal out of piss-poor nothing."

"I don't want to hassle with you, Frank. I'm just beginning to see how hard it is for you to risk working with me. It even seems rough to stay with me on the same topic. I think I got a glimpse of what a tough, lonely battle you must be fighting inside all the time."

He is silent a minute or more, a rare thing in itself. He is looking stonily straight ahead at the wall. Suddenly he bursts out, "Shit, that's just the crutch I have to bear!"

Did he really say that? Of course, but I doubt he heard himself. "Frank, can you say again what you just said?"

"I said I guess I'm just stuck with being that way. Why?"

"Do you remember the actual words?"

"Are we back to playing word games again? I thought you said you were tired of that shit."

"You're right, Frank, I am."

Once again, Frank's unconscious humor and insight has spoken in a remarkable phrase. It is indeed the crutch/cross Frank feels he must bear. I wish I could show him that part of himself, but not yet. Still, today marks a really important movement in Frank's therapy. He risked conceding his need to pull away, and he didn't have to fight openly my reflecting his inner struggle and misery.

Eight

"Show Me Your Legs."

Frank. The rain is continuing, and Frank hangs his coat in the hall readily, comes in with something approaching a smile — but not quite that extreme. Let it stand that he's not manifesting anger today; rather his face is serious and relatively open.

"Last time you said I threw away my opportunities here, and when I asked you what you meant, you said something about there being more in that deal with the old lady than I had said. Well, I thought about it, and I went over the whole thing, and I can't find anything more." Slowly, Bugental. As usual, he's saying you were wrong, but he's also saying he heard you and tried to use what you said. Don't get caught in his defensive ploys.

"It didn't seem to have anything else in it that you could see, huh?"

"No, I mean, I sort of went through the whole thing again in my mind, and I think I told you everything that was important about it, and I can't see any dramatic lessons to learn in it or anything." His talk is different — less profane, more substantial. He's still putting bait out for me: That bit about "dramatic lessons" is strictly to get us off. Underneath he is really terrified of closeness.

"Well, maybe so. Now, looking back on the whole thing with the old lady, what do you think was working in you to make

145

you do what you did?" Is that too much? It's awkwardly phrased; I'm so anxious not to crowd him into flight.

"How do you mean, 'back on the whole thing'?" He's cautious too, but he's not pulling out yet.

"Just however it seems to you, Frank, why you decided to do what you did with the old lady."

"Aw shit, it was raining buckets outside, and that fag Berman gives me a pain in the ass anyway. So I figure, what can it hurt to let the old bag dry off and get warm? I don't know why you want to make such a big deal out of it."

"Seems pretty matter of fact, eh?"

"Yeah, sure. Why? Do you see something else? I mean, if you see some of those big opportunities you talk about, let's hear them." This man is like a person who has been burned all over. However I try to touch him in order to help him, it hurts, and the pain makes him pull away.

"No, I don't see anything big right now."

"Well, do you see anything more than I said?" Hmmm. That feels different. He's coming out toward me a bit.

"Not really, Frank. I guess the biggest thing I'm aware of is that you risked something for a complete stranger."

"Aw shit! What risk is that? The fucking job is a stink anyway. They can shove it up Berman any time for all I care."

"I think it makes you angry if I suggest you have any kind motives."

"What 'kind motives'? I don't give a damn for that old bag. For crying out loud, you're making a huge big deal out of piss-poor nothing."

"Wow! You sure need to turn on a lot of power to deny that rather mild hunch of mine."

"Look, just don't get the idea I give a damn for some dumb old dame or anything like that."

"That seems very important to you."

"Yeah, well, I think you better not get some screwed-up idea of my motives if you're going to be any help to me."

"Okay, so the message is: Frank has no kind motives toward old dames. Is that it?" Uh-uh. Too much sarcasm: I had to strike back. Shouldn't yield to the temptation. He really knows how to get to me.

"You're deliberately twisting what I said. That isn't the message, and you know it. I can have kind motives where it means something. Why the. . . . "

"You're right, Frank." Interrupting, urgently. "You're right. I did twist your meaning. I'm sorry. I think you just got to me a bit, and I hit back."

"Oh, shit, it's okay. Don't make a big deal out of it."

"Maybe you understand about. . . . No, I don't want to do it that way. Frank, try to hear this, please: I started to make a parallel between the way I needed to twist your words a few minutes ago and the way, it seems to me, you need to twist mine at times. I started to do it in a subtle way that would have been kind of a dig. I don't want to do that. We've both done that too much, and I think we both would like to use our time more to work on the problems that are deeper for you. Do you see what I'm saying, Frank?"

"Yeah, yeah, I get it." Pause. "You know I hate it when you get so intense and emotional. Why can't you just say things straight?"

"For a minute we met just then, but I think it was too much for you, and you had to find something to complain about to push me away."

"No, I just don't like all the melodrama that you seem to go in for."

"I feel kind of stung right now, and one part of me wants to hit back at you or to defend myself. Another part says, 'Frank needs to see melodrama in anything that involves emotional closeness.'"

"Why would I do that? I just don't like being talked to in big. . . . "

"Wait, Frank, let me answer your question." I pause, he stops and listens. He's gaining, and I'm moved by seeing it. "I think you do need to push away emotional closeness because you really haven't much experience of it . . . except as hurt. The little you've told me about when you were a kid is mostly about being disappointed or hurt by your mother and, maybe, your brothers and sisters — and almost everyone else you were with."

"Yeah, mostly it was pretty shitty."

"That's sure the picture I've formed. And if that's the way

it was, it's no wonder you're uneasy when someone seems to be trying to get close."

"Well, I had some good things with my older sister, the one who kind of took care of me after my mother was put in the hospital."

"Will you tell me about that? I don't know much at all about those early years."

"Sure. I just thought you didn't like to get into ancient history."

He needs to make a thrust, of course, but he's not following up on it. Instead I think he's waiting for me to encourage him! He's never needed that before. Once he lets go of his adversarial posture, he is uncertain how to proceed.

"I'd like to hear about how it was with your sister. By the way, what was her name?" This should help him get started.

"Nancy. Well, it was mostly the pits for us, but once in a while we'd get a little extra money. You know, more than we had to have to eat."

"Mm-hmm."

"Well, anyway . . . you know, we swiped stuff. Nothing big. Just the change in a newspaper box or a cigarette machine."

He's testing me with this confession, really risking.

"I see." Neutral tone.

"This one time, we had a little extra, and we went to this stupid street carnival. Spent it all on the dumb rides. I won a screwy Kewpie doll throwing balls at milk bottles. We both were kinda drunk on just throwing around money like that. I never saw her laugh so much, and . . . I guess I never laughed so much either."

Frank goes on with little need for my help, talking in a less complaining and more sharing fashion. Today he's making a further shift. I need to go very carefully now, not push too fast, yet not let the tempo slow — if possible.

Shortly before our time is up, I find a place to recommend that Frank come into the therapy group. I'm encouraged by his gains to think the group may be right for him. On the other hand, I realize that it might drive him further away. No sure things in this work, alas.

"So you think I ought to meet your other nuts, huh?" It's actually more teasing than hostile! I think he's pleased. He's known I had a group, and I've never suggested he be in it before.

"I think it'll give you a place to try out being with people in different ways. What you've told me today about your life in the past makes it evident you didn't have much chance to experiment with relationships."

"It was all one big experiment — and mostly it was a lousy failure."

"Not totally, Frank. You're here, you're growing, and you're ready to move on to the next phase." Uh-oh, that got away from me. Too much, too much.

"What next phase? You got something you want me to do, tell me. Don't get mysterious."

"Frank, I don't want to get into a wrangle. What the next phase is is not something I know but something we'll have to find out together. The group will be a place for that."

"Yeah, well, okay, I'll give it a shot."

"More than one shot, Frank. If you come in, you're committing yourself to at least six sessions."

"Jeez, you've got more little rules, haven't you? Okay, okay, I gotta go now."

I thought we were going to have a skirmish. Astonishingly, he passed up that chance. Well, he's going to be an interesting addition to the group's mix.

Jim. As Frank begins to risk reducing his angry defense, I see better how essential it has been for him. He has used the only means he knew to try to preserve himself against being captured and destroyed by an unfriendly world. Only by constantly being ready to fight against whatever threatens to overpower him can he be reassured that he has any power. It's a sad, self-defeating kind of strength, though, for it is tied to the other — whomever or whatever that other may be. It is never truly free and self-owning. The person who relies on anger for safety very likely suspects, even if not consciously, how bound to the object of the rage he is. Thus he continually redoubles his fury in the vain hope of breaking free.

Using anger as a defense, as a way of life, is a terribly

vulnerable path, usually impelled by a conviction of ultimate weakness. For any of us, anger is the emotion triggered when we feel we have been made helpless, have had choice — and, therefore, power — taken from us. The more completely we feel powerless, the greater our rage. The person who feels totally impotent is the one likely to commit terrible, senseless acts of violence, such as a random killing rampage.

Frank was so fearful of the power others might have over him that he tried to wall himself off from them. Frank has needed not to please as strongly as Louise needs to please. I have a grudging admiration for the perverse skill Frank has in countering anything that is directed his way. Of course, Frank is very lonely in the tight little one-passenger life he has constructed for himself. He has stocked it with books and ideas and has tried to subsist on the company of distant authors. But ideas have a way of growing and escaping the bounds individuals (or governments) try to put around them. Because of his reading Frank came to therapy and to a new and wider living. Now he is risking emerging even more. Of course, he feels in danger.

Recognizing how his life has been prompts me to appreciate the guts and determination of this man. He has somehow kept alive a small flame of hope; he reads endlessly and ponders, alone, on philosophy, psychology, ethics, and religion. He reads, at first barely understanding, then more reading and his understanding grows, and still more reading and he is truly thinking.

Group Psychotherapy. Not surprisingly, Frank is the last to arrive at the group. The group knows only that a new member will be coming, so talk is desultory as they wait for him to arrive. How sadly typical that Frank makes it more difficult for himself by being late! When he arrives, I see he's doubled his disadvantage. He has chosen to be even more ill-kempt than usual. I suspect he needed to go to the other extreme from making himself "presentable," to announce by his appearance that he doesn't give a damn what anybody thinks about him — which is to say that he cares so much that he can't risk being seen to care at all.

Additionally, Frank's features are locked in a surly expression. When Hal sees Frank, his own expression makes a grim complement to the younger man's. Storm warnings!

If Frank notices Hal's reaction, he gives no obvious cue. He nods rather curtly in response to introductions and, with evident difficulty, says his own name. Then he pulls his chair back a bit from the group's circle and slouches in it with elaborate casualness. As the group begins talking, he follows the conversational flow with apparent intensity of attention, turning his head continually to stare at each person who speaks. I feel as though he's putting on a performance rather than actually listening. I suspect Frank is so panicky inside that he can scarcely hear clearly, and I resolve not to press him unless he shows some signs of being ready to be helped into more active participation.

The group, sensing his discomfort, and perhaps put off by his angry visage, has been making no efforts to involve Frank for well over a half-hour. Then, during a pause, Louise turns to him.

Louise: "Have you been in therapy long, Frank?"

Frank: "No, I mean, yes. I. . . . What the fuck's 'long'? I started about seven or eight months ago. What's it to you anyway?"

Louise: "Oh, nothing. Just curious. I've been coming for about a year."

Kate: "You sound mad at her, Frank. Are you?"

Frank: Troubled, frightened, and thus angry. "No, why should I be? Anyway, why make a federal case out of everything? Christ!"

Kate: "Now you sound angry with me."

Frank looks into a distant corner of the room, his face portraying bafflement at these strange creatures with whom I have put him. Hal watches him intently. There's an awkward pause which Ben ends.

Ben: "You just sound pretty snotty to me."

Frank whirls, looks at the other man: "Who asked you?"

Ben: "No one has to ask me. I just think you're a sourball to anyone who talks to you, so I might as well get on your shit list right away."

Frank: "Big deal." His eyes go back to his corner.

Kate: "Frank, you do seem ready to be angry at every-one. Is there some reason for that? I'm often angry myself, but I don't show it. But it makes me feel sympathy for anyone else who has those feelings."

Frank: "Who needs your pity?"

Ben: "Hey, you forgot to cuss her, tough guy."

Frank (to no one in particular): "What a creep!"

Kate: "We all seem to annoy you, don't we?"

Ben: "He's just a big ball of anger, this boy."

Louise; "Ben, why do you pick on him so much?"

Ben: "Aw, Louise, you're such a bleeding heart. Can't you see he's just one of those drifters who give the counterculture a bad name? He just substitutes nastiness for really taking a stand against all the things that are fucked up in our world. I've seen a lot of his type, and they're not worth our sympathy."

Frank turns to look at Ben, obviously sizing him up. I have a hunch he's being goaded toward some kind of showdown, and I'm about to intervene when Hal, who has said nothing to this point, bursts out.

Hal: "For crying out loud, Ben, and the rest of you! Can't you see that this guy's scared stiff? Weren't we all scared when we first came into the group? I sure as hell was. Why do we have to demand that he play our game right away?"

I'm dumbfounded. I thought Hal was seeing his son in Frank and would join the attack. Instead, he seems to have recognized the scared kid under the blustery exterior. His effect on the group is instantaneous.

Louise: "You're right, Hal. Frank, I'm sorry we were nee-dling you."

Frank: "Yeah, well, you didn't. . . . And besides, oh hell, I don't. . . ."

Ben: "Okay, so he's scared. So were we all, but we didn't talk so foul-mouthed and mean to everyone. (Turning to Frank) Look, Frank, I don't like people who don't wash and who talk the way you do all the time. I won't pretend I do, but I do ad-mit that I came off pretty sudden on you."

Frank: "Don't do me any favors, jerk."

Ben: "Watch it, buster, I don't take cute talk from punks."

Hal: "Stop it, you two. Look, Frank, I know you're scared, but try to idle back on the cracks, will you? And you, Ben, we're here to try to use the group to deal with our hang-ups — not to act them out. If the two of you punch each other around, you'll only prevent yourselves and us from using the group for the reason we're here. Now talk all you want, but quit acting like a couple of twelve-year-olds playing chicken with each other."

Hal's good sense — plus, probably, his size — seems to persuade Ben and Frank to cool their antagonism. Both make pro forma growls, but they readily let others in the group take over the conversation. I speculate to myself whether some more direct working-through of the hostility would have been more helpful, and decide Frank just isn't ready for that yet. Ben is so judgmental that he needs help in recognizing the self-deception hidden in his self-righteousness, but now is not the time for that either. I feel a combination of chagrin and relief — chagrin at the neat way Hal handled the situation without any need of my intervention, and relief that I didn't have to move in authoritatively. For the therapist to do so nearly always means that the group overgeneralizes about his intent, with the result that members are hesitant to confront each other for some time after.

Tuesday, October 18

Louise. "I keep thinking of Cynthia, a student I counseled yesterday." Louise is getting settled on the couch with practiced familiarity that contrasts with her first tentative and self-conscious trips on that strange conveyance. "I want to tell you about her, and at the same time I don't want to even think about her, let alone bring the whole thing up." She adjusts her pillow and smooths her modest skirt carefully over her legs. (Lately, I have the feeling the skirts are shorter than they used to be, but I'm not sure.)

"You're pulled to talk about her and at the same time to cover up what she stirs up in you?"

She wriggles around, trying to get comfortable, but it's as though her body won't relax today. Again she adjusts her skirt, half rises on one elbow, and kicks off her shoes. "Yes, I just don't know whether it's worth using up our time on what is not really something in my own life." She lies back as she speaks and then goes through the whole routine of getting settled again. "It's probably not important."

"All your trouble getting settled and your ambivalence about talking suggest that maybe it is about something in your life. Better take a look."

"Oh, I'm all right now," she smiles (politely?), as she adjusts herself yet again. "I had a dream last night that I was sure I'd remember because it was so vivid. It woke me up, and I went over it in my mind so I would remember it. But it's totally gone now."

"Louise, you're still restless, and you've just changed the subject. I think you'd better pause a minute, listen inside, and find out what's going on in you right now."

She quiets, shuts her eyes, and is silent briefly. "I guess I know what's going on, but I. . . . Well, I just find it uncomfortable . . . embarrassing to talk about."

"Mm-hmm."

"Cynthia had a little adventure with a medical student, and she told me about it, and it's . . . it's the thoughts that I find I'm thinking about it, and. . . . " She pauses, waiting (I think) for me; so I wait also.

"Yes. Well, Cynthia and this boy — young man, really — have been going together and the other day he asked her to come to his apartment (pause, deep breath). Then he asked her to pose for him — he's an amateur photographer. She liked that, but when he wanted her to . . . to take off her clothes, she was uneasy, but. . . . Well, anyway (speaking quickly now), she did, and then after a while they made love." She stops, waiting again.

"Mm-hmm. And what happens in you right now?"

"Nothing (pause). I was just thinking of Cynthia's little incident. I mean . . . I mean, I'd rather not say." Again she waits.

"Mm-hmm. Want to just drop it and run, huh?"

"If I could, yes (pause). But you won't let me, I know."

"You'll only work with what's stirred up in you, because I insist. Is that what you're saying?"

"Oh, damn. No! I know I need to work with it. It's just that I'm embarrassed, and don't you say 'hmmm-mm' to me that way one more time!"

I'm mightily tempted to say "hmm-mm" right now, but that will take us in other directions. "Your being cute and playful is a way of distracting us also."

"Ugh!" She's silent, once again adjusts her position and her clothes. "I suppose so. Anyway, Cynthia's little story kind of stirred up a lot of . . . a lot of sexy feelings in me. So there, are you satisfied now?"

"Are you?"

"No! I'm acting like a shy, virginal spinster, and I'm not! I'm not virginal, anyway. I told you about my affair with Ralph; so I don't know why I'm so uneasy with these feelings. It just doesn't make sense."

"Are you going to bawl yourself out so you don't really have to deal with those feelings?"

"Ohhh! I don't like it that Cynthia's little incident upsets me so much."

"It isn't Cynthia's 'little incident' — as you keep calling it — that upsets you. It's Louise's feelings and thoughts."

"Jim, they really do make me uncomfortable, and I wish they didn't. I'd like to be more grown up. Like Kitty was in the group. When the group talked about sex, she could join in and talk about herself so . . . so easily, it seemed. And I just sat there tongue-tied."

"Talking about what happened some months ago in the group is easier than talking about what is happening in Louise today."

"Well, all right!" She pauses, once again tugs at her skirt, adjusts her blouse. "Cynthia took off her clothes and posed for him, and then he began touching her, and — . You know, I just realized what I was doing. I was going to tell you about Cynthia; so I wouldn't really get into those feelings here. But it wasn't working. Oh, damn."

"It's so frightening to have your feelings right here and now. You keep trying to avoid them every way you can."

"Yes, yes, I do." She's close to tears. "I want to try though."

The courage she and others have to face their own demons! it always gets to me.

"Go slow, but try to be with whatever you find inside." I didn't really need to say that, but I wanted to support her.

"Cynthia . . . Cynthia said. . . . "

"Tell me about Louise, not Cynthia."

"Louise hasn't had anyone touch her—but herself—for so long (sadly). I'm so hungry for that closeness, and I wonder if I'll ever have it again." She is quiet, tears sliding down her cheeks.

"So hungry . . . will it ever be again?" (soft voice).

"Yes. It was so good when Ralph and I held each other." Her left hand plays with the buttons of her blouse. "Just to lie together without any clothes on. Just to feel our closeness." She sounds dreamy, recalling. Her hand moves from button to button, touching and fingering each.

"It was so good. . . . " At thirty-seven, Louise talks about herself as though her days of romantic possibilities are over. But she is far from the gray old lady that she portrays.

"Yes, and though I touch myself . . . masturbate, there!" She's saying the hard word, she wants me to know. "Though I masturbate sometimes, it's not the same. Oh, it's nothing like the same." Her hand is now pushing a button part of the way through the buttonhole and then pulling it out again.

"You long for someone to be with you."

"Yes, oh, yes (pause). That's what is hard to say . . . hard to know. After Cynthia talked to me, I kept wanting to just let go and imagine myself in Cynthia's place, and maybe touch myself, but I was afraid. I kept telling myself, 'You'll have to tell Jim everything you think and do, so be careful.' And I guess I'm still being careful." A small, rueful laugh.

We wait quietly, but I can sense much tension in her. Her hand has actually unbuttoned the top button of her blouse, and now it refastens it.

"Can you let those thoughts come through now, Louise? Just as you wanted to do?"

"Oh, I don't think . . . don't know whether. . . . It would be so . . . so . . . so naked. That's the feeling. It would be like being naked in front of you."

"Would that be a bad feeling?"

"Oh! Oh, my, you are making it difficult, aren't you?"
She hesitates. Her hand leaves her blouse, starts to adjust her
skirt, stops. "No, and yes. I mean, mostly yes . . . I think. It
sounds nice . . . and it sounds very frightening."

"Your left hand has been trying to unbutton your blouse
most of the hour today." As I say that, the hand has indeed
returned to its work and pushed a button half through the hole.
At my words, it freezes. Louise lies very still. I wait. She seems
to be holding her breath.

"I . . . I don't know. . . . "

"Louise, you were trained — as I was and as most of us
were — to see your body and the feelings and wantings connected
to it as in some way shameful, dirty, bad. Though that training was well-intended, it has cost us many hours of shame, misery, and frustration. To disregard any limits on how we use
our bodies, as some are urging these days, is as wrong as blindly
following the old teachings. Right at this moment, you're facing this issue." What a speech! I wanted to help her get perspective, but I think I may have helped her distance from her
feelings. Damn! Now can I help her get back to them?

She has listened silently, unmoving. Now she stirs very
cautiously. "Yes, I can feel how I keep from letting go here,
how I'm afraid you'll be Mrs. Colten, how I'm avoiding feeling
warm. Oh, damn it, I'm no child: I'm avoiding getting hot . . .
horny — oh, I've never said that word before. I want to discuss
all this academically with you (pause), and I know that doesn't
work."

"Unbutton your blouse, Louise." Inwardly, I gulp, and
a part of me shouts in astonishment, "What the hell are you
doing, Bugental? Do you want to get hauled before the ethics
committee or a court or something?" I stop these thoughts, push
all that aside, and try to keep focused on this moment. This
is high-stakes poker, but being proper now would be a cop-out
on Louise and on myself.

She has not spoken. She is lying very still, hand unmoving
as she wrestles inwardly. Then her hands come to her blouse and
slowly, deliberately undo the first one, pause, then the second,
another pause, and they move to the third and stop. "All of them?"

"It's your blouse, your hands, and your life. You know what we're trying to do." I wait.

The two remaining buttons are unfastened, and her hands have reached her waist. She hesitates again, and I remain silent. I imagine she's debating a further step, importantly one I haven't suggested. Is she thinking about unfastening her skirt? How far can I let her go? Uneasy feelings. Wish she'd go further. Wish she'd stop and cover up. Wish we'd never started this. Shut up!

Now Louise opens her blouse wide and puts her hands at her sides with the palms up, a movement and position that are so appealing. Her simple white bra covers her breasts more demurely than most swimsuit tops today. Still, her full breasts are very evident . . . and very attractive.

"I want to cover myself up and run out of here." Voice taut, breath shallow. "I suddenly have the awful feeling that I've failed some test you were giving me and that you never meant for me to really open my blouse this way." She's closing it as she speaks. "I'm afraid I've made myself a fool, and the nice warm feeling I had a minute ago is all gone. I'm so chilled I'm starting to shake." She is indeed trembling and crying. Her arms are wrapped around herself and her knees drawn up.

"What you've just done is very frightening to you, Louise. You've made a statement about yourself that you've feared to make before — except when you were sure the other person was so involved he couldn't stand apart and judge you. But now you're standing apart and judging yourself."

"Oh, it makes me so damn mad. I know you're not judging me, but in my head you're all the people who would be shocked if they saw what I did." The tears are still coming, but now she is beginning to take hold again.

"Tell me what's happening inside you right now." Voice tender, supportive.

"Oh, that's hard to do . . . I'm doing so many things. I'm trying to keep aware of where I am, and . . . to keep aware of why I am . . . was half-dressed in front of you. . . . Still it all keeps slipping away, and then I want to run away from here, from all this . . . or to be angry at you . . . or at me. Then it swings back and I'm angry at myself for giving in to feeling bad or ashamed. After all, I haven't done something that awful. I'm sure you've seen a woman in her brassiere before. To make such a fuss is quite ridiculous."

"You're not making a fuss about showing yourself to me in your brassiere. That's not keeping faith with yourself to say that. You're frightened by the fact you *chose* to do so, by your letting me know you feel sexy, by your violating all the taboos you were taught from your earliest years."

"Yes, that's so! And that makes me even more mad. I feel like tearing off all my clothes and dancing down the street saying 'Nuts' to the whole stupid world."

"That would show them, huh?" Then my unwitting pun hits us both and we laugh—probably more than the humor warrants, but as a release of the tension we've both been feeling.

"It's so strange how just opening my blouse could create such a storm of feelings." She opens it again, testing the feeling. "That's funny. It doesn't happen now."

"You're thinking of yourself in mechanical terms, as though opening the blouse was itself the cause of your feelings."

"Yes, of course. It's when I was risking doing something forbidden. It's just like Mrs. Colten always saying, 'Keep your skirt down. Don't sprawl and show your legs.' That seemed one of the important things that separated nice girls from bad girls, not showing our legs."

"Show me your legs, Louise." In for an ounce, in for a pound. How far you going to go, Bugental?

Instantly, on hearing my words, Louise's animation disappears. She's holding her breath. Now she takes hold of her skirt with both hands and raises it several inches. She is still poised, tense.

"They look very pretty, what I can see of them." Oh, oh, that's not the therapist talking, that's the man who wants to see more. Keep alert!

"Don't be so impatient." She's caught on to me. Now the skirt comes up slowly until most of her thighs is exposed. Then her arms come up to cross over her chest.

"Is that the right place?" Double motivation in that, I can

feel. One part is teasing, asking for more; one part is telling her to accept responsibility. I'm not convinced about the second part's reality.

"Oh, I don't know!" She's annoyed, probably feeling a similar conflict. "You know as well as I do that there's no 'right place.' Why ask me such a question? I'm certainly not showing something you haven't seen before."

"That's where you're wrong."

"I know, I know. Don't tell me." She is more animated now. "What you haven't seen before is my choosing to be in myself this way, showing you not just my legs but my excitement as I do so."

"Yes, Louise, that's so."

"Jim, I'd like to take off all my clothes and show all of me to you. I don't think I can do that today, even though I'd like to. But maybe one day I will."

"I hear you, and I feel the same way."

And the hour is over.

Jim. After Louise leaves, I feel emotionally — even physically — exhausted. I realize now how tense I've been, but I didn't register it at the time. I'm still tense when I think of what I've just done. My defense counsel leaps up, "You didn't touch her. You didn't hurt her." But the prosecution says, "But you enjoyed encouraging her to open her clothes. It isn't what you saw that is your crime; it's that you enjoyed it."

The mid-sixties are times of experimentation in overthrowing cultural taboos. Typical of our time is "streaking," in which individuals of both sexes and a range of ages run naked through public places, sometimes alone, sometimes in large groups. Similarly, mixed nude swimming in pools and bathing in hot tubs is becoming frequent. Nudity on the live stage and in motion pictures is increasingly accepted.

Nor is nudity the only realm of venturing. Premarital sex is more open and commonplace all the time; homosexuality is no longer a name to be greeted with opprobrium; coeducational dormitories — and even coed bathrooms! — are being urged on campuses across the country; contraception is no longer a word to be whispered. Miniskirts approach the minimum possible if they are still to retain the name "skirt"; see-through blouses are worn without brassieres, and nude beaches have arrived.

These things go in cycles. The twenties and thirties saw a general loosening in codes about such matters; the forties and the early fifties swung toward more conservative styles, now the sixties are opening new frontiers of permissiveness. I expect future decades will swing back again. Glad I'm in this period.

Thursday, October 20

Louise. Avoiding my eyes as she enters, Louise is subdued and distant. She settles herself on the couch, still not looking at me directly; then she lies silently.

"What are you thinking?" My tone is neutral.

"Nothing. I mean, I'd rather not say."

"Can you say what makes you hesitate to tell me?"

"I just want to get on to something important and not waste time on trivialities. I think I should talk with you about whether I'm going to go back to graduate school or continue working at the agency. It's getting close to time to apply for admission, if I'm going to do it. I've been thinking that I might be able to get some kind of fellowship or assistantship. Dr. Clifton would give me a strong recommendation, I'm pretty sure, and. . . . " She pauses, seeming to lose momentum. I say nothing, and in a minute she starts again.

"I mean, I think that at my age I ought to finish going to school. If I went to UCLA, I could probably get a doctorate in social work in about two years, maybe three. Then I'd be in a good position to teach someplace or maybe get to be the head of an agency, one of the smaller ones, and. . . . " Again she pauses. She is clearly pushing herself to keep talking, but she seems to have little enthusiasm for the topic. Still, I keep silent.

"I'm just not sure I want to spend two or three years at it, even though it's really worthwhile." She grinds to a stop.

"Louise." Quietly. She tenses as soon as she hears my voice. "Tell me what happened the last time you were here."

"Oh, that was silly. Let's not waste time. I do need your help to decide. If I get accepted in another city, will I be ready to leave therapy in September?"

"You are very anxious to keep our attention away from what happened last time. You're trying to push yourself and me into this other matter, even though you have a hard time concentrating on it." Insistently, slight challenge.

"I don't want to talk about it. I behaved in a very silly fashion, as you well know. And you were certainly letting us get away from our concerns here too. So let's just. . . . "

I cut in sharply, "We did not get away from our concerns here. That's what you're trying to do today." I'm peeved with her for denying what we shared, and I recognize that I'm also a bit guilty for my enjoyment of her. Thus I'm anxious to prove that what we did is not a violation of her trust in me.

"I really do have to make some decision about graduate school, Jim; no matter what you say and no matter what happened the other day. So please help me pay attention to what's really important today."

"Louise, when you appeal to me that way, I'm moved to go along with you. But when you say you want to pay attention to 'what's really important,' I know that is your feeling about our last session and not the nice, safe topic of whether or not you will go to graduate school next fall."

Suddenly, I am aware that she is crying quietly, making no immediate response. I feel a wave of tenderness and then a pang that our experiment with sexiness set her back. Even as I think this, I know it's not so, but again my guilt for enjoyment is displayed to me. (I must work this through further, especially if I am ever to encourage anyone else to violate taboos in ways that are also gratifying to me. Something in me reacts with shock! Do I plan to do *that* again?)

"I don't know what you want me to say about last time." She is still crying quietly, but it is evident that she trusts my interpretation and is trying to go along with me. I feel warmed by her confidence and silently resolve that I'll never let her down. And I realize I can let her down either by being too risky or by being too conservative.

"Why don't you just tell me what happened during our last time together?"

"I'll try. I told you about how Cynthia's romantic, sexual experience had aroused me. Then we noticed that I was restless with my clothes and so we . . . and so I. . . . You suggested that I. . . . Well, you know what happened. Why do I have to say it?"

"Louise, you can feel right now how very hard it is for you to talk about what happened here. That is a simple fact. And that simple fact points to the conflict within you. And that conflict is what we need to bring out more — right now, while it's raging inside of you."

"Well, I'm embarrassed, I guess, and kind of ashamed, and. . . . "

"And?"

"Well, I don't ordinarily go around opening my clothes and showing off my body to men."

"What's that got to do with anything?" Voice sharp again.

"Oh, I don't know. I'm just kind of upset, I guess."

"And you're angry with me a bit, but somehow hesitate to say that too."

"Well, yes, but I really have no good reason to be angry with you. You didn't make me do anything. I did it. You didn't do anything to me."

"I suggested you unbutton your blouse and lift your skirt."

"Oh, I know. But you. . . . "

"Louise, you're acting as though we committed a great crime here the other day, and now you're being noble and taking the blame."

"Oh, I know. I know I'm being very silly. That's why I didn't want to even talk about it."

"Damn it! Louise! You persist in treating your emotional response to our experience as a triviality to be gotten past as quickly as possible. It's so clear that you have a strong reaction that is interfering with your work here. That's no triviality."

Abruptly, she sighs heavily. "I'm sorry, Jim. No, I'm not! I mean, it's a great relief to have you say that. I guess I thought you'd be disgusted with me, that you hadn't really meant for me to do what I did but were just testing me, and so. . . . "

"Louise, you double-crossed yourself and you expected me to do so too. You also know that we experienced real closeness and did some important therapeutic work here Tuesday. Yet you so fear to trust your own knowing that you deny it."

"Yes," she weeps softly. "Yes, I do double-cross myself (growing angry), and I do it again and again. If I think someone might be displeased or find fault with me, I jump over on their side against myself. It makes me so mad to see how I do that."

Louise works well for the rest of the session, reviewing her shame and fear around her own sexuality, recognizing how much she still lets the narrow morality of her foster parents control her, and then returning to her yearning for love — and, somewhat hesitantly, sexual relations. The recurring theme is how she learned she was most apt to please others when she closed off awareness inwardly of her own needs and wantings.

As she leaves, Louise gives me a quick hug at the door, something she has done before but not with the hint of sensuality that I think I detect this time.

Jim. In our Western, basically middle-class, religiously based morality and value system, we accord the erotic a unique place. Although we are not apt to make it explicit, still we show that we regard it as having special — perhaps even magical — power and significance. And I think we are right to do so.

That instinct and magnetic pull that links us to the divine function of creating life is not like any other in its power to affect our lives, our relationships, our self-esteem, our uses of our powers. In our culture, we fear this power, knowing it can overthrow high intentions and inspire low acts. Out of this fear we seek to imprison the erotic, to force it into the straight-jacket of convention, and to limit it to a tightly fenced compound. That the erotic continually escapes these limits should surprise no one.

Indeed, it doesn't really surprise as many as pretend to be shocked. Our public, explicit standards demand a verbal and performance allegiance, regardless of our private policy and, at times, of the costs in misery and frustration. Yet we know no other way to handle this explosive potential.

Working this way with Louise is like walking a tightrope. I am balancing between her therapeutic needs and our sexual responses to each other; between what is acceptable socially and ethically and what is needed therapeutically; between using her need to please through ready compliance and the opportunity to turn that need to account by showing her its effects in distorting the reality of what we went through with its consequences for our work.

And I'm resigned to not being able to carry off this task without slips. Those slips could be near fatal — literally and figuratively, in terms of our therapeutic goals. But they have been only minor so far, and I'm determined that they will not be more than that — for Louise's sake and for mine. Happily those are not opposed considerations.

The question recurs in my thoughts at all sorts of odd moments these days — when I'm driving someplace, as I go to sleep, while I'm waiting for someone or something — what are the appropriate limits of therapeutic actions? What is definitely out of bounds? Paul Bindrim, about whose work I know very little, has been conducting nude psychotherapy, usually in groups. He is very strict about banning overt sexual actions, but encourages participants to get their fill of showing their bodies and seeing other bodies. I don't think I'm ready to do that with my groups. Why not?

What are my limits? Would I have sexual intercourse with Louise if I felt it really appropriate to her needs? Umph! That's the $64,000 question for sure. Would I hit her? Hard? Knock her out? Would I risk my own career? Would I take her home to help her? A thousand more questions such as these. Then the realization comes: If I'm truly honest with myself, I can't answer them, any of them, in the abstract.

Wow! That's scary. I mean literally frightening. It would be so much more comfortable, less disturbing, to have some predetermined limits. Well, I wouldn't kill her. Great! That's not much help. Then another voice inside me: There are many deaths other than the ultimate, physical one. If I don't help her really claim her life, that's killing her. No! Not true. If I don't help her really claim her life, I might — at most — be letting her kill herself.

Ah, but this "killing" stuff is all playing with words, using melodrama to make a point, isn't it? Is it?

What about the personal and subtle drama of all this? Some part of my impulse here takes satisfaction in the image of the lonely, courageous contender with society's constrictions and against the killing of possibility. Well! That takes care of the matter.

No, it doesn't. A human life is much more than a physical span of existence. Louise is living a partial life — a hollow life, to use her own word. Much that is truly Louise is in a suspended state and will be, for all intents and purposes, dead if she is unable to breathe life into those parts of herself. She has enlisted my help in doing that. Where shall I draw the line in fulfilling this trust?

Now, in the sixties, we are seeing many challenges to the established codes of the way it's always been done, of what is right and proper, of good taste, of "appropriate" conduct. There is no doubt the reaction against these folkways and mores overcarries in many instances. Such is the way of change; it takes so much energy to break out of the past that once we push through we are carried past our original mark.

Have I overcarried with Louise? No doubt many would say so. I hope I'm right in insisting that I have not.

Nine

"I Felt Motherly!"

Thursday, October 27

Kate. The hint of smoke in the air as I drove in this morning has such contradictory associations. First, it is threatening. Five years ago, fire in our hills destroyed more than six hundred homes around mine, which suffered a lot of smoke damage. Is that what I smell? But then the aroma of burning leaves brings back my Middle West boyhood delight of running and jumping into piles of leaves, of burrowing in them and being completely (we thought) covered, and of the delicious perfume of their burning.

"Hello, Kate." I motion her into the office ahead of me.

"Good morning, Jim." She says my name a bit awkwardly as she enters with a market bag held with her purse and deposits both beside her chair. Then, without any of the preliminaries typical with most clients, she speaks with a businesslike tone.

"You have told me that I need to discover what emotionally matters to me, and. . . . "

I nod, curious what this prelude will bring. She seems to be more present today, a hopeful sign indeed.

"Well, I thought about that a lot after we talked last time, and I realized I've never told you about my work. It is really quite interesting — although perhaps not so much so for someone not in the field?"

She's asking my permission. Shall I call her attention to that? No, that would pull us away from what she's taken thought to bring to our work. I want to be receptive to that, and I hope it's something I can understand enough not to distract us by my ignorance.

"I'd like to know about what interests you, Kate."

"Yes." She's pleased, but she barely lets that show. "Yes, well, I've been working on the properties of carotene. You know, these isomeric red hydrocarbons are in a lot of our foods, especially in carrots, and. . . ."

Kate continues for several minutes, describing her work. Much of what she says is beyond my understanding; although she is making a determined effort to put things so I will understand. Usually I would interrupt a client who talked about matters so removed from her inner experience; but I can see that, though the words are abstract, Kate is really trying to share something important to her.

After several minutes, she pauses, and I realize she is embarrassed. "I hope I'm not boring you. I forget sometimes how specialized is the work we're doing, even though it has a lot to do with foods everyone eats." Her hand goes to touch her purse and the market sack.

"I didn't understand it all, Kate, but I think I have the general idea. I can see why this is such an interesting project. And I really liked your sharing it with me."

"Yes, hmmm." She's weighing this, not sure how to respond. She glances at her purse and the bag beside it, then looks up. "Well, as I said, carotene has many values. I just don't understand why people don't eat more carrots and other red and yellow vegetables. It is really important to vision, and—"

"I want to interrupt to ask a question."

"Yes?"

"I notice that several times you've touched your things there on the floor. Is there something about them that is concerning you?"

"Oh, I didn't realize—." She stops, embarrassed.

"Can you tell me about it?"

"Well, really it's unimportant, I had just thought. . . . I stopped on the way here to. . . ."

"It's hard to say what you want to say." Voice careful, uninflected, open.

"Yes, and of course that's silly of me." She shifts in the chair, takes a breath. "I picked up several bunches of the kind of carrots that are especially rich in the nutrients I was telling you about, and. . . . "

"Uh-huh?"

She grimaces slightly. "And I thought you might like to have them." It comes out in a rush.

"Kate, that's very thoughtful of you. Yes, of course, I will like to have them. Thank you."

She smiles a cautious little smile, reaches down, and passes the bag to me in such a way that her hand is letting go almost as soon as I take hold. She seems to fear that we might both hold it at the same time.

What a daring step for Kate to take, and how much it expresses the growth of a bond between us — a bond that she still would surely deny and flee from if it were to be made explicit.

The rest of the hour passes quickly as we work together in our separate ways. Kate fears the dawning involvement that is intrinsic to our efforts, rightly sensing it will open up new parts of her life, something she has long avoided. Her security has always seemed to lie in keeping each aspect of her life closed, final, requiring no further changes.

Jim. Today's session with Kate is typical of where she is in her therapy: She cautiously acknowledges that her emotions and other parts of her inner life must be influential in how she is living and how she works professionally. But having conceded that much, she is determined not to cede any more territory to what she has long regarded as her enemy within. Thus she will discipline herself to tell me about feelings that she has about external matters, carrots and research — the further from this room the better — but she resolutely suppresses any emotional promptings that may arise and be directed toward me.

Kate is a mountain hiker unexpectedly finding her route takes her along the face of a sheer cliff, the path agonizingly narrow, the yawning chasm continually clutching at her feet. She inches along, clinging to the reassuring wall even though it hurts her hands and projects outward in a horrifying way from time to time. Still she keeps going, hoping for some wider place in the path where she can rest; but repeatedly finding the space too narrow, so that she must keep moving one foot and then another. She knows how heavy is the pack of avoidances she carries, and how their continually increasing weight pulls her toward collapse. Yet she cannot risk letting go.

Still she continues on the path! That is the wonder of Kate's courage. She truly dreads the task she now realizes she has undertaken by entering this kind of therapy. She is continually beset by yearnings to give it up. Yet she continues!

Kate has tried to be safe in life by finding the solid stopping place of a fixed way of being. She earned the highest academic degree our culture offers in a field that is immensely demanding, but one in which there is the prospect of reducing all pertinent phenomena to factual terms. She has never had any romantic relations, since they threaten disruptions. Her brief marriage was intended to be a "sensible arrangement" rather than a love match. She has few friends, mostly fellow professionals, and she spends much of her non-working time in reading—either professional literature or nineteenth-century novels celebrating the orderly Victorian life.

"Change" is not a welcome word to Kate. "Unpredictability" ranks with the four-letter epithets she never would consider using. "Ambiguity" is a sin against knowledge, and "incompleteness" a moral failing. Kate wants to feel that she has found a way of being which will last her out the rest of her life. When she has thought she found components of such finality, she elevated them to near sacred status.

Kate is frightened, close to panic, wanting to give up the whole terrifying enterprise of therapy; but Kate is also persisting, trying to do the dreaded things, facing up to her lifelong fears. Gradually, she is winning through to a plateau with more space and less imminent threat of disaster.

I'm impressed with how she keeps going, how so many of my clients keep going straight through the center of their personal hells to try to claim more of the richness sleeping within them.

What courage! What courage we all have. Come on, let's say it: What a magnificent species is the human!

Does that make your flesh crawl? Is that maudlin? Soupy? New wavey? Dumb? Untrue? Superficial?

Or is it true, but only a partial truth?

It's not fashionable in these times to celebrate ourselves and our potential. That was Victorian, provincial, and certainly verges on being racist — since for far too many humans, their condition is anything but *magnificent*. It's almost obscene to use such a word for a species that permits such degradation of its own members.

But perhaps our unwillingness to claim our achievement is the other side of the coin of suppressing knowledge of our failure. Pascal says someplace, "It is dangerous to show man too often that he is equal to beasts, without showing him his greatness. It is also dangerous to show him too frequently his greatness without his baseness. It is yet more dangerous to leave him ignorant of both. But it is very desirable to show him the two together."

Why should we not be proud that we have sent our space vehicles to land on the moon and will soon have humans there, discovered the secret of DNA, produced Beethoven, Mozart, Mahler, Martin Luther King, Einstein, Schweitzer, Byron, Yeats, and a list that can go on and on?

If we claim that right, then perhaps we'll be a step closer to picking up our responsibility for Ethiopia, Hiroshima, Auschwitz, Duvalier, Lee Harvey Oswald, the extermination of so many species, and all that breeds our despair.

After seeing Kate, I am swept with strong feelings. How the current vogue of cynicism about our human nature becomes a self-fulfilling prophecy! Occasionally, a session fills me with a kind of holy fury, an urge to stand on street corners or mountaintops and shout like an Old Testament doom-sayer.

The book I wrote last year says some of it; but I still haven't put the message over strongly enough, loudly enough, to reach enough people. Damn it, human lives are being lost by our culturally sanctioned, crippling view of ourselves.

My shouted message has various themes, but there is a single underlying message: *We don't know who we are.* We don't appreciate what we can do. We're messing things up for ourselves and each other and for our beautiful world because we don't know.

So how come I think I'm the one who really knows who we are? A bit inflated there, Bugental? On a Messiah kick? Maybe, but I don't think so — principally, because I don't find how to get my message across. (Messiahs have that problem too.) Oh.

The bottom line is Paul Tillich's: "Man resists objectification, and if man's resistance is broken, man himself is broken." We are unaware, we do not know. We are blind and deaf to our own nature. Like the broken and bound feet of Chinese women in an earlier time, our blindness and deafness are deformities much in style in this century.

Trying to have more aliveness and less deathfulness while yet we are alive is what it's all about. But we are handicapped in this effort because we have had too shrunken and paltry a view of our potential, and we have not known how to claim the life that is our birthright. Seeing ourselves as objects, as impotent midgets in a world of gigantic forces, pushed heedlessly by powers from the outside, and driven by blind forces within ourselves, we've learned to disregard our own inner living and so lost connection with the real sources of our aliveness.

We make ourselves objects. Objects have no intrinsic power, no intrinsic values, no intrinsic purposes. Power, values, purposes are applied to objects, not discovered in them. This is no big news.

The big news is that *we* are the ones who bring power, values, and purposes to objects. Power, values, and purposes are human attributes. Why the hell do we try to pretend it isn't so?

Answer: Because we don't know what to do with how many billion units of power-value-purpose running loose at the same time.

So what we do is pretend each of those human units is

an object and only a few are entitled to use power, value, purpose.

(You know any better way?)

No, dammit, I don't. But we sure better be looking for one. It's more important than any of the other "world macro-problems" that make the headlines.

Group Psychotherapy. Frank's fourth group session is the first in which he takes any real part in the discussion.

Kate: "Frank, you haven't said very much since you've been with us. In fact, I know almost nothing about you."

Louise: "Yes, that's right. I've been watching you, and I realize I don't have much of an idea what goes on in you. I get kind of shy and self-conscious the way you look at me — at us — but I can't decide whether you think we're freaks or what."

Frank: "Aw no, I don't think that. I mean, I just don't have anything to say. I just kind of listen, you know. It's all kind of new to me, see, and when I. . . . " He stops, uncomfortable, not knowing what to say.

Kate: "Frank, I wasn't trying to put pressure on you. I just would like to know more about you — if you want to say something, that is."

Frank: "Yeah, I dig. What do you want to know?" Surly tone.

Louise: "You sound like you're angry with Kate."

Frank: "Hell, why should I be angry with her?"

Kate: "I don't know, but it does sound like you're angry with me. Are you?"

Frank: "Oh, for Christ's sake, you keep pushing me, and, of course, I get teed off. Aw, I'm sorry, I shouldn't have said that."

Louise: "You don't have to apologize if you feel that way. I don't think Kate meant to push you, though."

Kate: "Don't worry about it. I know how it is to be angry inside and to have it spill out."

Frank: "I just feel lousy all the time, and I probably shouldn't even try to be with people and. . . . " Again he runs out of words, embarrassed by his self-disclosure.

Hal: "How do you mean, you feel lousy — physically or
emotionally?"
Frank: "Uh, I dunno. Both, I guess. Why?"
Hal: "I just wondered."

I feel a heightened alertness as I listen to Frank take his
first hesitant, stumbling steps toward relating to others without
relying on his anger to shield himself. I know I have to watch
a tendency to be overprotective at this point, but he seems so
vulnerable — that he could easily be frightened back into rejecting all possibility of being with people in any mutual way.

Friday, November 11

Louise. "I thought that after we talked several times I'd let go
of that session where we experimented with . . . with my opening my clothes." Uncomfortably, Louise looks for encouragement. I'm quiet.
"But, well, it keeps coming back in my thoughts (pause).
You know, I'd rather not talk about this, and you're not mak-
ing it any easier by being the strong, silent one."
"You want help so you can talk about what concerns you?"
"No, dammit, I don't want you to do anything for me!"
The words hurtle out of her, seeming to surprise her as much
as me. "Oh, uh, I mean. . . . (pause, swallow) I mean *that*. Well,
not 'anything,' but not that."
"What do? . . . " I stop myself from asking a question that
would help her. Now, by stopping, I've muddied the waters.
Damn.
"You just be quiet and . . . listen." She sits up, looks at
me squarely. "I keep thinking about when I opened my clothes.
I . . . uh . . . I liked doing that. I'd like to take off all my clothes
with you . . . uh, in front of you. I'm not about to do it, but
I want to say it right out that I liked doing it and remembering
doing it. That's all. Now you can talk."
"You're doing your job. I don't need to add anything."

Friday, November 18

Kate. Gray clouds and hazy sunshine compete for the day but cooperate to reduce L.A.'s notorious smog. The restless wind always makes me feel vaguely uneasy, and I think it affects the patients' moods, but maybe I just project that on them. Gotta keep alert to that possibility.

As Kate comes in with her face tightly set, I nod to myself. Just what I was thinking. Well, maybe so; but go slow; maybe is not surely.

"I want to . . . I need to talk to you about something that happened yesterday," she says, as she sits in her usual position on the end of the couch, as far away from me as she can get. Lately, I think, she has sometimes moved closer to the center. She's never lain down; although several times I've suggested it. Clearly, she can't risk the intimacy and possible loss of conscious control that lying down would signify — and that would be one of its benefits.

"Kate, I'd like to hear whatever you need to talk about, but it is most useful when you talk about what you are discovering in yourself right here as much as possible."

"Yes, I know. However, what I am trying to tell you about is influencing what I'm experiencing 'right here.' *Yesterday,"* her firm tone announces she plans to continue, "I had to go to the children's ward at County Hospital to compile some data we need. I was working in a nurses' station, going through charts, when a child in a wheelchair came up and began talking to me."

"Mm-hmm."

"You must understand that I generally do not like children, and I suppose I might as well admit that I'm usually uncomfortable around them. When this little girl came into the station in her wheelchair, my first thought was one of annoyance. I had much to do, and I didn't want to be interrupted. Oh, I suppose I sound like a witch in a Walt Disney story, but I really don't think children are all that delightful and interesting. Generally, their minds are undeveloped; they are only interested in their own worlds; and they are often inconsiderate

and messy. I don't usually go on like this, but you must understand this about me to realize what an unusual experience this
was."

"Kate, you sound as though you are giving a speech about
some strange creature you had dissected, rather than talking
about your own experience."

"You are always telling me things like that, and I suppose that is what you think you should do, but I can't see what
help it is supposed to be to me. Anyway, I don't want to get
distracted now." She moves ahead, coolly pushing aside my in-
trusions. "I was telling you about this child, and. . . . "

"I don't want to hear about the child. I want to hear about
your experience," I cut in. I'm challenged. Come on, Bugental, face it.

"Yes, yes, of course. I'm telling you about my experience
as best I can under the circumstances. And now will you listen
to me, please?" Kate's acerbic manner is not unusual for her,
but today it seems to have some additional edge.

"Go on, Kate." Conceding. I am challenged, I know, and
tempted to press the point, but to do so would be more for my
need than for hers.

"Well, this child — her name was Tanya, a ridiculous name
for a nine-year-old — somehow engaged me in conversation. And
do you know, I was really quite enchanted! I found her simply
charming and very intelligent. In no time at all I was explaining to her about our research program — imagine explaining that
to a nine-year-old! But I do think she understood! She seemed
far beyond her years, but then that's not altogether so. . . . "
She pauses, musing. I sense a change in her mood. She seems
momentarily, incredibly, vulnerable.

"She seemed older in some ways, but then in others. . . . "
I let my voice trail off, open-ended.

"Yes, in other ways. . . . " Still engrossed in the feeling
within her. "In other ways, she seemed even younger than her
nine years. I mean, perhaps it was because she was so crippled
and so helpless. Some way I could feel her helplessness physically. And it made me feel. . . . " Suddenly, she breaks off, and
I realize with a start that she is close to tears. Kate has only

cried once or twice before, and then there was more bitterness than sorrow in her emotion. This is clearly a different Kate.

"She made you feel? . . . " softly, ever so softly.

"Oh, I don't know." The tears are near, but anger is threatening to replace them. Oh, delicately now.

"It would be easier for you to be angry now than to let your true feeling through, Kate." Voice even, no challenge.

"I felt motherly! There, I said it. Are you satisfied?" She pulls her head erect and stares defiantly at me. Looking into her hot, hurting eyes, my own steady, seeing, not pulling away.

"You still want to use anger to get away from your tender feelings." There's a subtle shift in her.

"Oh, what's the use of them anyway!" But she softens, and the tears well out of the corners of her eyes. "A lot of good it will do me now to weep about children! I'm too old. Too old, and you know it. So why take on about it?" The anger is thin; the pain shows through starkly.

"You're trying to tell yourself you are too old to have any children of your own, so why feel the grief. Is that it?" No lead now. She's with herself.

"Yes, yes." The tears are coming faster now, and the anger is weakening. "Oh, it just isn't any use doing this."

"Kate, you're doing the very thing you need to do. Quit getting in your own way." Firmly but warmly. I feel like comforting her but know that she can be frightened into total retreat by too much tenderness. A surge of feeling rises in me.

"I had the ridiculous thought that perhaps I could adopt that child! Oh, it makes me so mad to carry on this way!" Now she is sobbing.

"It's so hard for you to just be with your own feelings and not try to order them to be unemotional and reasonable." Insistently, but with understanding.

"Yes, yes. Oh dear!" She stops talking and gives herself up to her crying. I sit silently as the sobs shake her. She cries for several minutes, and then she looks up, shyly, the anger gone from her manner. In a wondering voice she says, "It feels like I had a child or children, and they are dead." My eyes are hot, filling.

"Yes, Kate, the children you would have had are dead. Just as surely as though you had had them and then lost them. And you are doing what you need to do — grieving for them." This triggers a whole new wave of sobbing, and she seems so hurting that my own hot tears can no longer be restrained. I reach for a tissue from the box she is using, and she suddenly looks up to see my weeping. This renews her crying. She has been sitting on the edge of the couch, and now I move over and sit beside her. She leans against me, an incredible action for stiff, formal Kate. I put my arm around her, and she collapses against me, crying bitterly, while tears stream down my own cheeks.

Jim. Kate has been gradually emerging from her granite cocoon for some time now, but today marks a major change. It is not that the little girl triggered long-stored pain in Kate. It is that Kate has done the hard, emotionally costly work of opening her closed life sufficiently that the child could represent for her all the lost years and never-to-be-realized mothering impulses. If she had seen the same child under the same circumstances a month or two ago, it would most likely have been only an annoying interruption.

This is an important difference and one too often overlooked by whodunit therapists. Only as the inner life of the patient is ready will any form of outer experience elicit a release of emotion or a change of perception about oneself or one's world. Using hypnosis, role-playing, Gestalt techniques, primal screaming, or any other draconian measure to force emotion before clients are internally ready usually yields only superficial relief and shallow increases in awareness. Not infrequently, the product of such assaults is greater resistance to genuine opening of the clients' inner living. Of course, truly therapeutic practitioners of each of these methods know this truth and respect it. They employ their techniques with measured patience until the clients are ready for emergence. It is only beginners and those who, for whatever reasons of their own, need to try for quick and dramatic changes that abuse the client with their heedless pressures.

Kate tried to be safe from pain and disappointment by being like granite or ice inside. In her scientific work, she was forced to recognize her reduced effectiveness. This was unacceptable to her. Thus she came to therapy to have that one part of her life repaired so that she could resume being stone and "safe." She had no wish or intention to be changed in other ways. But life is a unity, and change for isolated parts is not to be had.

So today the granite-ice is beginning to melt. I am not surprised. What does surprise me — and encourages me — is that Kate is yielding so trustingly to that change.

Jennifer. Jennifer seems tired as she comes into the office. Her costume, as always, proposes bright colors in unexpected combinations, but her spirits don't accept the invitation. Instead she sinks down on the couch, absently slips off her shoes, and lies back with a sigh. She's wearing high heels, and I notice her good legs again. Ah, the eternal delight of women!

"A big sigh," I observe.

She pulls herself together like a good student who has been found woolgathering; then, apparently reminding herself that here she doesn't have to be a good student, she slumps back. "Yes, I suppose so," tonelessly.

"'Suppose'?"

"Uh-huh (pause). 'Suppose' means I don't know what I'm feeling or what to talk about."

"And you don't sound as though you are trying to find out." There is reprimand in my voice, I realize with chagrin. How readily she invites that and how quickly I oblige!

She stirs in mild irritation, and adjusts her position on the couch to find more comfort. "I guess you're right. I am not really looking for something to talk about. I know I should, but I just don't want to. I shouldn't say that, but. . . . "

"But that's what's real right now, isn't it?"

"I suppose so."

"Still supposing, eh? Is that what you want to do now?"

"I . . . uh . . . I . . . . " She bursts into a brief laugh of genuine amusement. "I started to say, 'I suppose not.'" Again she laughs, and she seems roused from her lethargy.

"Sounds as though you were stuck in a rut."

"I was — am — no (pause). I'm not now. I guess seeing it and laughing at it helped me get out of it."

"Nice to see you more here."

She rouses herself to sit up and look at me directly. "Jim, will you tell me something honestly?" She stops, startled, then, "Oh, I didn't mean that the way it sounded. I know you'll tell me the truth, but I . . . I mean . . . I mean I want your . . . uh . . . your best opinion."

Quietly, firmly, "I'll tell you my best opinion if it feels to me the best thing to do right now, or I'll tell you honestly that I won't answer now. Until I know what it is you want to know, I can't answer better than that."

"Oh, I don't know, I—." She stops, uncertain.

"It's hard to ask the question. What's that like for you?"

"No, it's all right. I mean, I can ask it. It's just that I'm having trouble because I don't want to put you on the spot."

"Ummm."

"What I want to know is this: Do you really think you can help me? I mean, do you think I can help myself — that I can use therapy, that is? I just seem to be so stuck, and. . . ."

"It seems to you that you're not getting anywhere, huh?" She's so uncomfortable. Shall I deal with that or with her question now? Let's see where she leads us.

"Yes. I mean, no. I get so confused. I don't want to complain or anything, but it seems like I'm still right where I was when I came to you. I mean, I've been coming for five months now, and. . . . Well, not really 'nothing.' I'm sure not about to go kill Bert — or myself now. That's a big difference. And I think I understand a little bit more about how I confuse myself by being so critical. That's good, but I still do it. Well, not as much as I used to, I think. But then I can't be sure. (pause) Oh, damn it, I'm doing it right now, aren't I?" She's not amused; she's discouraged.

"It's hard to tell your mother to let you change ways you've used for so long, isn't it?"

"Yes! It's so damned hard. And yet. . . . Well! That's what I'm talking about, I want to change the ways I've been, and I'm unhappy because it's so hard, because it's taking so long."

"Mmmm."

"I suppose. . . . Oh, there's another 'suppose,' and I want to change those too. Anyway, I was saying that it's not been so long that we've been working. At least when I think of what we have done and what I want to do."

"What do you want to do, Jennifer?" Softly. She's got her direction; keep out of her way.

"I don't know (pause). I mean, I know I want to get over . . . or least cut down on chopping myself up so much, and. . . . "

"And?"

"And I'd like to feel differently about Bert." Startled, she sucks in her breath. "No! I can't feel any differently when he's done what he did. I won't give in! I won't!"

Jim. Jennifer reveals she has made more progress than she can yet recognize. But her struggle is a difficult one, and she's not ready to take the big and frightening step of giving up her right to blame Bert — although, remarkably, she even considered that for a brief moment.

The patterns we develop for dealing with disappointment are usually pretty firmly cemented into place. They give us what seems to be a solid footing when otherwise important parts of our worlds have been shaken. The more central the part of our life pattern that is frustrated, the more determinedly are we likely to clutch our familiar modes of dealing with the failure of our expectations.

As so often, I'm reminded again of Karl Wallenda and his balancing pole. Karl Wallenda's story is Jennifer's story, is my story, is the story of everyone. The very ways of being that have made life possible, that may even have rescued us in the past, must sometimes be discarded if we are to survive and have our lives. But in a time of crisis, rather than letting them go, we are apt to clutch them more tightly.

Jennifer tried always to be absolutely right, to know and obey all rules, to prove herself innocent whenever things didn't go as they should. When Bert had his affair, he violated the rules, he threatened Jennifer's world. She had to blame him totally, and so she was the victim. The more she felt the pain of the separation and the more she felt unable to do anything about it, the more she had to clutch her balancing pole, blaming. When she first came to therapy, it was on the verge of killing her, as literally as Karl Wallenda's pole brought him to death.

Friday, November 25

Hal. When he finally got in touch with his tears and his pain about his son three months ago, Hal emerged into a realization of the fact and importance of his inner sense. At first, he thought this was the culmination of our efforts. Then, as he tried to put into living practice the new perspective, he came to see that it was only a way station on the road, not the end.

Since then, Hal has determinedly tried to get in touch with his inner sense, and has found that this is not a simple matter of flipping some subjective switch. There are days when he has clearer awareness of his intentions, feelings, hopes, and apprehensions than he has ever known before. Then he is optimistic and enthusiastic. But there are other days when he feels skeptical that he can ever really maintain such knowing or put it dependably to work in his life.

"You know, Jim," he says, as he settles on the couch (now his chosen working site), "Tim just doesn't bug me the way he used to. He's still pretty nutty, but a lot of what used to get to me — like his hair — just kind of amuses me now. Well, it is upsetting sometimes when I have to introduce him to some of my straight colleagues. But even then, I'm amused when I see them react to the way he looks."

"Mm-hmmm."

"We're not really close like we used to be. But then maybe it's hard to be close with late teenagers anyway." He smiles wryly and drifts off, musing.

"Hal, you started out with a tone that suggested some misgivings. What happened to that?"

"Oh, I don't know. I'm just feeling kind of . . . kind of unsure what we can do now. That's not really so, either. There's a lot I need to work on here, but somehow I don't have much energy for it."

"That's what needs your attention, then."

"Huh? Oh? Oh, I think I see what you mean. Yeah, yeah, I suppose so." His tone is dispirited.

"Not much energy."

"No. Not really. It just feels like too much work."

"Does that matter?"

"Yeah, I guess so."

"Doesn't sound like it."

"Yeah. It's like you're pushing me to wake up, and I want to stay asleep."

"So? . . . "

"Jesus, Jim, I don't know," but there's more energy in his tone.

"So? . . . "

"So I need to find out, I guess. Uh-oh, I heard that 'guess,' which means I really don't want to. Why am I sitting on my can this way?"

"What's your answer?"

"Oh, shit, I've forgotten what I started to say. You know, something's going on in me, and I'm damned if I know what, but I'm not into myself. I can tell you that."

"So? . . . "

"You're in a rut, Jim."

"No, you are, Hal."

"You're right. And I'm getting kinda pissed at it. Wait a minute. Let's see if I can get with it more."

He's silent, shutting his eyes, deepening his breathing. Such a contrast to his former need to fight off going inward.

He begins, his voice dreamy. "Jim, there's so much . . . so much piled up that I really want to look into (pause). So much. I can't begin to think through all the implications — in my practice, at home, in my relating with Greta, and with Tim. In my teaching — . . . oh, boy! . . . in my teaching. Hell!" He opens his eyes and sits up.

"No wonder I don't want to work here. I mean, in some ways I don't want to work on any of this stuff ever again. Do you know, my friend (turning to me), what you've led me into? You sonofabitch, you've just brought me to a place where my life is turned upside down. Thanks a lot, buddy." He's being sarcastic, but he means it too.

"Tell me, Hal."

"Well, you've helped me discover this whole subjective experience business, this whole world inside of myself. What the hell am I going to do with that when I'm doing the kind of research I'm paid to do? When I'm teaching the courses I teach? Just for starters, tell me that. And those are just the easy ones."

"I see what you mean."

"Again, thanks," he says ironically, then pauses. "No, I mean it, Jim, I do thank you. And equally straight, I'm overwhelmed what all this means for my life. How can I keep on with our research when I see it's just on the surface of the problems we're supposed to investigate? How can I teach what I've always taught when my whole view of psychology is changed?"

"I don't have any answers, Hal, but I'm here to help you think through these questions. One suggestion, though, you've just entered the world of your subjectivity. Everything is apt to seem to be in black-and-white contrasts. Don't do anything drastic in the way of changes until we talk it through, at least for a month or two."

"Uh-huh! That's interesting, and it's reassuring. Yet, you know, this is strange, it's also a little disappointing."

Never one for little steps, Hal is overwhelming himself with his urgency to use his new insight to revise his whole life. It's one of his great strengths that he seldom does things by halves. It is also one of his failings. We have our work cut out for us.

Jim. Just a month until Christmas! The years go by so quickly now. I wish I could feel the excitement that Christmas used to rouse in me. Instead too often, at home, I seem flat or inert emotionally. I think I look to my work to enliven me. Not good!

It's my task to keep my own emotional issues clearly labeled as mine . . . if that's possible. Again and again I've seen how my clients' concerns seem to cluster, to be similar. Then those clusters often relate to where I am in my own life. I pull, unconsciously, for some themes or emotions, and those of my clients for whom those themes or emotions are currently more accessible are likely to surface them. It works the other way, too; the themes they are processing induce parallels within me.

These days I'm very aware of the way our lives are limited by a variety of influences — especially customs and the continual struggle to be "right." I'm finding satisfaction in the way my clients wrestle with what limits them and in how they are beginning to get free. Clearly, I'm feeling my own constrictions and my own promptings to make changes, become freer. This doesn't negate what they're doing; it does alert me to what I'm most tuned to respond to and encourage. All well and good, but let's keep on top of it so that I'm not trying to get my clients to take the steps I fear to take myself.

Thanksgiving yesterday. Don't usually come in on the day after a holiday, but I feel the need to keep in touch with Hal and Jennifer and, less so, with Kate. Though these are the middle phases of our work, when there are fewer times of great relief or of dramatic breakthroughs, I know the danger that can suddenly explode when we least expect it. This all relates to what's called the therapeutic "honeymoon." When someone begins depth psychotherapy, there tends to be a first guarded period, which typically soon gives way to a spurt of productivity. Once therapist, place, and work are familiar, the initial hesitation is replaced with a zest for catharsis of pent-up emotions, secret thoughts and shames, and cherished but suppressed hopes.

The honeymoon is a time when so much emerges that previously was present in our subjectivity but not brought out into the light of full consciousness. Once that pent-up store is largely exhausted some therapists and clients stop. Useful emotional relief has been achieved, some insights gained, and a more hopeful attitude toward life has been achieved.

All well and good, but too often those gains come apart over the next months or years. The real work of deep, life-changing psychotherapy only begins when the honeymoon is over. Just as the real work of making a lasting relationship, a true marriage, begins after the honeymoon.

This "real work" — the working through — involves discovering and truly accepting the recurrent patterns through which we conduct life, deal with disappointments, relate to others, contribute to our failures and hurts. Then we need to identify these patterns over and over again, in as many of life's venues as can be examined. Knowing the truth is the first step, but putting that truth to work is the necessary second step. And it is hard work, humbling work, painful work, and ultimately growth-inducing work.

As Carl Rogers and Barry Stevens wrote, "Ye shall know the truth and the truth shall make ye free, but first it shall make ye miserable."

Ten

"What Is Death?"

Jennifer. "Jim, I hope you know you've been a great help to me in my work. Now I have twice as much trouble making a decision." She lies on the couch in her favorite position, one trousered leg hooked over a bolster and her hands clasped behind her head. How small her breasts are! Her sarcasm is a way of asking for my help without taking responsibility for doing so.

"You're pretty complacent about this increase in trouble."

The leg comes down, and her voice becomes more sober. "I'm not really complacent. I think we're finding what's back of my irritability and headaches. I think the pain is having to discipline students. That's what I need to work on. Okay, let's try it a different way." Then Jennifer takes a step I've often urged, but this time she takes it on her own: She lies down and gets in a relaxed position. She is silent for a minute or so.

"Uh-huh (pause). I think of Molly who came to see me today. She's in trouble for cutting chemistry lab too often. She wants me to help her get back in good standing with Professor Young. She has lots of good reasons, but they all boil down to the fact that chem lab comes the same hour as her boyfriend's free, and they've been making out in his car when she should be in the lab."

"So what does this all mean to you?"

"Well, frankly," she's up on her elbows already, "I sympathize with Molly. I'd rather make out with a good-looking man than with a Bunsen burner and test tube any day. But I can't let Molly know that, so. . . . "

"Why not?"

"Well, what kind of thing would that be for a dean of women to say?" She giggles, enjoying the image. "On the other hand, why not? But if I said anything like that, how could I ever enforce any discipline? Umm. . . . " She drifts off, silent.

"Mmmm?"

"Oh, I suppose I could. Still, if I don't preserve a certain amount of . . . reserve, I guess you'd say. If I don't have some reserve, how will the students respect me? Well, it isn't respect that's the issue, but they have to know there are limits, and that I'll. . . . When I think again of how some of the faculty would react if they heard I'd told a student I'd rather make out. . . . " She chuckles again. Then she calls herself back to the job.

"The dean of students absolutely insists we get tough when the violations are willful, and Molly's sure were that. I don't know why I can't just. . . . Once it all seemed so simple, but now. . . . I think I ought to go back to teaching or get into some other work. I'm not the right person to be in charge of discipline." She squirms with the tides of her thoughts.

"What sort of person should be in that job?"

"Well, one thing's for sure. She should have her head on straight so she wouldn't get her personal feelings all jumbled up with school policy and go home and feel like biting her husband's head off the way I do with Bert . . . uh, the way I did."

"Bert's still at home in some part of your feelings."

"Oh! No, he's not. I don't want him there." She stops, pulls back up on her elbows. "Oh, damn, I don't know. I wish he'd never fucked that damn Ellen. I wish. . . . Oh, never mind. It's all too late now." She drops back down, face tight.

"Want to explore that?"

"No!" She pauses, her face works, her eyes seem close to tears. Then more quietly, "No, Jim, I'm not ready yet."

"When?"

"I don't know. I've got to get myself straightened out first. This whole thing at my office is giving me headaches — yes, I hear, and I mean it. If I were more like I should be there I wouldn't have so much confusion going on inside of me all the time. I know my mother was like that. She had everything under control, so serene and untroubled (pause). I hated her for it! (Another pause.) And I loved and admired her for it. But nothing could ever really get to her."

"Including you."

"Including me," sadly.

Louise. Santa Ana, the Mexican general, is memorialized in this part of the world by the hot, dusty winds that blow in from the desert and can lower the humidity to three or four percent. It is said you can't risk stamping your feet in the hills lest you send a spark that can generate a firestorm. The "Santana" is blowing these days, and we sniff the air and cringe when we hear a siren.

Louise arrives windblown and a little breathless. Her hair is straying, and her clothes are awry as she comes into the room. I'm irritated with myself and with her that I find this stimulating too!

She makes some perfunctory apology and then catches herself. "Yes, I'm not tidy. If you disapprove, that's just too bad." She pauses, then grins a bit sheepishly. "I know you don't disapprove . . . probably . . . but I wanted to show you I wasn't trying to please you." She pauses, shrugs wryly. "But, of course, to tell you that I didn't care if you disapproved was a way of pleasing you too. It's all so damned confusing."

"Like right now?"

"Uh, yes, I guess so (pause). I'm not sure how you mean?"

"How do *you* mean?"

"Well, I . . . I don't know. I don't know what you mean and. . . . Oh, damn, and so I don't know what I mean! There it is again. Honestly, it is so maddening. All the time nowadays, I see myself trying to take my cues from everyone else. When I'm in a store, it's the salesclerks; when I'm with friends, it's what they want; at the agency, it's what the students, the other workers, and the director want (pause, voice rising). What do *I* want?" It's not a question; it's a cry of protest.

"You seem to want something right now."

"Well, yes, I do! I want to know what I want. Not what salesclerks, friends, agency people, or . . . or even *you* want." She pauses, listening to the echoes of what she has just said. Then her face, which has been intent, almost angry, falls, and her voices changes.

"I'm wondering what you're thinking about me and what I've been saying!"

"Why should you be different here?"

"Why should I (angry, ironic)? I guess I do it here too."

"That's the right answer. That will please me, eh?"

"Oh, I wish you wouldn't do that!" It comes out angrily. Now she stops, tasting the echo of her voice. "I really don't know what to say when you do that. I mean, I see what you intend, but. . . . " She pauses, confusion plain.

"Louise, you're swirling around now, entirely outside of yourself, finding only thoughts of what I've said, testing to see what they mean for you, trying to read my intention, wanting to make the right answer, but trying to reject that compulsion. All of this is going on so busily that you can't hear your own inner voice at all."

"Yes, yes! I am doing that." She is crying, angry, and seems dazed. I wait quietly, but focus my attention on her in a way that demands response.

"I was surprised you brought it right in here, but, of course, I must do it here too. And I *hate* that. I absolutely hate it!" The last is shouted at me.

I make no reply. She pauses, uncertain.

"So?"

"Well (pause), I . . . I really do hate it, and. . . . " She stops again, hesitating.

"Now you've said how much you hate it, but then you don't know what to say next."

"Uh. Yes. I guess so."

"Are you waiting for me to say something; so you'll know what to do next?"

"Awrrgh!" It's a cry of rage and distress.

"As far as I can tell you haven't yet taken time to feel within yourself, to find out what your own thoughts and feelings might be. You're totally focused on what I'm doing and what I may expect and what you should be doing. It's no wonder you are all tangled up." It's so important for her to feel the loss that her compulsion to please exacts. She's come far enough now to use that in a way she couldn't have earlier.

"Ohhh! That's right!" She's furious, realizing how caught she is within her own skin of being so outwardly focused. She wants to tear her way out but is unable even to do that.

"You're agreeing with me. What motivates your agreement? You're angry. Will that prove to me how well you're learning?"

"Wait! Let me think. Did I just agree with you because I really agree with you, or because I wanted you to see me as understanding? Wait! Wait! Oh, I can't — I really can't tell the difference. After all, you're trying to help me, so why would you tell me something different. . . . No, I can see where that's taking me. I don't know, Jim. I don't know!" The last is a wail, and the tears are streaming down her cheeks. She looks miserably unhappy.

"Louise." Voice quietly insistent. "Louise, tell me how it is inside of you now, right now, while you're feeling so miserable."

"Oh, awful. I'm kind of whirling around inside. It's like I'm dizzy. Yes, like I can't get my balance. When you keep pressing me that way it's like I can't . . . I can't. . . . It's like the floor is tilting, and I'm falling, but then before I land it tilts again another way, and I fall another way, and. . . . Oh, damn it, Jim! It makes me so mad!"

"Do you think that description of the way you feel is what I was looking for?"

"Huh? Oh! You're doing it some more. Well, frankly, right at this moment, I don't give a damn! Uh! Oh, my, oh!" She pauses, her face twists. She darts glances at me, pulls herself back. Suddenly she stands up, tears streaming down her face. "Oh, God!" Gasping. "I can't stand it! I want to run, to run right out of here. I want to run away from you and from myself."

"Tell me, Louise." Still quietly, quietly. Important to convey by my manner that what she is doing is all right, is necessary. Yet is that reinforcing the dependence? Don't think there's any other way. She has to go through this.

"For a minute I knew where I was. When I described the tilting and dizziness inside of me . . . I knew then. I didn't think what you might think of it, or me. Then when you asked, it felt good to tell you I didn't care what you thought. But I suddenly got so scared. I was sure you were going to be furious at me, and yet right at the same time I knew you wouldn't be. And still, at the same time, I thought you'd be pleased that I knew you wouldn't and then I knew you wouldn't like it if I thought you be pleased, and then. . . . And I started to feel like I was suffocating. I mean really suffocating, like I couldn't breathe. So I had to stand up, and I wanted to run, and right now a part of me still wants to run right out of here. Oh, please don't do that anymore right now." She sinks down to sit on the couch, hand to throat, catching her breath.

Okay, enough, I tell myself. "I hear you, Louise." She is so shaken that she is literally panting. Am I doing this as an erotic thing? The answer is clear: No way. What we have been doing has no sensual quality whatsoever.

"Jim . . . Jim, I know sooner or later we've got to do this more. I hate it, and I hate you when you make me so dizzy and frightened, but we must do it as many times as I need to break out of my pleasing straitjacket. I hate that even more."

I silently salute her courage and determination.

Monday, December 19

Hal. I miss the hearty, kidding Hal whose appointments I used to look forward to. He's more sober, struggling with the changes he is making, not sure how much he really wants them, but knowing that he can't go back to his old way of being either. Now as Hal comes quietly in and sits lumpishly on the couch, I feel again the disquiet that has been an undertone in our hours for the past several weeks.

"Hi, Jim," his greeting lacks its former energy.

"Hi, Hal. You sound kind of low."

"Oh," he seems to collect himself. "No, no, just thinking a lot. Been thinking about my practice. Since we've been working together, it's changing a lot, and yet I'm not satisfied that I'm really able to make the transition from my old approach to what I want to do now. I wish I could come to you for supervision, but I know that wouldn't work. But I'm not content or. . . . (sigh) I don't know."

"Confused."

"Yeah, confused. I've been thinking it might be good if I could go back to the Post-Graduate Center and get some really top-notch training in group therapy. I've never used groups much, and I like the way your group works. But I don't know whether that's right for me or. . . . " He stops again in mid-sentence, looking into space.

"You're not sure what's right for you, huh?"

"No, I'm not. I was reading in one of the journals last night, and there's a lot of stuff I've never covered that I guess I need to catch up on, but still. . . . "

Hal goes on in this limping way, starting a topic and then losing momentum, pausing, and switching to something else. He tells of being driven to hunt through books and journals, planning to attend workshops and institutes, seeking to end the incompleteness and frustration. His work is not fulfilling him these days; instead it seems continually to show him what he lacks and to call on him to make changes in a life pattern that once seemed set and promised a steady future.

Late in the session, he sighs deeply and says, "And so I've been thinking of going into full-time research or teaching, or sometimes. . . . I've been having these thoughts that . . . well, maybe if I got into teaching . . . I mean, I've got a pretty good place at the college, and I think I could get on full-time there, and then maybe. . . . It might be pretty nice teaching a moderate class load and having some time left for thinking and. . . . "

"Hal, what's going on with you? You can't seem to let your thoughts go. You keep running dry or cutting off or something."

"No. I mean, I don't know. I guess I'm just kind of unsure or something. I mean, I kind of wonder whether. . . . " He drifts off, leaving it incomplete.

"Is there something you're reluctant to say?"

"Huh? Uh, no, not really. I'm doing a lot of wandering around. Anyway, I wasn't really serious about it; so there's no use wasting our time. Besides, I'd like to think with you about this idea of going into full-time teaching. I know you used to be on the UCLA faculty and I wonder why. . . . "

But his manner prompts me to cut in again: "I have the impression, Hal, that you're quite uncomfortable with this idea you don't want to talk about, even though you say you're not serious about it."

Now the pause is very long before he answers. He is obviously struggling with himself, and when he does speak, his words come out slowly and with much strain. "All right. I'll level with you, but I want you to know this is just one of those fantasy-thoughts that everyone gets. I've just thought of stopping, that's all. There's nothing to it, really."

"Stopping, Hal?" (persistently.)

There's an edge of irritation — or is it desperation — in his voice when he replies. "Yes, stopping, you know. Just stopping. Stopping practice, stopping psychology, stopping — uh — anything."

"Anything?"

His voice is very faint this time. The fight seems gone as quickly as it flared up: "Anything or everything — stopping living."

It is very quiet in my office.

My inner thoughts are strangely relaxed. It is not that I doubt the sincerity of Hal's suicidal impulse. When I think about that, I am on the verge of anxiety about it. He means it. He might well do it. I can't dismiss that. No, the curious relaxation is one of closure. During the past two weeks, I've felt the presence of some threat in him again and again, and yet I never could discover what it was nor even find suitable leads in what he told me so that I could work with my intuition. Now it's out in the open. Hal thinks of killing himself. And he thinks very seriously about it.

I have been silent, busy with my own thoughts. Hal rouses himself now.

"I don't mean to threaten you, Jim. I'm not about to do anything right now. If it ever happens, I'll not mess you up . . . or my family . . . or anybody else, if I can help it. I know what it can mean to a therapist if a patient suicides. In fact, I didn't want to tell you. You were just too fast picking up the cues."

"Maybe you were slow in covering the cues because you wanted me to know."

"Well, yeah, that could be, but. . . . "

"It's a pretty lonely place you're in."

"Yes, it is. But I can handle it." His chin is trembling, but he's struggling to keep the calm, sad facade he's had all along.

"For some reason you need to suppress your loneliness and pain even now."

"Jim, Jim, it won't do any good. I know, man, I know. Get all the emotions out, eh? Yes, it does help, but only if there's something more going for the person. It's too late, or I'm too confused, or something. I don't know what I'm saying. It's just no use, no use." Now the tears push through his tight eyes. Abruptly, he relaxes and sits limply, letting the pain have its way with him. He makes no effort to reach for the tissue box close to his hand, but simply cries quietly without any sobbing, his big frame slumped, his face drained of expression.

I wait quietly, feeling a mix of apprehension, affection, and determination. I've got to keep faith with Hal now in a way that he may try to resist.

When Hal sighs heavily, takes several tissues, and wipes his eyes and blows his nose, I lean toward him, put my hand on his knee firmly, and look into his eyes. He attempts a deprecatory smile, but it doesn't work. As he starts to speak, I interrupt.

"Look, friend, we've got to talk very straight with each other right now. You know that, don't you?"

"It's okay, Jim, I won't do anything now. What with Christmas and all. You don't have to worry."

"Damn it, Hal!" I'm angry, and I want him to know it. "What kind of shit is that? I 'don't have to worry.' Well, I damned well *do* worry, and you can't dismiss it. I want you to really level with me and not try to smooth things over or dodge what we need to do."

"Yeah, sure, I understand. But, like I said, I'm not about to do anything now. I just had these stupid thoughts, and you picked up on it, and. . . . "

"Hal, I'm not interested in all that. I want you to make an absolute, flat-out agreement with me. You have got to promise me that you'll do nothing about killing yourself or even radically changing anything in your life until we've talked it over thoroughly."

"Sure, Jim. It'll be okay."

"Goddamn it, Hal, you're not playing straight with me. We've been through a lot together here in this room, and you owe me. What you do, and what you feel like doing, matter very much to me — not just professionally but personally too. You owe me this, and I want you to stand up to it with me. You are not to do anything radical, of any kind, without our talking about it for at least five times." My tone is strong, angry, demanding. I've got to break through his lethargic distance. I may have to anger him to do that, but that's all right.

"You're really mad, aren't you?" He's becoming more aware.

"You are damned right I'm mad, and I'm calling in what you owe me."

"I hear you, Jim. All right. I'll agree to hold off on doing anything until we talk it over."

"At least five times."

"At least five times."

"And you damn well be here tomorrow."

"I'll be here."

I stand up and put out my hand. Standing, he takes it. I hold his hand firmly and look into his eyes. "You matter, Hal, don't forget it."

He returns the look and the firm handclasp. "I hear you, Jim. I'll follow through."

Tuesday, December 20

Hal. Hal is still in a subdued, inwardly focused mood. He's not really depressed, so far as I can sense, but he seems resigned, and to lack energy or his customary forward thrust. As I watch him, I feel a heightened sensitivity, not anxious but alert.

"I almost canceled today, but I remembered what you said; so here I am." He smiles wanly. "I really don't feel like working much today. It's like I'm too tired or something."

"Too tired to do much here, huh?"

"Just like I'm played out, like I don't have any energy."

"I'm glad you came in anyway, Hal. You're right, I would have been concerned. Should I be right now?"

"No, I don't think so, Jim. I don't feel like doing it, like killing myself. Even that would take too much energy. Anyway, I promised you: If it comes to that, I'll talk to you first."

"That promise means a lot to me."

"I know it. And to me also." We're silent for several minutes. He seems strangely empty. I keep a horde of thoughts from intruding on the open sensitivity I need to maintain.

I wish he'd give me more to tune into to try to read him and his needs better. "What's it like inside of you right now?"

"I don't know . . . it's like I'm waiting . . . but I don't know for what."

"Waiting? . . . "

"Yeah. Maybe for something to let me go. I don't even know what I mean by that. Maybe to do it, to end things. Maybe something that will release me from the need to do it. I don't know. I just don't know, Jim. I'm just waiting."

"I'll wait with you."

"Yeah, I know you will. I value that a lot."

"So do I." We're silent together for a bit.

The hour goes slowly, low key. Hal's heaviness contrasts with the holiday season. Christmas/Chanukah is a rough time for clients as general happiness contrasts with their inner misery.

I'm worried about Hal's being in such a low place, but I don't have a feeling there's an immediate danger of his acting to kill himself. I do want to understand, as well as I can, what is going on for him.

His discovery of his subjectivity and its range and power challenges him to modify and partially let go of the perspective in which he was trained and to which he's devoted much of his adult life. That's a major confrontation beyond doubt.

Yet my intuition is that there's more involved in Hal's present situation than a change of his theoretic perspective and working orientation. These are conscious to him now and he's already begun to confront the needed changes. As much as they entail sizable efforts, they don't appear to have hit him so centrally as to make him question whether to continue living.

With some clients who have worked to greater than usual depth within themselves, periods of inertia and vagueness are parts of a rite of passage. To oversimplify, they are times of confronting necessary relinquishments and grieving over inexorable losses.

If I'm right about this—and the more I think about it, the more it seems to fit—then in a very real way there is a death confronting Hal. A way of being is coming to an end. It's no melodrama to call that a death. When one makes a major change in his life program, the self that might have been—that life one has implicitly and over many years anticipated having—that self is killed. The old way must die to make room for the new. That death calls for grieving, and I think Hal is grieving now.

Most likely Hal is in the process of letting go of subtle and fundamental aspects of his conception of himself and his world. To give it a name, Hal's in an existential crisis, the crisis of existence. Letting go of one way of being alive, not yet able to create/discover another.

Right now, he speculates it might be life itself that he needs to let go of; but so far that's only speculation, not impulse. I've got to keep in touch, though; it can change. I know it's not physical life that must be ended, but I also know it feels that way and that this mistaken perception can be acted on if it isn't resolved. I'm going to stand by.

Jim. Christmas everywhere. My kids, now grown, will be home. We'll have a big day. I'm into it more than I was last week. Each year it takes me longer to catch the spirit. Lurking in the background now is Hal. I don't think I have to be anxious—yet—but I still carry thoughts of him, concern, sympathy for him.

Christmas is my birthday. As a child I felt cheated, having only one day a year for getting presents, when everyone else had two. My favorite aunt solved this by making my "second birthday" the Fourth of July. No wonder she was my favorite.

I'll be fifty-one. Who is it that will be fifty-one? Hal is younger than I but is feeling he may be through with life! I've never seriously thought of suicide as a path I might choose. I never have felt fully hopeless for myself. I've certainly been down, way down. But ending my life didn't invite me.

During the Depression, when I was desperately trying to earn enough to get married, I was lucky. I got a job as a paid trainee office machine salesman! Twelve and a half dollars a week was not enough to set the date; but more was promised when I began selling, as I was sure I would. After all, I had sold magazine subscriptions successfully for two months the summer before.

After three days' training, I went door-to-door in a commercial district: Ask for the purchasing agent or owner, present my product, get turned down, on to the next place. Over and over. In four months, I sold one cheap machine. I hated that job!

I despaired about myself because I so dreaded making each call. I would sit in my car, near tears, getting up my determination to go make the next call. Sometimes I just drove away from my territory and went into the park and sat with my misery. I feared I was going crazy, but even then I never thought of suicide as an alternative.

Thinking back to that time, I know now it was not just the pain of so many rejections that tormented me. It was the discovery that I was not who I had thought myself to be. When I began work for the office machine company, I was not just one of six new trainee-salesmen, I was the star—the one the manager thought the most promising. I thought so too.

I was special. That was my secret, but I knew it was so. I was a "gold palm, Eagle Scout." I had been editor of my high school yearbook. I was on the debate squad and associate editor of the junior college newspaper. I was special, surely.

I remember hearing that the other trainees dropped out too—1938 was a bad year for sales of any kind. But my failure was what mattered to me. I had thought I could do it, that I was different. What that job did was to hold up a magnifying mirror in which I was forced to see that I was not special. As most of us do when confronted with that recognition, I went from being special in a good way to deeming myself special, deficient. I really couldn't do anything and never would be able to. I had to be special, or I'd be nothing. Now this job had proven that I was, indeed, nothing.

Recalling all this and thinking about Hal and most everyone I know, I'm struck again with how much we all tend to think of our identities, our worth as tied to what we do, what we achieve.

Who and what am I? I have tried to deal with my fears — of death, of being nothing — by collecting titles, achievements, recognitions. It didn't work. Still, I pursue these substitutes.

Substitutes for what? What I am. What am I?

I am alive only in the process of my being. I cannot find my life in what I do, what I achieve, what titles I hold, what others think or say of me. Only in the instantaneous moment of being aware, of experiencing, choosing, and acting do I most truly exist. Therefore I cannot see my own being, for I am the seeing and whatever I see cannot be me. I am the seeing, the moving, the awaring.

But that's so vague, so wispy, so insubstantial. Yes.

If I allow my identity to become bound up with objective thing-ness, then I am hopelessly vulnerable to external circumstances and contingencies. Identity based on what I have done, how I have been seen, what others think of me, is past-bound identity. It leads to stale and repetitious living. Only truly finding identity in the living moment answers the terrible questions. Hal hasn't found that out yet, and there is really no way I or anyone can tell him. I know it, but I know it always incompletely, need to learn it again and again.

Thursday, January 12

Frank. Frank enters with anger flowing off him in waves like radiations from a hot engine. He drops in the big chair, stares bitterly at his usual spot on the wall.

"Well, I'm fucked! I mean but good. Shit! Shit! Shit! I don't know how I can keep coming here either. You're just as greedy for money as anybody else. What the hell's it matter anyway? I don't think we're getting anywhere anyway. Oh, goddamn it! I can't see what. . . . "

"Hey! How's about filling me in?"

"I'm fired, canned, have been given the good old sack, am out on my ass, am informed that the great Cosmopolitan Hotel can stagger along without my services."

"How come?"

"Awghh! It makes me sick. Because Berman is a prick, that's how come. Because Gambel, the resident manager, is an even bigger prick, that's how come. Because. . . . "

"What happened?"

A different expression quickly flashes across Frank's face. I can't read it, but it doesn't fit with all the noisy anger that he's spouting.

"Last night, this guy and gal check in, see. They have only one suitcase, and it isn't heavy. I figure they just want to shack up. Nothing new about that. Except the doll is really something. I mean she *is stacked!* He is one of those shirt-ad types, all good clean young American middle-class creep. They're both high on something, not giving a damn about me. The big playboy gives me a lousy two-dollar tip and tells me to get lost, and he's reaching for her before I'm out the door.

"Well, I go down to the bell station, but I can't read or anything, thinking about them up there balling. It's been weeks since I had a piece. Then, after an hour or so, the elevator door opens and the guy comes out, his face kind of foggy, dazed. Y'know? He doesn't say anything, just goes out the street door."

Frank pauses, and again I see that quick change of expression. I think he's enjoying telling this story. I wonder if I can get him to recognize that. While I'm trying to decide what to say, he goes on.

"Then I get to thinking about that woman upstairs. First, I'm thinking there she is all alone in that bed, and then suddenly I'm wondering if that creep did anything to her. I mean, he was so spaced he could have carved her up or something. The more I think about it, the more I get worked up, half wanting to go up in the hope I'll see some more of her without the dude being there, and half afraid of what I'll find if I do go up.

"So finally I just go on up and knock on the door. It takes a couple times before she answers. Then there she is, leaning against the door because she's pretty near out herself, and she's mother-ass naked. I mean, she's got a body that doesn't quit. I just stand there kind of dumb, staring at her. After a minute, she pulls back and says to come on in.

"So I go in, and she kind of falls on the bed and just looks at me, but her eyes don't focus too good. She reaches her hand up, and one thing leads to another, and pretty soon I'm as naked as she is and on the bed with her. Then, just when everything is going great, the dude walks in! Christ! What a time for him to come back! The girl doesn't see him at first, but I do. He just stands there looking at us, and then he starts laughing and tells me to get the hell out of there. So I grab my clothes and dress in the hall and go back downstairs.

"When I get there, there's old shit-head himself all puffed up like God Almighty. 'Get out of that uniform, and out of this hotel,' he says. 'Your check'll be mailed to you, but don't ever come back in here.' So I start to tell him what he can do with his crummy job, and he says he'll give me ten minutes to be out of the building or he'll have the cops come for me. So that does it, and I haven't any job, and what the fuck do I care anyway?"

"Wow, Frank, you had quite a night!"

For just a second the smile flashes, and I know he's secretly pleased with the adventure and the story. Then he grunts, and his usual sullen visage returns. "Yeah, I guess so. But now what the hell am I going to do? You're going to want me to pay you, and jobs are hard to come by."

"Frank, you've referred several times to my wanting to be paid; so let me be straight with you. Yes, I do want to be paid. And I don't have the reserves to be able to carry much of an unpaid balance. So. . . . "

"Okay already. I said I knew you wanted to be paid. Don't get uptight and give me the big lecture."

"Slow down. I want to tell you that it's ok if you need to

get behind on your bill for a month or so, but I can't continue much more than that. After you size up your situation, fill me in, and we'll work out a plan together so that we'll both be clear."

"Sure, sure. Don't sweat it. I'll find something."

I have mixed feelings about this session. I didn't do much to get Frank to recognize the feelings he had about what happened and about telling me the story. Yet it was a kind of sharing that I think was unusual in Frank's life. He's been so alone that there would be no one to tell of both the adventure and the letdown. I note that in his account he has included a lot of his subjective feelings without his usual protective coverings of devaluing or distancing. His growing trust of me and of what we're doing is becoming more evident.

And, of course, I enjoy a sexy story.

Hal. Hal is regular and prompt in attendance—physically. It is hard to characterize his emotional, subjective state. He alternates between periods of wordless inner contemplation which has a melancholy but not truly miserable quality and times of low-key review of events, relations, and life issues that are open questions.

Today he is engaged in this process, so I ask, "Hal, what's it like as you look at various parts of your life in this way?"

"I dunno, Jim. It's as though my desk were covered with a lot of things needing attention, and I was getting things in order. No big rush, but the job needs doing."

"You know, the phrase 'getting your papers in order' is often used in a particular context."

"It is? Oh. Oh, yes, when the patient is dying, huh? Well, maybe that's part of it, but I don't feel that I'm dying—at least not yet."

"At least not yet" echoes in my mind. Don't get lulled into complacency, Jim. He's not on the brink of doing it, but it's still very much a present possibility.

Jim. Hal has a contract with me not to kill himself unless we've talked it over at least five times. He could abrogate and do it today or tonight or any time. I don't think he will. I think he'll respect our contract.

I have an implicit contract with . . . with whom? Probably with society — to keep him from killing himself, if I can. I too could ignore that and let him go — even give him the support of passivity. I won't do that. I will respect my contract too.

Why this nearly unanimous agreement that we must do nearly everything we can to prevent — no, forestall or delay, death? I also belong to the Hemlock Society, which lobbies for the right of suicide and the right to aid the suicide of terminal patients who are suffering. Many in our culture look on that as anathema or downright evil. I see as obscene needlessly prolonged suffering or the extension of physical life by heroic means when the person is gone.

What is death? Well, for starters, tell me what life is, and I'll take a try at telling you what death is. Whatever your answer, mine will be the end of how you've defined life *as we know it*. It seems pretty clear that whatever else death means, it is an end to our familiar experience of being.

But wait, not necessarily. These musings make me think of *Outward Bound,* a movie that made a great impression on me when I was quite young and quite terrified by the specter of death. In that film passengers on a ship slowly discover, as they go about their familiar routines, that they all died when their ship sank in a storm. Now, they realize, they are in an afterlife and still aboard the ship. That story was so reassuring that I went home and wrote another story on almost identical lines. It was one of the few writing projects, of many begun in those days, that I actually completed.

Death is mystery. It's open season on this mystery. All of us can — and do — create our own scenarios for what happens or does not happen after we die. And the range is tremendous, of course. Oblivion (always, for me, the most terrifying), pearly gates and harp-playing angels, another round on the wheel, purgatory — you name it. I mean, you do name it. No way you can avoid doing so in some way.

Sound familiar? I've been saying that each of us creates his or her own life — defines his own world and himself within it. That's the way we each define what we mean by "life." Perhaps, it's the same, we also have to create our own "deaths." Seems logical. Seems as good an answer as any.

Just in case it is so, why not create the one that most suits you? Nobody who could prove you wrong is apt to do so.

Group Psychotherapy. Since Frank entered the group and was championed by Hal, the two have seemed to have an unspoken alliance. This has never been openly discussed, but when Frank does volunteer anything — which is not often — he almost always looks to Hal more than to anyone else. For his part, Hal can usually be counted upon to make at least a mildly affirming response to what Frank says. Tonight I notice a difference, though, when midway through the session Frank takes what is for him a rather big step.

Frank: "I lost my damn job today." He particularly looks toward Hal; but Hal, who has taken little part, being sunk in himself, doesn't seem to notice.

Louise: "Oh, Frank, that's too bad. What will you do?"

Frank: "Oh, it was a shitty place anyway. I'll find something else." Again his eyes flick to Hal, and again Hal seems unaware.

Ben: "What happened? You diddle the boss's wife?"

Kate: "Ben, what does 'diddle' mean? Oh, oh, I think I understand." She's embarrassed.

Ben: "That's rough, I know, Frank. Got any possibles?"

Frank: "No, nothing right now. I haven't been down to the employment office yet or checked the papers. I don't . . . don't have much . . . training, you know. Oh fuck!" He looks embarrassed. "I'm sorry. I just meant I have to take such dumbass jobs that —"

Ben: "You know, Frank, I think I can give you some leads."

Frank: "Yeah, thanks." He sounds distant, which tells me how much Ben's offer means to him and how afraid he is to show it.

The talk goes on for a bit, and then Hal sort of shakes his head as though he's waking up. He speaks directly to Frank.

Hal: "Sorry to hear about the job, Frank. Our college has

an employment office you can use even if you're not a student. Let me know if you'd like to be steered to it." His tone is impersonal, but I can see Frank is relieved to have some response from him. Interestingly, it is Kate who senses something of what this interaction is triggering.

Kate: "You wanted something from Hal, didn't you, Frank?" It's too direct, too explicit.

Frank: "No, what would I want? You get the screwiest ideas, Kate. I just. . . . Yeah, I just was glad to know about that employment office. That's all."

Kate: "You make me think of myself, but I'm not sure I could tell you how."

Aha! Kate *is* getting it.

Eleven

"I Am God!"

Monday, January 16

Jennifer. Our steady focus on Jennifer's life patterns is shocking her with the recognition of how essentially alone she is. The relation she and Bert had with Ellen and Dan, the main other-than-work friendship she had, is gone. She is surprised to realize that most of her friendships were made through Bert. The only others are more accurately acquaintances at the college. She sometimes lunches with them there, but these are group affairs, and she has no one-to-one times that aren't work related.

"Jim, since we've been talking, I've started thinking: How is it that I don't have any more friends? I mean, I have friends, of course, but . . . but not real close friends or. . . . Well, with Bert away, I guess I'm lonely. Well, not exactly 'lonely,' but like I need . . . or want . . . someone to. . . . "

"It's hard to say that you might be lonely."

"Well, yes, I suppose so. I mean, I have a lot of people in my life; so what right have I to. . . . Well, that isn't what I mean. It isn't a matter of 'rights'; it's just that. . . . "

As we explore her feeling of lacking companionship, it becomes manifest to her that she is indeed lonely, but that this is a mark of having failed in some way. Thus she has resisted facing it — or doing something about it.

This line of discussion gives me an opening to propose

207

that she come into the therapy group, a recommendation I've had in mind for several weeks. She is reluctant, however.

"I'll go into the group, if you really think I should, but I just don't see what being with a lot of other people and hearing their troubles is going to do for me. I'm mixed up enough without having somebody's else's problems added on to mine."

"The group is not a place to trade problems. It's a place for you to try out being who you are without hiding behind rules or anything else."

"Do you think I'm 'hiding' (pause)? Well, maybe, in a way, but . . . but not really. Well, I suppose. . . . ”

"Sounds as though that's another thing you're not supposed to be or do."

"Ummm. Yes, I guess so. I didn't realize how many things like that I had."

"That's what we're talking about, isn't it?"

"Well, yes, I suppose so. I do have a lot more rules than I realized. Not just at my office, I'm coming to see. And you think I hide behind them, do you?"

"What do you think?"

"Well, maybe."

"Do you think there's any connection to what we were talking about — your feelings that you haven't many real friends?"

"Oh! Oh, the rules keep me away there too, you mean?"

"Do they?"

"I didn't think of that. It could be, but. . . . ”

"Jennifer, don't try to work it out rationally. You and I know that that seldom helps. I suggest you come into the group and see what that shows you. The group is a place for us to understand better what threatens you in being with other people and what we need to explore so you can be yourself more genuinely. Rather than arguing about it abstractly, why don't you come for a half-dozen times, and then we'll see how it feels to you?"

"Okay, if you think it'll help."

Hal. Today Hal's mood is restless, smoldering anger.

"Do you ever wonder why you got into this stupid busi-

ness? Well, I do. I was just asking for it. Just asking for everybody to dump on me. Mrs. Kanowsky wants to know who
should make the decisions about money in the family. Should
she or should Herman have the last word? Come on, Doctor,
what's the answer? Don't they teach that in graduate school?
Then Mr. Bayard asks me with tears in his eyes — asks *me,* mind
you — what can he do to help his teenage son who's running
around with the wrong kind of kids. And young Bill Lewis looks
at me respectfully and wants me to use all my great knowledge —
after all, I was his college psychology professor only last year —
use all that great store of knowledge to tell him whether to marry
little Betsy Carter or just screw her since she's a *shiksa* and his
family would have a fit if he married her. That's a simple question, is it not? Surely the statistics on interfaith marriages would
make the answer easy for anyone, especially for a professor and
doctor. Then there is dear old Ben Fowler, a lush in the making if there ever was one. But Ben is so repentant after every
binge. 'Doctor, how can I get myself to stop drinking? I know
it's ruining my life. I'm going to lose my family. Doctor-lah,
tell me from all your studies of psychology.' Well, *Doctor* Bugental,
what do I say to them, hah?"

"What do you say, Hal?"

"Oh, and I almost forgot Mrs. Palmer, dear Mrs. Palmer.
'Please to give my son some tests and tell him what field he will
be a big success in.' Oh, Mrs. Palmer, never use a preposition
to end a sentence with. You see, I am a doctor. I know how
to speak properly. What's that about your son? Well, he better
look out for prepositions too, and propositions also, you Jocasta,
you."

"Wow! They really get to you, don't they?"

"Oh do they ever! All those good people. All those good
questions. Like Mr. and Mrs. Green. 'Doctor, why do we fight
so much? We really love each other. Tell us how to stop hurting each other.' So stop, already! Enough! Enough! I can't do it."

"And you hurt because you can't."

"Hurt, schmurt. They pay their money. What am I supposed to do? Say 'Don't feel bad' and pat their hands, like the
old family doctor did? No, they won't buy it. Their message

comes through loud and clear: 'You're a doctor. You've studied these things. You teach at the college. A psychologist! You must know. You *must!* Tell us. Help us. We're giving up things we want and need in order to pay you. Help us. Our lives are being messed up. Help us. Help us!' And so what do I do?"

"What do you do?"

"I say, "Tell me about it, Mrs. Kanowsky.' I say, 'Now, Bill, let's see, are you the eldest in your family? And what is Betsy's birth order? And was your father orthodox, conservative, or reformed? And how strict was Betsy's Christian upbringing? And did your parents have a stable home life? And did Betsy's? And how long have you known each other? And what degree of intimacy have you shared? I mean, do you screw her just on the weekend or every night? But not on *Shabbas!* No, no.' Oh, hell, Jim, I'm acting the fool, I know. But it feels good to pour it out to someone. Now, you be the doctor and fix me all up, will you? I'll just lie here on the couch and cuss quietly to myself while you check any books you doctors use and figure things out for me."

He falls silent, having not really heard me up to this time. I am overwhelmed. "My God, Hal, you really feel the weight of every one of those questions as though it were a ton of rocks right on top of you!"

"You're damned right I do, and I'm sick of it. I'm about through with the whole fucking bit. I'm going to quit. I'm fed up."

"So fed up that you want out, but the only way you can see out is to kill yourself."

"If that's what it takes, okay! I mean it, buddy, in spades. I've had it up to here. You can take the whole thing and shove it right up the world's ass."

"You're not depressed; you're mad as hell."

"Amazing deduction, my dear doctor!"

"And you. . . ."

"No, Jim, I don't want to give you any shit. I'm sorry. I'm just so fed up, so tired, so sad." And abruptly the rage passes, and he sits slumped in his chair.

"Hal, where the hell did you go? You didn't hurt me. I know you, and we know each other. A few fast words aren't going to get to me."

"Yeah, yeah, I know. I'm just sorry to mouth off at you. I hope you don't feel hurt."

"Oh, for Christ's sake, Hal. Who do you think you are — God? You don't crush me with a snappy retort. For that matter, it sounds like you think you're God with those people who come to see you too."

He sits up rather abruptly, looks at me in a strange way, and says with complete calm, "That's right, I do. I do think I'm God."

We sit and stare at each silently. He means it! He knows it, and I know it. He really means it! A quick shower of half-thoughts hits me: paranoid? hallucinations? delusions? dangerous? But this is Hal. I know Hal. Suppose it were true? Would I believe Jesus himself? Quit wasting time. Need to respond effectively right now. This is an opening. Now maybe we'll really break through. I want to. . . .

And then I shove it all away and read the invisible words inside my eyelids: "If you're not ready, shut up." And I shut up. Look at Hal. He's swamped with feelings himself, or is he? His face is strangely calm. I feel unexpectedly close to him. I've had a few deific fantasies myself. To myself: "There's not enough room for two Gods in this world, stranguh." What the hell's going on with me? Wisecracks at this point? I'm unnerved. Take time, breathe; let the quiet in. We are silent, briefly. Then I hear him sigh.

Hal is talking, almost talking to himself. "I guess I've always thought I was God. Or Jesus. Or something or someone like that. I never believed I would die. Still don't. Really believe I can do anything if I just put my power to it, just really focus in on it. Have done almost everything I really tried to do. Sports, grades, degrees, marriage, kids. . . . Kids! Tim sure doesn't think I'm God. He used to. I think he really did. I overheard him talking to the other kids one time when he was four, maybe five. 'My dad can fix it! My dad can fix it!' He was excited about something. I don't even remember what. 'My dad can fix it,' he shouted. 'My dad can fix anything!' And some place down inside of me I thought, 'That's right. I can.' But I can't fix it with Tim today, can I?"

"Tim doesn't think you're God anymore."

"No, Tim doesn't think I'm God. That's for sure. I don't know what I think. When I was little, my mother and father were in some religious thing in which they believed everybody was God. You know, we all have powers that we don't use, to heal the sick, to raise the dead, to move mountains. I don't know even today; maybe it's so. I'd guess I heard just enough to confirm my own ideas. I am God! It still feels like that's my secret, like I shouldn't tell you, or I'll lose it. But it still feels like it's really so. And I don't believe I'll die—or, at least, not until I choose to."

"It's hard for you to tell even now how much you believe it and how much you don't."

"Oh, I suppose my educated, adult mind knows that it's all a lot of crap. But there's another part of me. . . . "

Jim. The belief in being special, in being different in some mysterious or divine way—probably we all have it, or at least have had it. It's a secret—one we may have been conscious of in childhood but one that most of us gradually learned to hide and ultimately most to deny.

But the denial seldom is total. In some hidden corner of our psyche it persists. I am special. I am not just another person.

Of course, we each are special to ourselves. Only within ourselves do we know our inner experiencing. No matter how close we come to one another, no matter how open we try to be to someone, still there is the unbridgeable gap between us. We are separate. We are unique.

Nor is this a delusion or a defect. We are most human when we are at once most uniquely ourselves and at the same time genuinely in relation with others. Thus our intrinsic duality confirms both our commonality and our individuality.

Louise. Louise is working well on her need to be pleasing. She traces its influence with the director of her agency, her colleagues, and even her students. She finds it pervading all aspects of her life, and now she is increasingly furious with its domination.

"Really, Jim, I feel as though I'm possessed. You know,

as though there was an alien presence in me forcing me to do things I don't want to do, forcing me to listen to what the other person needs, and shutting off my awareness of my own wants."

"It's like something has taken you over, huh?"

"Yes. I say something to someone, and right away, I see that I never even thought about my own views. Don asked me at lunch whether I'd also like the crab salad he was thinking of ordering. Just a simple question. Instantly I told him how good that sounded, and he was pleased. Do you know? . . . " She pauses, lets the force of her feeling mount. "Do you know, *I didn't even check with myself for one second?* I just said yes."

But the very fact that she is more constantly aware of this compulsion to agree means that she is beginning to catch it sooner, and sometimes even before it occurs.

Late in the hour Louise tells me with obvious pleasure about her developing relation with a Dr. Don Webber, a psychiatrist who has recently joined the staff of the agency where she works.

"He's such a nice person, really, Jim. He was divorced a couple years ago and has just decided to move to the west coast. He seems to like me, and, though we've just been out together twice, I find he's in my thoughts a lot these days."

"You must be pleasing him."

"Oh!" She pauses, considers this, then looks at me very soberly. "Yes, I am. I am pleasing him. And I'm glad." Now she stops again to think before going on. "I just don't want to sell myself out anymore—to please him or anyone."

"Mm-hmmm."

"And I find I do it so quickly. I can hardly catch myself. It happened again—or almost happened at the office." She looks troubled but determined.

"What happened?"

"When Dr. Clifton asked me to take on another supervisee, I started to say, 'Of course,' just the way I always do; but I caught it before the words got out of my mouth. I sort of stumbled, and then I told him that my workload was such that I just couldn't do a responsible job with even one more."

"How'd he take that?"

"Oh, it was all right with him. He said he was sorry, since he'd like this student to have what I uniquely give to my trainees, but he understood. That almost got me. I started to say that I could rearrange things and add the student after all, but . . . I didn't!" She's pleased. So am I.

Our good-bye hug today is quick but joyful. I like those hugs. Too much?

Jim. There's no doubt about it, Louise gets to me as a person and, very much, as a man. I have given this a lot of thought. Am I too turned on by her? Should I do something about it? If so, what?

I've had a couple long lunches with Al, my dearest friend and confidant, and pretty much laid it all out for him. He is concerned but not alarmed, he says. Together we think through what is involved.

I'm not as authentic at home as I am with my clients. I've known that for some time now, and I worry about it. That has advantages for the work, and disadvantages. With Louise, for example, to pretend not to have any reaction to her, to try to hide all my feelings, would make for inauthenticity in our relation. And it would dull my necessary sensitivity to her way of being.

Traditional wisdom is that I should transfer her to another therapist. I've talked with Al about taking her if I should decide to do that. He's willing, but he thinks it's premature and risky.

The big risk is that if I transfer her now it will be a replay of the transfers she had from her parents' home to her uncle's to the Coltens' and ultimately to the older lady whom she took care of. It will be another rejection based on her not pleasing (by overpleasing)!

I've simply got to keep as aware as possible, for the time being at least.

Friday, January 20

Jennifer. "Well, Jim, I went to your group last night, and . . . and I . . . uh, I think it's probably not the thing I need right now. I mean, I'm sure that it's fine for some people, but. . . . "

"But?"

"No, it's just that. . . . Well, I don't think. . . . " She pauses, uncomfortable, debating what she will say.

"You keep starting to say something and then stopping yourself. Can you tell me what that's like inside you?"

"Well, it's that the group. . . . you see, it's sort of. . . . Well, they seemed so kind of emotionally troubled . . . and mixed up. I mean, take the big man, Hal, for example. He just sat there, and he didn't say much of anything, but he felt so tense and. . . . And then Louise, who seemed like such a nice woman, but she was so upset about something I didn't understand."

"Mm-hmm."

"And Ben seemed kind of mean about most everything. And the other one, I mean the man who . . . the one who was out of work. His name is 'Frank' or 'Hank' or something."

"Frank."

"Yes, well, Frank frightens me. Not because he's kind of angry, but because he seemed so far down, like Hal. I kept thinking of them. I kind of worried that one of them — Hal or Frank — might. . . . I mean, they all seemed to have such bad things happening to them, and. . . . "

"And? . . . "

"And I suppose I ought to learn from them that my problems aren't so bad and quit feeling so sorry for myself, but . . . but anyway, I don't think I need to go back. Besides, I have so much to do right now for the college, and. . . . "

"Jennifer, so far you haven't really leveled with me about what is stirred up in you by being in the group."

"Well, yes, uh, I suppose so. You see, the thing is that I was kind of disappointed that you didn't say more and give the group more guidance. We just seemed to wander all over without any plan." She pauses, musters her resolve. "And frankly — I don't like to say this — but frankly, I didn't think the others would be so . . . so . . . so sick. I mean, those people really have serious troubles."

"They seem so much worse off than you are?"

"Well, not exactly. I don't mean really that their troubles are so much worse. I mean, the thing between me and Bert and this problem I have in being so confused about my own thoughts and feelings. . . . Well, I suppose those things are not so different. But these people seem so broken or torn up or something. I mean, I didn't know they would be so bad off about things, if you see what I mean."

"I think I do, but why don't you tell me more so I can be sure."

"Well, like Frank, you know. I thought a lot about him last night after the meeting. I wondered if maybe I should say something and see if I could buck him up. He really sounded pretty bad. Weren't you worried about him? You know, the way he talked about wanting to just close his eyes on the freeway and all?"

"You found Frank's misery sticking in your thoughts, eh?"

"Oh, yes! I just wonder whether he got home all right. Oh, I suppose I'm being kind of ridiculous. You probably know what you're doing, and besides it's none of my business really."

"But it does kind of make you wonder, doesn't it, whether it was wise for me to let Frank go off alone that way?"

"Well, not really. You know Frank a lot better than I do, and I don't want to butt in on something where I have no business, you know. . . . "

"It seems to make you uncomfortable to express any doubts about me."

"Yeah, I guess it does. But that's not the main point anyway. The main thing is that I just don't think the group is the thing I need right now."

When a new person comes into a psychotherapy group, her frequent reaction is that the other people in the group are much sicker or much more disturbed than she and that the therapist has probably made a mistake in placing her in the group. This reaction is, of course, what Jennifer is expressing. She is actually responding to the manner in which group members talk about their subjective experiences. In most of our day-to-day lives, we express our inner emotions and impulses in front of others only when in great stress or personal disruption. So Jennifer mistakes the openness of group members for signs of severe psychological disturbance.

Now I must help Jennifer to face her misgivings. Gradually, she recognizes that she is not so different from the others, but that the "rules" for herself made it hard to accept her likeness to them. This leads us to her recognizing that the group is a good place to work on these rules and on her fear of being who and as she really is. We agree that she will return for at least five more sessions before again considering dropping out.

I've learned the hard way that putting new people into an ongoing group can be disruptive of their therapeutic work and sometimes of the alliance I have with them. Thus I now insist on at least a six-session commitment before they enter the group.

Jim. Damn it! I'm mad at Hal. Yes, I'm concerned about him, but right now I'm pissed. He's canceled twice. That's not being straight with me, and I'm going to tell him so.

For whose benefit? Mine or his? For his, of course, he needs to know that he matters. And, of course also, for mine. I need to feel I can count on him, especially at these times. For my own peace of mind. Our needs come together, and we both need to be in regular touch.

Listening to my own thoughts, I wonder if, like Hal, I think I'm God and am responsible for all my clients — and my family, and everyone else I have anything to do with? Yes, and no. No, mostly, but some yes. Am I my brother's keeper? Tough question. I've been a poor brother to my real brother. That bothers me. But it bothers me more that I might fail my clients who put their trust — and their lives, in varying but significant degrees — in my keeping.

No, I can't *keep* their lives. I can only do so much, not take care of all that matters to them. They know that — at least, I hope they do. I know that, and I'm growing in how surely I know that. It's too much indeed, as Hal is miserably recognizing, to try to do it all, have all the answers. If I can just help people use their own resources, help them see how they block their own purposes, that's enough. No, it may not be enough, but it's all I can ask of myself. A realistic answer; I'm not altogether content with it.

It's the difference between what is objective, reasonable,

and explicit and what is more implicit, subjective, and perhaps
not so reasonable. I'm much concerned with how we all deafen
and blind our inner sense, our subjective knowing. I'm trying
to be more inwardly aware myself and to help my clients to be.
But that's a loaded enterprise.

Hal has really entered into his innerness, and it's brought
out some startling, explosive recognitions; but it's also stunned
him, pushed him to reevaluate his expectations of himself, his
commitments to his clients, and his life generally. So overwhelming is this recognition that he thinks of ending his life!

The eruption into consciousness of long suppressed thoughts
and feelings can come smashing into our view of ourselves and
our world. Ideally, this emergence is gradual, and it is possible
to integrate what is learned as we go. Sometimes, as with Hal,
it is explosive, and we must be prepared for damage control.
Still, that opening has life-renewing, potential benefits so great
we need to continue to encourage it. We don't give up dynamite
because it's dangerous; we try to use it wisely, with caution.

Monday, January 23

Hal. Last Monday, Hal uncovered the belief that had been hidden even from himself: that he was God and therefore was required to know all that was needed by those who consulted him
and almost everyone else in his life. Tuesday he left a message
that he wouldn't come to his appointment Thursday but would
make the group. Friday morning the phone-answering service
called me early to say Hal had left a message that he was out
of town and wouldn't be in for his appointment that day. Now
it is Monday, and I've had no individual time since last Monday and the shock he (and I) experienced then. I don't like it.
I don't like it one bit.

It's briefly reassuring to see him in the waiting room, but
only briefly. His manner is distant, and the usual surface joviality
is absent. He enters with a brief nod, tosses his coat on a chair,
and sits on the couch.

"Sorry to have missed seeing you. Needed to get away.

Probably should have stayed longer." Flat, matter-of-fact. I notice the absence of any subjects for the verbs. Is this significant or picayune? I decide to play it.

"Who?"

"Who what?"

"Who needed to get away? Who should have stayed longer?"

"I did." No rise to the bait. No response to the implicit message.

"Tell me about it."

"Last time here kind of shook me up. Figured I better think about it. Told my wife I had to go on business. Went to San Diego. Stayed in a motel. Didn't do much real thinking."

"Hard to find your sense of 'I,' of being the one who did those things."

"Yeah, think you're right."

"Who does?" Wanting to needle him, to bring him out of that deadness.

"Sorry I didn't give you more notice. No time, really. Just needed to get alone." He doesn't seem to even notice the needle.

"What the hell's therapy for, except to give you a chance to think things through for yourself?"

"Yeah, I know. But I couldn't do it. I'm sorry, Jim. I know you care, but I couldn't do it."

"You had to do it your way, Hal. The point is, did you do it? Where are you now?"

"I don't know. I don't know if I did it; whatever 'it' is. I don't know where I am now. I just don't know."

"Lost."

"Lost. Right, lost."

"And so alone."

"Always been alone. Always will be alone. Don't really belong with people. Can't really be with them."

"What's that mean?" Needling again. Something in this withdrawn, dead mood triggers an attack from me. Feels right for what Hal needs.

"How do you do it, Jim?" Sudden burst of feeling; not hearing my question or caring about the needle. "How do you — or anybody — do it? How can you carry all the load? The people who come to see you — like me and the other poor slobs — and your family and all the others. How do you do it?"

My impulse is to say "do what?" but let's risk going more directly: "So many, so heavy, and you're so alone."

"So goddamn alone. So goddamned alone. I am God damned. I mean just that. I am God damned. Do you know what I mean?" Deadness gone, dreadful urgency. Not panic but anguish.

"You're no God, but God damned, damned by God, huh?"

"Yes, yes. Oh, Christ, I sound like a madman. Am I mad, Jim? Am I psychotic? Have you thought . . . of course you have. What do you think, am I nuts? I mean, give it to me straight. Have I flipped out? Do I need to be hospitalized? I almost hope you'll say 'yes.' Come on, Jim, level with me!" The last is harsh, commanding.

"You're not God, and I'll level with you in my own way! Just idle back. You're not psychotic, but you're playing with it. You could work yourself up to be hospitalized, but I won't be part of it. I won't help you cop out on being human."

"But I can't do it. It's too much. I don't know how you do it. I don't want to cop out, but I don't know how to carry this load. Really, I don't; can't you understand that?"

"What you're saying is that you can't be responsible for your wife and your son and your daughter and Mrs. Kanowsky and Bill Lewis and the guy with the drinking problem and the couple who fight and all your students and all your friends and everybody else in the whole damn world. You can't do it because you're not God and because you don't know enough and because you can't read enough or take enough courses or whatever. You're just an old ex-jock who tries to get along as best he can but who can't live up to all everybody else expects of him and who sure as hell can't live up to all he expects of himself."

"That's easy for you to say, maybe, but it's not for me."

"What the hell is that supposed to mean?"

"I mean, you never thought you could take care of everything, and so you never set up your life and all your relationships so that people expected you to take care of everything. So you don't have to suddenly face them and yourself with the fact that you can't do a damned thing for them or yourself or anybody else."

"You're still playing God and telling me how special you are and how different I am and have been. Well, let me tell you, buddy, you don't know what's in my life and my relationships."

"You know, that's right! I don't really know, do I? Maybe you're as nutty as I am! *The Christs of Ypsilanti,* eh? How many were there? Three? Six? Maybe you do know what it's like. Do you?"

"Hal, sometime I'll be glad — more than glad — to talk with you about this, but not now. Right now, you stay with your need to take care of everybody and everything, and how you can't do it because you're only human."

"It sounds dumb to me right now, but a minute ago it seemed absolute truth, the way it really is. I don't think it's really gone, either. It's like I can feel it in the back of my mind someplace."

"Don't use energy to fight it, Hal. That will just keep it there."

"Huh? Oh, I see. Never thought of it that way. So what do you think I should do when it starts up again?"

"This sounds easy, but it's damned hard; still, it's the only thing that will work in the long run: When you recognize the god-feeling coming on you, just take note of it and set it aside."

"'Take note of it' — I don't know what that means."

"What color sweater are you wearing today?"

"What color? Oh; blue; why? Oh, I think I see."

"Tell me."

"Well, I can take note of that, the color of my sweater, but I don't have to dwell on it. That the system?"

"Pretty much. As you can imagine it's not as easy as your sweater color, but the principle is the same. You want to recognize that the god-feeling is one you have — you might say, you wear — sometimes, but it's not you. It's a thought you learned to have and that comes up sometimes, but it's only one thought among many."

"Whoa, whoa! I think I'm getting it, but I'm afraid I won't remember all of that."

"You're right, it was too much; but that's okay. Let yourself just keep the general idea. Then you'll work with it as you need to, and you'll probably give it your own twist."

"Yeah, I hope so. It's not my usual way, but what is these days?"

"One more thing, Hal, and it's a big thing—a thing between us." He looks surprised, sobered.

"Don't stand me up again," hard voice. "I mean that. You may not feel you care much about life or whatever, but I do and having you cut out on me is not acceptable. *You be here* when we have an appointment. I really mean that."

"Yes, I hear that you do." He pauses, his eyes moisten, then he looks me full in the face. "I'll be here, Jim."

Jim. After Hal leaves I bring myself back to a question that has been hovering: Why do I always unload so much—too much—on Hal at once? I must want to play God with him by having lots of good answers—and answers he didn't know. Yes (embarrassed by this), answers he didn't know. That's the nub. I'm showing him how rich my perspective is—in understandings his didn't have. Yuck!

Monday, February 6

Louise. Finally, Blacks are refusing to stay second class. I feel real sympathy for their cause, and have contributed to CORE often. A small act, but it is doing something. Yet I'm uneasy when protest turns to riot. My clients have taught me how impotence gives birth to fury, and there is so much stored up racial rage.

It seems to contradict my formula—impotence $\rightarrow$ anger— to see affluent younger people also acting out fury, until I realize that privilege bestowed is not power attained—indeed, can feel to the recipients like a demonstration of their powerlessness.

These thoughts are in the back of my mind as Louise tells me how the new director of her agency seems determined to turn the clock back and keep all traditions firmly in place.

"He found a student social worker and her client sitting on the floor for their interview, and he was outraged. When

I asked what they were doing — thinking they might be engaged in something unprofessional, you know — he didn't know what I meant. 'Conducting a social work interview, Miss Gowan, and sitting on the floor to do it!' His only objection was to where they were sitting."

"So?"

"Well, you know how the young people seem to like sitting on the floor, on the sidewalk, and so on. I don't see what harm there is in it, but Dr. Elliott was as indignant as if they'd been . . . been doing something they shouldn't."

"Have trouble saying the first thing that came to mind?"

"Yes." She purses her lips ruefully. "But it is so sad, Jim. We're just getting our program for teenagers going so well, and the whole staff seems to be pulling together as a team, and now Dr. Elliott is . . . is going to ruin it all, I'm afraid."

"How does he feel toward you?"

"I don't know. How would I know?"

I don't answer, just look at her steadily, confidently.

"Oh, I suppose I have some idea. We get along well enough, I guess (pause). I know what you're. . . . Probably I'm making sure he's pleased with me." She looks up in disgust.

"Now you've given me the right answer."

"Well, I. . . . Anyway, I just feel sorry to see what's happening."

"You'd like to change the subject."

"You're the one who changed the subject" (mischievously).

"Did you tell Dr. Elliott how you feel about a worker and client sitting on the floor to conduct an interview?"

"Oh, no (crestfallen). I told him I'd talk to the student to see whether there was any reason she felt it was necessary to conduct the interview that way. He said that wouldn't be necessary since he'd already reprimanded her. However, he told me, I should immediately inform all my trainees that there would be no further deviations from appropriate professional conduct."

"So? . . ."

"So I've been putting it off, but I suppose I'll have to do it." She pauses, looks at me almost beseechingly, and protests, "Well, he is my superior. What else can I do?"

"What else can you do?"

"Oh, I suppose I could. . . . "

"Louise, stop right there. You're about to respond to my question and even to the whole situation we're discussing as though you were a child, a pupil, and you haven't performed as well as you should, but now you'll try to come up with the right answers and perhaps even go try to put them into practice. But I have yet to hear from Louise Gowan, M.S.W., what her professional opinions really are and how she intends to deal with this professional problem."

"Ohhh! Yes, you're right! That makes me so mad. That's just what I do again and again and again. There is no Louise Gowan, M.S.W., professional. There is only a good child, trying to please the adults! I hate it!" She is quite genuinely enraged — and quite appropriately.

Jim. What can Louise do? It's not my job to answer that question, I'm glad to know. Yet it is my job to think whether I'm encouraging her unrealistically. She needs her job; she does good, useful work in it. If I push her until she gets fired, what will be accomplished? If I slack off confronting her, do I conspire with Dr. Elliott to keep needed change from happening?

Well, let's not get grandiose, Jim. If you do your real job with Louise, you're not going to push her or not push her; so you won't be making the decision for her. My job is to help her see clearly the choices she is facing and their likely consequences.

That takes some of the god-load off, for I sure don't know the best answer for her situation. Still, I wonder if I'm also providing myself with an answer that relieves me and obscures the subtle ways I may influence her decision.

Can't tell right now. Need to keep thinking about it.

Tuesday, February 7

Hal. Yesterday, Hal was still in his slump; and today he comes in as though he's in some suspended state. It gets to me and arouses far echoes in my unconscious. I don't like it; he's staying down too long. True, it's no small thing to yield up the deep, primitive conviction of divinity and immortality. His adult mind always rejected such thoughts, yet subtly they framed his conscious life. (Nor is Hal unique in this. Many of us hold miraculous beliefs deep in our being, beliefs that we would deny or ridicule if suddenly they were made explicit and conscious.)

Now he sits on the couch, talks vaguely about changes for the course he teaches, pauses silently, and sighs unawarely too often — his eyes vague, not fully focused; body heavy, sagging.

"I'm thinking of dropping the appointment at the college. It's a drag, and the kids are more interested in rebelling than learning. I don't see much point in it." He drifts off.

"What's going on?" Irritation, sadness, apprehension creep into my chest and stomach.

"Huh? Oh, I don't know. Where was I?"

"Where are you now, that's more important."

"Just kind of wondering . . . about you and this work we . . . you do. What's it like for you? How do you see it?"

Quick estimate: Will it help him for me to answer or will it feed his passivity? I'll go with his question; at least it's a step out of his inner preoccupation.

"I've a sort of fantasy that comes to me at times, imagery about our work. Would you like to hear it?"

A bit more alive, Hal smiles slightly. "Yes, thanks, Jim."

"I see us all — you, me, all humans — as people climbing on a mountain. We climb day and night. Sometimes it's bright and sunny, sometimes it's foggy and easy to lose our way or our footing; sometimes it's night, and in the dark we just sort of blunder along, tripping, bruising ourselves. When one of us falls, then — " I'm a little embarrassed as I choke up; this image always moves me.

" — When one of us falls, I realize that none of us has arms or hands; so the only way for someone to get back up is for someone else to come along, get down, and put his shoulder against the shoulder of the one who's fallen. Then they push together and both can get up. Of course, there's always the possibility that the one who stoops to help will lose his own footing and fall. So those are scary times, but they're close, good times too.

"And so we go on climbing. Often we forget why we climb, but then occasionally the fog lifts when we're on a high place and in the distance on a peak we see the city of our fondest hopes. It cheers us to keep climbing even though we know the night and fog will come back, and we will wonder whether we just imagined that city. Still most of us keep climbing and keep trying to help the others."

Hal and I sit silently for several minutes. I get no clue to what my words have meant for him. Finally, when the buzzer announces the next client, he rouses himself. "Yeah," he gets up and puts on his raincoat, "yeah, Jim. Gotta think about it. Thanks, huh?" And he's gone.

I sit back a minute letting my inner workings have their time. It's a corny image . . . or is it? It means something important to me, and I don't want to analyze it any more than I want to analyze my doodles.

It means something for me, but it didn't seem to do much for Hal.

Kate. "I woke up this morning with such a good feeling." Kate smiles with an odd little twist to her mouth. She seems childlike in her pleasure. "It's been years since waking up was a good feeling. I can't really say how it happened, but I just know that I felt so much more ready for the day. I haven't looked at my mail in days, and now I'm curious to see what's in it. I've collected a whole batch of mail, you know, and it's like I'm going to open up those envelopes and find interesting things and hear from people I've practically forgotten about but now I want to hear from."

"Um-hmm." I'm trying to get a better sense of just where her feelings and thoughts are coming from. In some way, she seems to be skating on the surface, and I feel troubled as I listen to her. At times it seems that the secret of a psychotherapist's task is to be perverse. When clients are unhappy, the therapist suggests there are other possibilities; when clients say they are happy, the therapist sniffs around for the hidden unhappiness; when clients talk about other people, the therapists urges focusing on one's self; and when clients deal with the past, the insatiable therapist asks that attention be directed to the present.

"I have so many plans, so many things I want to do. All of a sudden, I find my work interesting again. I've gotten a new assignment on some of the amino acids, and I really think I'm going to like working at it. Imagine that! I'm going to like working at it!" She smiles with delight at her own feelings.

"It's really good to feel your interest in your work . . . and in life itself coming back."

"Yes. It really *is* good."

This uncharacteristically happy mood persists for nearly a half-hour as I supply only bridges so she can express herself. It's plain that she is delighting in the freshened appreciation of her life, but it becomes more evident as she continues that she is also pressing herself to keep this mood, and only this mood. Her spontaneity lessens, and she begins repeating things she's already said.

Finally, when she pauses, apparently spent for the moment, I judge it's time to help her be more aware.

"Kate." My voice is very gentle, for I really hate to puncture her balloon of delight. "Kate, it sounds as though you're all through with the bad feelings."

She is silent, but the smile drains rapidly from her face. I wait. She seems to be holding quite still emotionally. I have the impression that she is avoiding any movement of thought, of feeling, or even of body. "What's going on, Kate?"

"Nothing, nothing at all." She tries a smile, but it isn't the same. "I was just thinking about what you said."

"Uh-huh. What are you thinking?"

"Oh, I suppose I'll have some times that aren't as good as right now, but. . . . "

"But?" She knows, but she doesn't want to know.

"Well, I really don't see why I need to. And besides I don't want to think about it now. I'm feeling better at last, and I'm going to stay that way. Or at least I want to as much as possible. So why are you trying to worry me?" Her tone isn't as sure as her words. She is clearly trying to persuade herself as well as me.

"It seems hard for you to think of yourself as flowing."

"We have worked some things out (protesting), and now they are taken care of, so why should I go back to the bad feelings? Don't you think we got rid of some of the problem when I told you about that time my mother got drunk?"

"No."

"No? Well, what's the use of what we're doing if you say 'no' like that?" Annoyed, ready to obscure the issue in a fight with me.

"It makes you mad when I don't see you as some kind of machine where we can remove the defective parts and put in better ones and then let you run more happily."

"Oh, I don't know what you mean. You're just trying to confuse me."

"Kate, you still see yourself in terms of a machine, and you think that how you feel is a product of how the parts are working; you expect that the way you feel today is going to be the way you will feel from now on."

"Well, why not? Isn't that what psychotherapy is all about? Don't I come here to find out what has upset my emotions, then to correct that, so that I can feel better?"

"Phrased that way, the answer is, of course, 'yes,' but that's misleading. Think of it this way, Kate: Can you imagine yourself as a river, rather than as a machine?"

"A river?"

I think of myself as not believing in the merit of direct teaching in therapy; but when I truly confront my practice, I realize I often produce little homilies, medium-sized teachments, and full-scale lectures — although the last genuinely is quite exceptional. I recognize this with some chagrin, feeling that a truly good therapist wouldn't talk as much as I do. However that may be, after rapidly weighing the advantages and disadvantages of going along with Kate's penchant for rationality, I decide a modest instruction is appropriate at this point.

"Yes, Kate, see whether you can get the sense of being a river. A river is never the same; it is always flowing, moving on. The water in the river at any given point today will be gone tomorrow, and other water will be at that point. Moreover, the river runs sometimes in sun, sometimes in shadow, sometimes in the city, sometimes in the forest. The very essence of a river is change, flowingness. You, Kate, and I, and all of us are much more like rivers than fixed, relatively unchanging machines or even hills."

"That's all very poetic, I'm sure, but I can't see what it has to do with my feeling good." She's not ready to meet me on the implicit level.

"You're a river, Kate, right now flowing happily in the sun. There will be rain on other days, but there will be more sunny days as well. It will never be just one way."

"I don't like that. I don't like that at all. Why can't I do whatever needs to be done so that I can get past the misery and have a little happiness I can count on?"

"I'd like that too. We all would. But, so far as I know, life just isn't that way."

Jim. As Kate leaves, I reflect that two of my pet allegories — the climbers on the mountain and the flowing river — seem to have been unimpressive to Hal and Kate, to whom I offered them. Ah well, I'll just have to be content with them by myself.

For some reason, this leads me to think about the poor bastards in Vietnam. They don't have the option of poetic metaphors; life out there is nasty, uncomfortable, depressing, and all too apt to be brief. Why the bloody hell are we still out there? I'm ashamed of my country before the conscience of the world.

Frank. Frank is more neatly dressed than I've ever seen him, although there still is that scruffy quality that I first noticed. He's clean, but his clothes look to be what they very well may be — thrift shop specials. They're not badly mismatched, but his unruly hair and beard detract from the ensemble.

"How's it going, Frank?"

"Shitty, that's how. I just got back from Hawthorne. Do you know that's way to hell and gone when you gotta go by bus?"

"What's cooking in Hawthorne?"

"Nothing. Goddam nothing. I went for a job interview,

and I blew it flat out. 'Sorry, Mr. Connelly, but this job requires dealing with the public, and frankly you look crummy.'
He didn't really say it that way, but I got the message."

"Were you surprised?"

"What do you mean, was I surprised?"

I just wait.

"Oh, hell, I don't want to play games. No, I guess I wasn't
surprised. But you know I hate getting all duded up for some
piss-poor job. What do they expect, white tie and tails?"

"Somehow you knew you weren't looking so great, but
you couldn't let yourself do anything about it."

"What's all this 'somehow' business? Damn it!" He stops
speaking, is silent, debating with himself. "I'm tired of doing
that, but when you do your mind-reading trick it pisses me off;
so pretty soon I'm back to our routine."

"I understand that, Frank, but I also understand you're
making a really sincere effort not to get caught in it so much."

"Yeah. Well, don't make a big deal out of it."

"Frank, listen, I want to level with you. I'm sorry that
when I talk personally — like right now — it gets you uneasy and
needing to push us separate. But, Frank, it's important to our
work that you let yourself be open to it as soon as you can. Now,
that leads me to what we were just talking about. And, Frank,
I do think it's a big deal — and a frightening one for you — to
begin to let down the guard you've depended on for so long and
really try to work with me."

He's silent, digesting this, frowning. Twice he starts to
speak; twice he stops himself. Finally, "Yeah, well, okay. I see
what you mean."

Whoa, Jim, don't jump in! He's just taken a major step.
Go slow, go slow. We wait quietly for a few minutes, which
seem nearly hours.

"You know that damn group really gets me down." He
needs to have something to complain about. It's okay, he just
has to have some time and space.

"What about the group?"

"Aw, they're always on me about being mad. What good
is that supposed to do me? I don't need any more people riding
my ass."

"Uh-huh."

"Take that Kate, the nosey old gal who's always asking questions, 'I don't know much about you, Frank' (mocking voice). Or the nicey dame, Louise, always trying to make everybody feel good. Or. . . . Oh, hell, I don't know. I just don't know whether I should be with people like that."

"Like what?"

"I don't know. Like nice, clean, middle-class jerks (pause). Well, not all of 'em are jerks."

"Which ones?"

"Hey, you know that mouthy guy, Ben? You know what he did? He gave me two leads for jobs. One was the one I busted today, but I'm going to the other one tomorrow. Who'd figure a smart-ass like that would do that?"

"It surprises you that Ben could be friendly?"

"Oh, shit, Jim, I don't know." His voice is almost a cry of pain. I think he's torn between using his old complaining escape and recognizing that he wants to get beyond it.

"It's tough, Frank. Give yourself time."

"Yeah, I suppose so."

"Is there anyone in the group you really feel positive about?"

"Oh, they're all all right, I guess. The big beefy guy, Hal, sure is in a tough place right now, isn't he?"

"You didn't say whether there was anyone you really like. I know that's hard for you, but see what you can do."

"Yeah (pause). Well, like I said, Hal's pretty much an okay guy, and. . . . "

"And? . . . "

"Oh, Christ, I just know you're going to make a big fucking deal out of what I might say about that one who's so knocked out, the one who's husband screwed some other dame."

"Hard to remember her name?"

"No, dammit. It's Jenny . . . Jennifer."

"What about her?"

"Well, I . . . I don't know. I guess, I think she's kind of special or different or something. If she weren't married I might. . . . Oh, shit, forget it. I like her. That's all."

"But it makes you uncomfortable to say it."

"No, it's just that you always. . . . Oh, all right. I guess it does, kind of."

Slowly, slowly, I tell myself. Frank has taken several big risks today and trusted me a great deal. He really expects that I'll laugh at him or tell him why he shouldn't have these feelings. That's all he's known in the past.

We don't talk more about his feelings for Jennifer. For me to force it would be highly counterproductive. Yet it's obvious that under the rough way he avoids her interest in him, Frank is hiding a strong response to her. And letting himself have that response is yet another big risk he's taking.

Twelve

"I'll Kill Her. I'll Kill Her!"

Thursday, February 9

Group Psychotherapy. Frank is talking about his feelings of misery. "For a long time I just felt constantly hopeless and like 'What the hell's the use?' Nothing mattered, and I'd just sit there feeling I was no damn good, and the world was no damn good, and why didn't I just blow the whole bit? But now, lately, I don't know quite why, but I get these restless feelings, and I can't sit still. I feel miserable as hell, and then I find I'm out roaming around, but I don't know what I'm looking for. Or I'll be as angry as though I'd just been robbed, and I'm not sure why I'm so teed off. I don't know whether I'm getting better or worse, but something's sure going on."

As Frank stops talking, Jennifer darts a quick glance at me, as though hoping to read whether these developments are a good or bad sign. Ben, who would like to take Jennifer under his wing in the group, picks up her action. "What are you looking at Jim for, Jennifer? Did you think he'd give us a character reading on Frank?"

Jennifer is flustered and just a little miffed. "I didn't know I looked at him. I was just going to ask Frank what made him mad these times."

But Ben won't be put off this easily. "I think you're dodging, Jennifer, and trying to get our attention off of you and back on Frank."

"Well, maybe so. But I really would like to know, if I'm not being too nosy. . . . " Pause, quick breath, turn to me. "I mean, if you don't think it would be . . . uh, the wrong thing, I mean, not so good for . . . uh, for you to say. I mean, is what's happening with Frank something you want or? . . . Oh, it's none of my business anyway. Skip it."

And so Jennifer struggles with her feelings, with her concern and fear, with her relatedness and separateness. She wonders whether Frank is improving or getting worse. She's uncomfortable to be concerned. She thinks she shouldn't be so "personal," and she pulls back from asking me for fear it might be wrong for Frank to hear my opinion. It is only slowly that she comes to see how much we are all involved in and with each other.

Thursday, February 16

Hal. Hal is back in the chair, sunk into it with a lumpish quality that contrasts with the animal-like grace that previously has been his. "I don't feel like I've anything special on my mind to say, Jim." He doesn't seem sad, angry, or anything else that I can discern. I remember his self-description, "waiting," and I feel a tiny shudder in my back.

"Hal, what's it like inside of you right now?"

"Just kind of . . . murky, I guess you'd say. I mean, it's hard for me to know or to describe. I don't seem to have many clear thoughts or feelings. I have a sense that it's 'time out' inside of me right now. I don't know how else to say it."

"Do you have any feelings of wanting, of yearning, of wishing for anything right now?"

"Not that I'm aware of. No, I don't think so. I sometimes. . . . " He stops, seems to be considering.

"Sometimes?"

"I don't know what I was going to say. I guess that some-

times I have sort of idle daydreams. . . . No, that doesn't feel
like what I mean. Sort of like I'm sorting through old pictures
in my mind, and seeing which ones I want to keep and which
I'll throw out."

"Like what?"

"Like the other night after Greta and I went to bed. I don't
know just why. . . . Well, yes, maybe I do. We haven't had sex
for quite a while now, and I guess my body was complaining,
but my feelings just haven't been interested. And she seems not
to mind too much and. . . . "

He pauses. I realize how little I know of Hal's ongoing life, how little any therapist can know. We know so much
about the people we work with, so much more than we know
about almost anyone else, but still it is so little. I ought to
recall that more often. It would be an antidote to my own
deific impulses. Attention back to Hal: He's just sitting there
like he's forgotten what he was saying. I feel impatient. He
scares me when he's that inert, that—Hmmm! I don't want
to say it even in my head, eh?—that dead. There. Impatient,
want to stir him up. I'm scared, scared of the deadness in him;
it's like slowly rising water that may ultimately engulf him,
take him away.

"What do you want, Hal? Right now, as you sit here in
the office, what can you find a wanting for? I mean inside of
yourself; can you locate any feeling of desire, of wishing, of
yearning?"

"No, I don't think so."

"You didn't even try, Hal."

"Well." He pauses; his face seems to take form a bit from
the inert expression it's worn so much lately. "I don't know, Jim,
I just don't seem to have much going on inside these days. Let
me try again." He passes his hands over his face, trying to wake
it up.

"Let yourself visualize things, Hal."

Hal stirs with a sigh. "Yeah, like I said, the other night
I was about to go to sleep when I found myself thinking of one
of the girls I see from time to time on campus. A secretary or

something, little older than the students, but dresses like one of the kids. You know, no bra, miniskirt, the whole thing kids do now that is so different than when we were that age. This girl, woman, is probably in her mid-twenties, cute, nice figure, and the shortest miniskirts you ever saw. When she bends over, she leaves nothing to the imagination. The kids seem to take it for granted, but an old guy like me. . . . " He lets it drop incomplete.

"What about an old guy like you, Hal?"

"Oh, I look. I'm not so far gone yet that I don't look. I think that's all I want to do, just look. Then the other night, just before I went to sleep, darned if I wasn't having a fantasy about this gal. Guess there's life in the old boy yet."

I feel the relief like a physical thing. Hal's sexy fantasy says exactly that: There's life in him, not just the deadly, rising water. Want to encourage this spark: "What did you fantasize?"

"Getting to know her, finding some excuse to take her away for a weekend, peeling that minidress off of her, going to bed with her, the works." He pauses, a half-smile on his face, more animation than he's shown in a couple of weeks at least. Then the smile fades, the empty look comes back. "But I won't do anything about it. It's just not worth the trouble. I wish Greta and I had more for each other these days, but we're so far apart. Not just physically; emotionally. She doesn't know where I am, and I don't seem to care enough to try to tell her. She has her own life, all the things she's wound up in, and I've had mine, and we seldom really see each other."

Pausing, he reflects, and his face enlivens from the blankness of a moment ago. "Sometimes I think we should get divorced. I don't give her much, and she doesn't seem to have much for me. The kids are at an age where they could handle a divorce without too much trouble. And then. . . . "

"Then?"

"Then, I might. . . . Oh, what's the use kidding myself?" The aliveness drains out of him, and he slumps in the chair. I wait, but he doesn't seem about to go on.

"What happened just then? You were thinking about what a divorce might mean, and then you suddenly seemed to go limp."

"Oh, nothing. Nothing, really. I just know damn well I'm just talking, just running off at the mouth. I won't try to make that chick. I won't divorce Greta, I won't. . . . "

"Won't what?"

"Oh, I don't know. I guess I was going to say 'won't do any of the other things I used to dream I'd do.'"

"Like what?"

"Like get in on some exploring expeditions. You didn't know that was my secret ambition, did you? Yeah, I always imagined that some day I'd have enough of a name that I'd be invited—or at least welcomed—on an expedition to some fantastic place, like up the Amazon or to the headwaters of the Nile or some other romantic and exciting place. You know, I always thought I'd see all the world. I mean, when I read about fantastic places—like Timbuktu and Afghanistan and Singapore—in some part of my mind, I kind of thought, 'One day I'll be there; I'll see that.' And now I know I never will. I probably won't see any of those places." He stops and seems to sink deeper into himself.

"Never . . . never," my voice is low, flat.

"I won't do any of it: get a sexy gal in bed, divorce Greta, go on an expedition, write the greatest psychology book, whatever."

"You sound pretty discouraged."

"No, no. It's not discouragement. Just kind of flat. That's just the way it is. No use sweating it. I'm an old jock with big dreams who just doesn't have it. I just dream. I don't do anything; don't do a damn thing."

"Nothing. You don't do anything about your life."

"Yeah, that's right. I just sit on my can and bitch." He is beginning to get angry. This is the opening we need.

"And time passes."

"Damn right it does. Time just goes along, and I'm not having a life. What kind of life have I had? I always used to dream I was going to do so many things; go exploring, have a great romance, write books, make a lot of money, see everything, do everything. All big dreams, but I haven't done anything; nothing, nothing at all."

"How old are you, Hal?" Trying to help him get to the slowly emerging feelings.

"Forty-six! Forty-six, damn you. You know very well. I'm forty-six God damned years old. Forty-six wasted years, trying to be God. Forty-six years of not having my own life. I'm still twenty-one or maybe even younger. I'm not ready to be forty-six! I'm not ready to be middle-aged! I'm not ready to be old. Damn! Damn! Damn!"

He is furious, but he is also hurting terribly, I know. He is pent up, beginning to be restless, rousing from his torpor, seeking an avenue of release.

"Hal, you're full of feeling and. . . . "

"Damn!" He shouts, cutting me off. "I just want to scream and cuss and. . . . "

"Go ahead."

"Aaaghh." He makes a strangled cry in his throat.

"You're holding it in."

He tries to scream, but it is an abortive sound. "You're holding yourself in, just as you always have."

"Aieee!" It is more a wail than a scream, but it comes out with surprising strength. "Aw hell, this is silly, Jim."

"Again!" Urgently. "No, it's not silly. Stay with your feeling."

But this time, Hal is self-conscious, and the sound is strangled again.

"You're choking yourself off, Hal. Just as you have for forty-six years. You're choking off your life."

"Shit! *Sheeeeeeit!*" He suddenly bellows so loud that, although I thought I was expecting it, I am startled. Now he begins screeching at the top of his lungs, the sounds becoming more open and full-throated each time. He pounds on the arms of the chair with both fists in tempo with the wild screams that burst from his throat. They are ear-splitting and terrifying sounds. Gradually they seem to be less constricted and tearing, yet even so my own throat is aching sympathetically. I find I am rocking toward him with each cry, feeling the sounds as though they were coming out of my own guts. Hal is screaming for me too, I realize, as I hear myself make sort of a half screech with him. I do it again, and it feels good and terrible at the same time.

I don't want to be in my fifties. I don't want to have my children grown and to have had so little real experience of them. I scream with Hal, and he looks at me, and the tears well up in his eyes. I don't want to have wasted so many years in hiding my own self, my own real feelings, in order to try to be the way I thought I was supposed to be. And Hal and I scream. My throat hurts, and some part of me is glad. And we scream. It is too late, and we scream. It isn't too late, and we scream. It is too late for so much, and we scream, and we scream, and we scream.

Gradually we stop our cries, and both of us are weeping. And we sit drained and strangely at peace. Each of us is within himself, and yet each is with the other. After a long time, Hal whispers, "You too, Jim?"

"Yes, oh yes." And we both weep anew.

Jim. I'm going to try to say once more the basic truths my clients patiently teach me. It always comes out differently, of course. That's the wonder of it; that's the frustration of it.

Humans are inherently hungry for life, greedy for having more and more fulfilling living. Yet so often we postpone or devitalize our living. As one patient said, "I don't experience my life; I tell myself about it."

Breaking out of old patterns, whether individual or societal, is frightening, exhilarating, liberating, dangerous, and vitalizing. Yet breaking out — such as so much of the current youth culture is caught up in — when done solely to break out, delivers only a brief jolt of energy and very quickly becomes deadening. Then we look for a bigger jolt, push the breaking-out further, risk losing the point of the whole thing.

As with any act taken only in opposition to something else, it is still motivated by that something else, having no energy of its own.

These thoughts emerge as I reflect on my experiences with Louise. Throughout the history of psychotherapy, the issue of what degree of involvement between therapist and patient is appropriate has been disputed. Similarly, the extent to which usual social taboos could be allowed to dictate the actions of therapist and patient (as opposed to what they might say) has repeatedly produced intense and self-righteous pronouncements — on both sides of the matter.

On the one hand, the social code born of Victorian morality and mechanomorphic views of human nature insists on a detached, antiseptic, and manipulative stance in the psychotherapeutic process. On the other hand, there is the existential reality of living human feelings, impulses, needs, and relationships. This body of vital experiences shines through the shabby garment of what is proper and makes evident what a betrayal of trust may be concealed by giving first priority to traditional folkways. Lived life often shows a complete disregard for such niceties and instead is involving, messy, and ruthless.

She wants more of life, risks much to go for it. I want more of life for myself . . . and for her. I too risk much.

I believe this wholeheartedly. Is it rationalization? Perhaps, in some measure; that doesn't invalidate it, though. It only traces one part of the motivation.

Monday, April 3

Louise. Is fate a player in our lives? Sometimes it seems so. Dr. Elliott, the new director of Louise's agency, is well picked to force her to confront the conflict between her values and her compulsion to be pleasing.

"I have to go in to see Dr. Elliott again today. That's the fourth time in the last two weeks. It's upsetting. I guess I still try to please him a lot — after all, he is my boss — but on the other hand, I'm always trying to get my students out of his bad graces. I was telling Don the other night that. . . . "

"You're seeing him more now?" (Interested, Jim? Why interrupt her?)

"Oh, yes!"

"Um. What did you tell him?"

"That Dr. Elliott's effect on the staff so far is to make us

more irritable with each other and yet to kind of draw us closer
together at the same time."

"How's it going with Don?" (I'm evidently more interested
in him than in Dr. Elliott. Watch it!)

"Oh, it's so nice to be going with someone again. Do you
know it's been almost two years since I've had more than a single date with someone?"

"How come?"

"I guess it's just that I don't believe in . . . in being intimate right away?"

"Intimate?"

"Oh, you know, getting all sexually involved right on the
first date. I mean, a lot of men if they take you out seem to
feel that you should at least pet a lot if not go to bed with them."

"And you don't want to?"

"Not right away like that. I might like to be tender a little, but I really don't want to get . . . to get more physically involved so soon."

"How about Don?"

"We've been getting to know each other gradually."

"How's that going?"

"Uh, it's nice. I mean, he's a very gentle and warm person. I really enjoy being with him."

"You sound very correct and formal."

"Well, I don't know why you want to know all of this."

"But you don't ask me."

"Well, all right, why do you?"

"Are you asking because I told you to or because you want
to know?"

"Oh, darn you! Wait a minute (pause). Well, why do
you?"

"I think it's a combination of wanting to have you keep
aware of how you are handling moving into a relatively new
area, and of my personal interest in you as a man."

"Oh!"

"What does that mean?"

"Uh . . . it means that I've felt this personal interest, but
I didn't expect you'd ever say it right out that way."

"Now I have."

"Yes, and I'm glad you did. Well, Don and I haven't had sex. No, that's not so. We haven't had intercourse. But we do kiss and touch, and oh, it is so nice. It has been so long. I don't know whether I really love him or not, but I do love being close and feeling our warmth. He is such a dear man, so caring."

Frank. Today, when I go to the waiting room in response to Frank's ring, I almost fail to recognize him. He is cleaner, neatly dressed in somewhat worn slacks and sweater, shoes not exactly shined but certainly cleaned, hair and beard trimmed to very presentable proportions. And he is very self-conscious. Neither of us says anything until he is seated in the office.

Frank lights a cigarette with undue concentration, making quite a business of getting it right and arranging an ashtray on the arm of his chair. Then he fixes his familiar spot on the opposite wall with a ferocious glare. I wait quietly. He stirs, draws deeply on the cigarette, busily taps the ash off, examines the burning end, draws on it again, taps it again.

"Shit!" What a wonderful word that is, capable of so many nuances. It is amazing how long we suppressed such a facile verbal instrument. Now, in a single syllable, Frank has conveyed intense feeling, exasperation with that feeling, and wanting me to break the silence.

"You look very different, Frank, but you sound pretty much the same."

"Yeah. I got a job."

"Good. At least I guess it is. Is it?"

"I feel like a damned fool. You know that, don't you? I mean the clothes and hair and all. I don't know why, but I do. And it pisses me off. I hate feeling this way."

"It really is miserable to feel self-conscious about breaking out of a mold."

"What do you mean, 'breaking out of a mold'? What mold?" Pause. "Oh, skip it, I know what you mean. Shee-yit! I feel like I want to start bickering like we used to do."

"Yeah, it would kind of keep us busy and. . . . "

"Same time, I'm tired of wasting my time and money on

that crap. Look, I got a job. You'd never believe it. Remember that old creep at the Cosmopolitan Hotel, the one who was threatening to have me fired for something I said to him? Gandowsky. Yeah, Ephraim Gandowsky. Anyway, I ran into him in the cafeteria, and the old guy was real friendly. 'How are you? What you been doing?' All that crap. At first I was suspicious of him, but by God, he was on the level. So pretty soon we're gabbing like a couple of old biddies, and he's filling me in on all the shit about the hotel. Seems Berman got promoted and Hicks — he was the bell captain — got fired, and a lot of other stuff like that. Fact is, it turns out, Gandowsky complained because I was fired. Imagine that! He'd heard the story of how I got caught screwing with that chick, and he was all turned on by it. Made me tell the whole thing, and he got so excited, I thought he was going to come right there in the cafeteria. He just laughed like crazy. Then he asked me what I was doing, and when I told him I was stony broke, he said he'd give me a job. Seems he runs a big printing business over on Kenmore. Said I had to clean up a bit though, so here I am. Shee-yit! What a screwy deal, huh?"

"Sounds pretty good to me."

"Yeah, I'm not knocking it. You know, he's a pretty good old guy. Told me I had to keep my hands off the women in his place, though. But you know, I never figured him to be that way. I mean, I never figured he'd give a guy like me any kind of a break. Don't know what's in it for him. Maybe he wants me to tell him sexy stories. Don't think he's queer. He didn't act like it anyway."

"It's hard for you to understand why anybody might like you or want to do something for you."

"Aw, I don't know. I just wonder. . . . Hell, skip it. I don't dig what his trip is anyway. He's all. . . . "

"You really get uncomfortable anytime there's a hint of any closeness or emotion in relation to you."

"Oh, for Christ's sake, you keep telling me that! It's all a lot of shit anyway. You know it. Everybody's really only out to get whatever he can; so don't come on like the Salvation Army."

"You'd feel a lot better about getting in a fight with me rather than dealing with this miserable feeling inside of yourself."

"What miserable feeling?"

"The one you'd be aware of if you didn't jump up and down and wave your arms to distract yourself."

"I don't know what you mean. You get these screwy ideas about. . . ."

"Frank, I'm starting to get caught into the old game, and so are you. I want to pull out of it, and I think a good part of you does too."

"Yeah, I don't want to waste my time on that shit anymore."

"Me neither."

"But, playing it straight, what miserable feeling do you mean?"

"Just wait a minute, Frank, and see what it's like in your guts right now. What do you feel right in the middle of you, apart from our bickering, apart from the details of your new job, apart from anything else? What do you feel in you right now?"

He pauses, sinks down in his chair, shoves his hands in his pockets so that his shoulders hunch up around his ears. Frank has come a long way; he's really trying to work with me now. Be patient, I tell myself; you should make as much of a change in your own hang-ups, Jim.

"Jim, I don't know. It's hard to get a hold of. Mostly I feel kind of like a bellyache; only it doesn't really seem like it's my belly or a real physical ache, and yet it is too. I mean, I think I feel bad, but I don't know why. Jesus Christ! I just got a job and at better pay than I got at the fucking hotel, why should I feel bad?"

"Wait, Frank. Don't get off on that for a minute. You really were in touch with your guts for a minute. Just stay with that, can you?"

Silence again. Then he looks up at me, and it's like the first time Frank and I have ever really looked at each other. His face is completely naked, all the surly, defensive look gone. "I am just so goddamned lonely I could shit."

Thursday, April 13

Group Psychotherapy. Spring is announced by budding flowers, leafing trees, and less concealing clothes on women. Ah, spring, beautiful spring!

In the group, the conversation suggests spring fever.

Louise: "I've been struggling at work, as I've told you all before, with our director. He's such a pill! I think he hasn't had a new idea since World War II. And you know how I'm always trying to please people? So I find myself doing it with him too. And I hate that. I mean I really do."

Jennifer: "It sounds a lot like what I'm having to do at the college. The dean of students wants us to be very firm — even tough — in disciplining the students who get out of line, and I don't like doing that."

Kate: "It must be very hard to do what you two have to do. I don't think I could do it."

Ben: "This is beginning to sound like a seminar of the academic council."

Kate: "Oh! Oh, I. . . . "

Ben: "Not you, Kate. Our two lady administrators are the ones who get off in their heads. You talked about feelings."

Louise: "I didn't mean to be abstract."

Frank: "You don't have to apologize to make him pleased with you."

Louise: "That's right, I don't. Well, Ben (sarcastically), I'm sorry you didn't appreciate the deeper emotions Jennifer and I were expressing."

Jennifer: "Yes, you missed the real point, the emotional point that Louise and I are having real emotional struggles."

Ben: "I guess I was distracted by Louise's tits. They're looking unusually good tonight." Kate looks uncomfortable.

Hal: "Ben, you are crude."

Ben: "Somebody's got to get us down to earth here. Now come on, hasn't everybody noticed what a great shape she has?"

Hal: "I've got to admit I have."

Frank and Jennifer make noises of agreement.

Louise: "You all are making me embarrassed."

Kate: "I think they like to do that."

Louise: "Since it's come up, I'll tell you that I've always been embarrassed about how large my breasts are. I wish I had a figure more like Jennifer's."

Jennifer: "What?" She stares at Louise. "You're teasing me."

Louise: "No, I'm not. You are so trim and slim. I feel sort of fat and dumpy compared to you."

Jennifer: "You really mean that (incredulous)?"

Louise: "Oh, yes (sadly). I really do."

Jennifer (looking to me): "You put her up to that, didn't you, Jim?" How she has to find someone to blame — even now!

Jim: "No, I didn't. What does this mean for you?"

Jennifer: "I just don't believe it! I look at you and think, 'If I just had a figure like Louise, Bert probably would never had had that affair.' If I had your figure (turning to Louise), I don't think I'd have any problems — with men anyway."

Louise: "Now I'm the one who thinks this is a setup. Are you serious, Jennifer?"

Ben: "I tell you what. Both of you strip to the waist and the rest of us will tell you which has the best pair."

Kate: "You can't be serious, Ben."

Hal: "He's just wishful thinking, Kate."

The session moves off into a discussion of Ben's continual need to sexualize the conversation whenever possible. He cops to this without apparent embarrassment. This leads to useful admissions and discussion of how inhibited most of the group is about sexual matters.

I'm intrigued with the way Louise and Jennifer presented mirror images of their idealized figures (and probably selves). The group gains when they bring out projections they have about each other.

Monday, April 17

Jennifer. "I've been thinking again about how Louise said she wished she had a figure like mine. I don't know whether I ever told you — the other night I thought maybe I had — how I've always been so embarrassed by my flat chest. I mean, I do have breasts, but they are so small; they're like a young girl's. I've tried everything to make them larger. I've even thought of having silicone injections, but I . . . I feel squeamish about it for some reason."

She's lying on the couch in her usual position, except instead of having her arms up and hands behind her head, she has hers crossed over the offending glands. She has not talked with me this candidly before, and I'm interested that she seems to be doing so now without apparent embarrassment.

"Ellen had nice full breasts, you know. I've thought that maybe that's part of what attracted Bert to her." She pauses; something is working in her. "I think I was doubly mad at him because by picking someone who had what I didn't have . . . Well, you know what I mean."

"Better say it out."

"Well, it added insult to injury. It was like he was saying I wasn't woman enough for him! Oh, I get mad just thinking about it, but. . . . " I realize that she's weeping.

"But?"

"But I'm not just mad. In fact, right now I think I'm more hurt than mad. Why wasn't I woman enough for him?" She's sobbing openly. "I wanted to be. It wasn't my fault my boobs were so small. Anyway he knew that when he married me. Why?" She cries more strongly. "Why did he have to go fuck with her? I like to fuck. I liked fucking with Bert. Really I did. I'm pretty good in bed. He said so lots of times. Why?" She gives way to sobbing, and I wait quietly, sliding the tissue box close to her.

Finally, the crying softens, she wipes her eyes, looks up at me with such heartbreaking sadness filling her features that I choke up inside.

"I miss him so, Jim. I think about him so much, every day. I want him to come home." She pauses, as though listening to herself. Then her jaw tightens, and her tears stop.

"No, I don't. I don't want to ever see him again. He hurt me. He betrayed me. He'd do it again. I don't care what he says. I can't trust him. I can't risk getting hurt again."

"You have such strong feelings both ways, don't you?"

"Yes, but I know what's best for me. I'm going to have to divorce him. Oh!" Another freshet of tears. Once more she yields to it briefly and then enforces a discipline on herself.

"You are determined to shove those feelings down."

"I *have* to. I absolutely have to."

"No matter what it costs."

"No matter what it costs."

Monday, May 1

Frank. Today's hour is distinguished by two things: Frank keeps busy almost the entire hour without mentioning his loneliness or anything close to it, and in the closing minutes — actually as he's getting to his feet to leave — he lowers his mask briefly once again.

"Oh yeah. Well. . . . Well, there's no time for it now, but. . . . "

"But?"

"Oh, I had a dream about Jenny. Not important. Just hot for her bod, I guess." He starts for the door.

"You sure want to dismiss this quickly."

"Yeah, well, I know you've got somebody waiting and — "

"And so you don't have to deal with the dream."

"Yeah, well, it really wasn't much. Or anyway I can't remember much of it. I was just kind of holding her, and she was letting me, and she seemed to like it, and. . . . " He pauses, hand on doorknob. I know we must end the hour, but I sense there's much more going on in Frank, so I wait silently.

"Jim, I really dig that woman. You know that? If I thought I had half a chance. . . . Oh shit! Gotta go." And he slams out of the door before I can say anything.

Frank is moving toward the very feelings he has taught himself for most of his life to avoid — emotional involvement with others. He is also risking letting me know about it, and I am warmly moved by that.

Jim. As Frank begins to emerge from his isolation and to let himself care about others, he also is beginning to know the grief of lost opportunities, of time past beyond recall. These are among the most poignant we can know.

- The shy young man who sees his imagined love carried off by someone else because he never had the courage to speak to her.
- The spinster watching with envious eyes the play of small children, which she denied herself in an excess of "virtue."
- The hourly worker who seeing his classmates move on to managerial positions he is unable to attain because he played away his chance for education.
- The business opportunity missed through timidity.
- The marriage ruined by hostility that never was open and worked out.
- The children lost in a divorce settlement because of an inability to control addiction.
- The novel never written, the music never sung, the garden never nurtured, the love never consummated, the invention never brought to reality, the hopes never allowed to become actual.

All these disappointments call out despair, anger, bitter sadness—the more so, the more we recognize how our own incompleteness of being brought them about.

Thursday, May 11

Hal. Hal is back to his old self—with a difference. He's not as boisterous, is quieter without being flat; yet he is gaining confidence, finding his way in a new identity.

"After this hour, if you've got the time, I want you to come out and see my new car. It's not just a new car, Jim, it's a new way of getting around—and I don't just mean in space. I don't think I ever told you, but up till now I always had to have a big car, at least a Buick. I had a lot of reasons why, but I think the real reason was that someone as important as I couldn't be seen in an ordinary car. Well, the new buggy is a brand new — are you ready for this? — Chevy! Yep, twenty-five hundred smackers. It's a lot of money, but not as much as if I still had to have a Buick or an Oldsmobile. This new life may save me money."

"You're really up today, Hal. It's great to see." (I think of the new Chevy I bought in 1940 for $865, complete. Wow! Prices have sure gone up.)

"Yes, I am up. It feels like I had a bad fever or something for a long time, and now I'm getting well again. It does feel good, and I know you're with me in that just as you were when I was down. Jim, I want you to know how much that means to me."

"I think I know, Hal, because I have matching feelings."

"Yes, I think you do too."

"What now?"

"I'm feeling like I'm getting ready to fly on my own. No, not yet, but the time is coming. I'm sorry to think of stopping our work, but I'm excited by opening up new possibilities."

"Such as?"

"I've arranged for someone to come in to take my place on the project I've been on at the Institute. My heart just wasn't in it anymore. I may set up another project, or I may just build my practice more. I've found a good supervisor who'll help me in my transition. You know Paul Kleiner?"

"I've heard good things about him."

"And Greta and I are going to take a week off next month and go off by ourselves and see where our relation is."

"You're not wasting time in getting things going."

"I've wasted too much time, Jim."

Thursday, May 18

Group Psychotherapy. Jennifer and Louise have developed a loose connection in which one usually responds when the other speaks, and occasionally they band together when Ben's teasing gets too much. Hal, freed of his agony, is very much part of the group now; although he still tends to be more reserved than I would have expected. Ben is absent tonight on a trip east. The conversation has again turned to love and sexual relations, a topic groups often find valuable after years of social inhibition on these topics. The younger generation would probably find many of our discussions mild, but for these people the talk is refreshing and supportive.

Louise: "I'm having feelings I haven't known for what seems like such a long time. I really am excited because I'm developing a relation with such a good man."

Kate: "How nice. I haven't had a man in my life for a long time."

Frank: "Is he a social worker too?"

Louise: "No, he's a physician, a psychiatrist, who consults at our agency. You know, I'm nearly forty years old, and I feel like I've never really been alive as a woman except for a few years. That's why this means so much to me."

Kate: "I don't want to pry, but have you had much experience with men?"

Louise: "It's okay, Kate, I don't mind talking about it. Maybe it will help me keep perspective. I used to date once in a while, but nothing more. I just didn't go for the ones who only wanted a roll in the hay."

Frank: "Have you ever? . . . I mean, are you a? . . . "

Hal: "Come on, Frank, don't be nosy."

Frank: "Aw shit, this is supposed to be group therapy not Sunday school. I just wanted to know. . . . "

Louise: "If I was a virgin? No, Frank, I'm not. I've had a little sexual experience, only one real affair and that didn't go anywhere."

Frank: "Why not?"

Louise: "He was married, and it just wasn't working out."

Jennifer's face suddenly grows intense. She stares at Louise as though piercing her with her eyes. She moves restlessly, a struggle is going on in her.

Frank: "When was that?"

Louise: "A couple of years ago. For a while it was so very sweet. . . . "

Jennifer: "Did you . . . I mean, I suppose it's none of my

business, but, . . . Well, I just wondered. . . . " She is pulled back and forth, hardly able to let herself speak; yet impelled to do so.

Louise: "It's all right, Jennifer, I don't mind talking about it now. What did you want to ask me?"

Jennifer: "Well, just, . . . I mean, was he married when you? . . . "

Louise: "Yes, but. . . . "

Kate: "Louise, how long ago was this?"

Louise: "Oh, it seems like just yesterday some ways; but then other times it seems like ancient history. It's so strange that it can still hurt so much."

Hal: "It sounds like it was very sad — for it to end, I mean."

Louise: "Yes, I'm afraid it was. I thought for a while that at last I'd found what I'd always wanted, but then . . . I guess there was no hope for me all along."

Jennifer: "What right would you have to any hope — going to bed with a married man?" Angrily, leaning forward intently.

Louise: "I don't know. That isn't what I meant." Startled, drawing back.

Jennifer: "You just screw with them for the fun of it and to hell with the wife, is that it?" Eyes blazing, hands clenching, opening, clenching.

Louise: "No, no. I just meant . . . I mean, I was thinking about my life and. . . . "

Jennifer: "Just thinking about yourself and only yourself. You don't care about anybody else. Oh, you bitch, you, I'd like to teach you a lesson."

Frank: "For crying out loud, Jenny, Louise didn't say she didn't care about anybody else. What's teeing you off so?"

Kate: "Remember, she's been on the receiving end of something like this."

Hal: "Jennifer," trying to reach her, "I'm glad to see you in here with your feelings, but you sure are laying a trip on Louise."

Louise: Crying and looking bewildered. "Look, Jennifer, I know what this means to you, but don't dump your load on me. What you said hurts, but. . . . "

Jennifer: "Oh, it hurts does it? You're lucky I can't hurt you like I'd like to. You dirty bitch! You lying, evil woman. You don't care about anything but getting laid by someone else's husband. You're not enough of a woman to get a man of your own. No, you steal somebody else's. Oh, I hate being in the same room with you."

Kate: "Jennifer, my husband went off with another woman too."

Jennifer: "I don't care. I don't care about anything. I just want to claw this bitch, and. . . . "

Frank: "Jesus, Jenny, you're a hellcat. Louise isn't like you're saying. You ought to. . . . "

Jennifer: "Kate, how can you sit there calmly and let this . . . this . . . this husband-thief talk with us?"

Kate: "Because I learned a sad lesson, Jennifer. No one stole my husband. The woman who 'took him,' as you would say, had my cooperation."

Jennifer: "I don't understand. Do you mean you wanted him to go off with her?"

Kate: "Not consciously, at least. It's just that I don't believe any person can steal another person. A husband isn't a pocketbook. I think I didn't give my husband what he needed, and so he was open to other possibilities."

Jennifer: "Well, maybe that's true for you, but I . . . I just hurt so much, and I get so mad. It was so unfair, so unfair."

Hal: "What was unfair?"

Jennifer: "He went to bed with my friend."

Hal: "What's unfair about that?"

Frank: "Hell, why don't you let her alone? Can't you see she's hurting?"

Jennifer: "No, I don't understand. Why doesn't everybody see that it's unfair? For him to go to bed with another woman? With my friend?"

Kate: "Of course, I see it. It hurt you."

Hal: "But what's 'unfair' about it?"

Kate: "It's like the rules of the game have been broken. I know the feeling, Jennifer, but I wish you could see what you did to help bring it about."

Jennifer: "I didn't do anything."

Hal: "I don't buy that. It takes three to make an unfaithful husband. And I don't think you want to face that."

Frank: "You all make me sick, just giving her lectures."

Jennifer: "Yes, you make me sick too. All of you. You don't care anything about decency and fairness. You're all so unfair. You take this bitch's part. You think she's so fine because she fucks with someone else's husband. Well, let me tell you," turning to Louise, "you filthy pig, I wouldn't spit on you; I wouldn't even be in the same room as you except that. . . . "

Louise: Shrieking, "Oh! Oh! You self-righteous bitch! I didn't do anything to you or your husband, and you're calling me everything nasty you can think of. Who do you think you are to talk to me that way?"

Hal: "It's good to see you come out and fight for yourself, Louise."

Louise: "I guess I'm a slow learner, but now I'm really mad. Lady," to Jennifer, "you've got a whale of a nerve passing judgments like that. I don't blame your husband for wanting someone more understanding if that's the way you were with him."

Jennifer: "Oh, you tramp, don't you dare speak to me like that!"

Kate: "Jennifer, Jennifer, you can't do it. You can't. . . . "

Jennifer: "And you! Don't play such an all-wise mother with me. I don't know what you did to drive your husband away from you, but don't try to tell me I did the same thing. I was always faithful in my marriage. I played fair. I played fair!" Nearly screaming it, trying to make somebody hear her.

Hal: "You're feeling very much alone right now, Jennifer."

Jennifer: "Of course I am. This bunch of . . . these people are all telling me it's my fault that Bert went to bed with Ellen. They're taking his side. And that's not fair. He's to blame. Bert's to blame."

Hal: "Jennifer, we're not saying that."

Jennifer: "Yes, you did. Don't try to back out of it." Frantic, furious, lashing out in all directions.

Frank: "Jenny, take it easy. You're off your nut right now."

Jennifer: "None of you cares about vows and faithfulness and marriage. You probably all screw anybody anytime. Well, I don't want any part of you. I think you stink! And you, Jim, is this your idea of what would help me? I told you I shouldn't be with these people. I have values. I'm not just a rutting animal. I. . . . "

Louise: "You have values, but you can't see people. You just pronounce judgment and want to administer punishment, all in your own self-righteous system."

Hal: "Jennifer, what Louise said sounds harsh, but she's right. You do sound terribly self-righteous."

Jennifer: "Oh, don't honor and promises mean anything to you people? Doesn't it mean anything that Bert broke his promise? It's so unfair! You are so unfair! Everybody says I'm to blame. I didn't go to bed with Ellen or with anybody else. It's unfair! He had the fun, and now everybody takes his side and says I'm to blame."

Frank: "Wow! You really feel sorry for yourself, don't you?"

Hal: "It sounds like you'd like to do something like that yourself."

Louise: "She couldn't let herself want anything like that. The rules are more important."

Jennifer: "You're damned right they are. I have principles. Principles, do you hear? Something neither you nor anybody else here knows anything about."

Hal: "And do you have any principles about judging people without having the evidence?"

Jennifer: "Oh, you're so sanctimonious and dignified, but you're probably just like the others. Have you screwed Louise yet? Why not? She's probably just itching to get another married man into the sack. Aren't you, Louise?"

Frank: "Jenny, you really can be a bitch when you want to, can't you?"

Louise: "You sound pretty jealous to me, Jennifer. Are you sure you don't want Hal yourself?"

Jennifer: "Oh, you . . . you . . . I don't go around spreading my legs for just anyone who comes along, the way you do."

Louise: "Listen, lady, don't judge me by your standards. You don't know anything about me. You just know what that sick mind of yours wants to imagine. And you must have a pretty filthy imagination."

Jennifer: "I don't have to be talked to that way by a slut. I'm going to leave, and go home, and take a bath, and try to clean off all the dirt that this group wallows in."

Hal: "Jennifer, you just want to lash out at everybody now. You don't care what you say or who you hurt or anything."

Jennifer: "Oh, I thought you were different, but—"

Kate: "Jennifer, you really are acting totally self-righteous, and though I want to be on your side, I'm getting mad at you."

Jennifer: "Don't trouble yourself. I don't need you or anybody." She's frantic now, reaching for her purse, dropping it, spilling its contents, crying, screaming.

Louise: "What's the matter, can't you take it? You can dish it out, but you can't take it. When the going gets tough, you want to pull out, run for home. No wonder your husband wanted a real woman."

Hal: "That's a low blow, Louise." Mediating, concerned for both.

Jennifer: "Piss on yoooouuu!" Screeching. "Oh, I hate you! I hate you! I'll scratch your eyes out." Coming out of her chair, heading for Louise.

Frank: "Whoa, Jenny." He grabs her, and they fall to the floor. She's spitting and clawing.

Frank: "God, you're strong."

Jennifer: "Let me go. I'll show her. I'll kill her. I'll kill her! Oh! Oh!" She hears herself, hears again the word *kill,* and suddenly she collapses. All the fight is gone. She lies limply in Frank's arms and sobs and sobs.

Frank holds her with surprising tenderness. The rest of the group sit slumped, exhausted by the storm of emotions that has swept over us all. Kate and Louise are weeping. Hal is sunk into his chair, face buried in his hands. I am suddenly so weary I feel I can hardly move. Although I've said little, I've been on the edge of my chair, ready to act if I felt it necessary, determined to try to let this play through if at all possible, sensing it was filled with meaning for nearly every one of us in the room.

Louise raises her head and speaks in a low voice to Jennifer:

"Jennifer, there have been times when I've called myself worse things than you called me, but I'd like you to know that it wasn't like you think. I mean, he was married, that's true. But he was separated, and at the time I was with him, he really thought it was all over in his marriage. It was only when his wife found out about us that she decided she wanted him after all. And I urged him to go back because I was so guilty. Now I wish I hadn't. They didn't make a go of it, and he went off someplace, and I've never seen him again."

"I'm sorry." Weeping, Jennifer barely lifts her head.

People talk in brief, half-whispered sentences to each other, gathering up their things, hesitant to leave. Usually the group has a post-session without me after the end of the formal period. Tonight there'll be none. Everybody knows, without it being said, that we're exhausted emotionally for now.

I sit quietly, waiting to see how it is with Jennifer. She may want a chance to talk with me. Louise, weeping, pats Jennifer's shoulder, smiles wanly at me, and goes out. The others also leave as Frank and Jennifer slowly and somewhat self-consciously sit up from where they fell in that last moment of struggle. I think Jennifer has been hiding in Frank's embrace, not wanting to risk looking at the other people. Now she turns to me with a face drained of all emotion but inward pain. Her eyes are red and smeared with mascara.

"I'm here, Jennifer, if you want to talk now."

Her voice is creaky from her strained throat and much crying. "No, it's all right. I'll go home. I have a time to see you tomorrow." She gets up and leaves quickly.

Frank looks at me questioningly.

"I don't know, Frank. I really don't. We'll have to trust her." Inwardly, I'm struck with the reversal: Once Jennifer worried about Frank.

"Okay, good night." He leaves, and I close up the offices, bone-weary.

Thirteen

"We Traded a Lot of Punches, Didn't We?"

Friday, May 19

Jennifer. Ben is out of town and I didn't fill his 9:00 A.M. time this morning. The clock slowly makes its way to 9:45, when Jennifer is due. Its snail pace serves to exacerbate the anxiety I've had since she left last night. With Frank, I was concerned how she might handle being alone after that orgy of fury. She doesn't have any close friends, and she has thought of suicide before. Should I have done more?

Since it's now morning it's too late to do anything. Can't tell what she may need until I see her. It's still not time? Five minutes yet.

Waiting for Jennifer, I am once again remembering Pete — Pete of the ready smile and the ready brooding moods. Some years ago now, he stopped therapy having made some gains but both of us knowing there was more that needed doing. Then one Thursday afternoon about four months after our last session he was on the phone, asking for an appointment. My first opening was on the following Monday morning; Pete said that was okay, and we hung up. Saturday he got drunk, took an overdose of pills, and died.

At times such as this when I'm unsure what a client needs me to do, Pete comes back in my thoughts. What could I have done? Did I overlook cues in the way he talked on the phone?

Was I too anxious to protect my weekend? So many questions; no truly satisfying answers.

It's 9:47, and Jennifer's not here! Where is she? Should I call her home? It's not like her to be late. She believes so much in schedules and agreements and formalities. That's been changing, of course. Oh, has it? Remember last night. Ugh! Yes, I remember. It's 9:48. Come on, Jennifer, get here!

Maybe I should go out to her home. Don't even know where it is. Where's her chart? Oh, she lives in Santa Monica. Fifteen, twenty minutes to get there. Or to get here from there. This time of morning, traffic could be a problem. Now it's 9:50. She's fought traffic from there to here often enough; that wouldn't do it. Unless there was a big tie-up for some reason. Wonder if I could get the traffic news on the radio. It's 9:51.

No traffic news, just advice to use Ban under my arms if I want to succeed in my work. Ban won't help Jennifer right now. Or me. Where the hell are you, Jennifer? It's 9:53. If I left now to go to her home, I might miss her here. If I wait too long and she's done something — pills, knife, gun? Was that the outer door?

My buzzer sounds. I stop everything. Whoa now, Bugental, take three deep breaths. Empty out. I don't know why she's late; don't take anything into our time that doesn't belong there.

She sits in the chair, rather than going to the couch as usual. Looking troubled, mouth working, she tries to find what she wants to say. Although I'm the world's worst judge of such things, it looks to me as though she still has on the clothes she was wearing last night.

"I'm sorry I'm late. I didn't come from home; so I didn't judge the time right."

"You look wrung out, Jennifer."

"I am." Barely audible. "I'm so ashamed."

"You seem to be judging yourself."

Pause. "Yes, I suppose I am. I judge everybody else, why not myself too?"

"Mmmm."

"I have something to tell you. I . . . I . . . I spent the night with Frank."

"Oh?"

"We didn't . . . we didn't have intercourse. But we . . . we . . . did sleep together. I mean, we slept in the same bed . . . without any clothes. Do you think I'm awful?"

"What do you think yourself?"

"I don't know." Weeping. "I don't know. I never did anything like that before. I wonder if Louise was right. Was I jealous? Did I want to . . . to be with a man? It felt so good to have him hold me. I haven't been with a man for . . . since Bert told me. . . . " Crying harder. "I don't know why we didn't make love. I wanted to. Frank wouldn't." The crying stops. "Do you think he didn't want me, just pitied me?"

"How hard it is for you to accept that maybe somebody just cares about you even though they don't do things your way."

"Oh!" Stung, pulling back.

"It hurts to hear that, doesn't it?" Kindly, insistently.

"Oh, yes." Tears starting. "I don't like you to say things like that. But it's true, I guess. Yes, it's true. I think Frank really does care for me too."

"And now you can let that in."

"Yes, and I care for him. I think he'd have liked to make love to me. I could tell, you know. . . . " Embarrassed.

"Yes, Jennifer."

"He just didn't want to do it that way. But, Jim. . . . "

"Umm?"

"I did. I wanted him to make love to me. And I'm still a married woman!"

"And it's against the rules for a married woman to want a man who's not her husband to make love to her?"

"Yes, I. . . . Well, no, not to just want it. But I would have. And I'm still married to Bert. Even though he doesn't live at home now. We're still married."

"Still married."

"Yes, and I want to be married to him, to Bert. Yet I wanted Frank to. . . . Oh, I'm so mixed up!"

"Are you mixed up about what you want?"

"Well, yes. I mean, no. I mean I want to be with Bert, and I really did want to make love with Frank last night, and. . . . Oh, I've made such a mess of things. Do you think he'll hate me?" And I wonder whether she means Bert or Frank.

She cries brokenheartedly. Gradually, the crying eases, becomes more relieving. Although the end of our journey together is many months away, Jennifer is beginning to accept the unacceptable, herself.

Jennifer's early training taught her to disregard her own unique inner being and to devote every effort to learning the rules and following them faithfully. It was so important to her to get things right that at times she could barely talk to me. She tried to hold in mind every possible consideration and to take account of all implications of whatever she might say; thus she ended up scarcely being able to say anything. Her life was very like her speech. Each thing she undertook had to run a gauntlet of self-criticism and ended up, as often as not, undone or poorly realized. Insistence on perfection is a sure route to aborting human efforts and to drowning out inner awareness.

Frank. Frank comes into the consultation room slowly, almost reluctantly, not meeting my eyes. I wonder if he thinks I'm going to be mad at him for taking Jennifer home and to bed with him last night. I remember how warmly she spoke of his tenderness during her interview a few hours ago, and how surprised I was to hear that he refused to have intercourse with her although they slept naked together. I feel a warmth and a strange kind of pride in this frightened, angry man and the big step he took last night, but I doubt that he could recognize or tolerate those feelings of mine right now. Maybe some day.

Again that spot on the wall gets one of Frank's grim stares. He makes a slow business of getting settled, lighting a cigarette, fixing the ashtray, the whole routine. Then he opens his mouth to speak his favorite word.

"Shee-yit."

"Hmmm?"

"Shit. Shit! Shit! That's all. Just plain shit!" He's angry.

"Wow! You really sound mad as hell. What's going on?"

"I don't know what the hell I'm doing here. I don't know why the flying fuck I ever came here in the first place. I don't think I've got a brain in my whole goddamn head, or I'd get the hell out right now."

I wait. Whatever's cooking with Frank is much deeper and more intense than anything I was expecting. He's hurting, and he's hurting deeply, but I haven't any idea why. So I wait.

"Ohhh, hell! Jim! Why didn't you tell me a long time ago to go back where I belong? What am I doing here? What am I doing with people like you and Hal and Louise and? . . ."

"And Jennifer?"

"All right, goddamn it, yes, and Jennifer. Poor Jenny! Jesus H. Christ, she hurts so damned much inside. Do you know how much she hurts? Oh, of course you do, but holy hell, what a double bitching life this is, isn't it? Poor Jenny! She told you, huh? Jim, I couldn't let her be alone. She was half out of her skull last night, believe me. I was scared for her. I just had to keep with her. I suppose you think it was shitty, huh?"

"What was shitty, Frank?"

"My taking her home and to bed. She told you, didn't she?"

"You tell me, Frank."

"I just have one bed, you know, and . . . I started to sleep in my big chair, but she said she couldn't stand to be alone and wanted me to hold her."

"Mm-hmm."

"So we . . . oh, shit! We stripped. I can't sleep in pajamas. That's not the point anyway. I wanted to have her . . . to fuck with her, but. . . ."

"But?"

"Oh, Christ! What do you think I am! I couldn't fuck her with her all torn up like that. That would be like screwing a baby or something."

"It seems hard for you to just let it be that you acted in a really caring and helpful way."

"Oh, that's all crap, and you know it. I'd love to screw Jenny, and I may just do it. I just didn't think I wanted to last night."

"To quote you, 'Shee-yit!'"

"You don't know how to say it right. I'll bet you never said 'shit' until recently."

"Frank, I think you're a very neat guy for what you gave Jennifer last night. Will you please hear that and quit the smokescreen?"

"What do you mean 'smokescreen'?"

"Uh-oh, we don't want to go back to that. We've left that behind."

"Yeah, you're right. But you know damn well it makes me uncomfortable when you say things like that; so how come you do it?"

"Like what?"

"Now you're playing that game."

"You're right. Okay, so I do know it makes you uncomfortable for people to see you as warm and caring, but Frank, I think it's time we dealt with that discomfort so you can get on with your life. I don't think you have to be hung up anymore — or at least not to the same extent — on the myth of being a tough guy who doesn't have feelings and doesn't need or care for anybody."

"Not so fast, Jim." He's really scared. His voice is as husky as though I'd pushed him to the edge of a precipice — and I guess I really have.

"Yeah, I hear you."

"Jim, for a minute I really could hear you then, all the way down to my feet. And you're right, but it scares the very shit out of me. Oh God, Jim, I'm really scared. I want to just run the hell out of here and just keep going and never stop. I want to forget all about what we've talked about and about all of the people in the group and especially about Jennifer." His voice trails off.

The hour is one of those magical times that can happen on occasion with some people and never happen at all with others, a time when a person finds himself open within and can know what he usually veils from himself, a time when I am trusted to enter the most private self of another, a sacred time. Toward the end of the hour, Frank surfaces.

"Jenny wanted to see me tonight. I told her I had to work. I don't, but I'm scared to see her."

"What scares you, Frank?"

"I'm scared for her. She really wants to go back to her husband, and if she gets hung up on me, she'll never forgive herself enough to make it with him."

"I see what you mean."

"So I guess I just won't call her or anything."

"But you'd like to."

"Yeah. Yes, I would."

"And that's the second thing that scares you."

"Yes, it is."

We sit silently for a minute, looking at the reality of Jennifer's and Frank's feelings, looking at the inevitability of his letting her go.

Monday, May 22

Louise. Red-eyed, sad-faced, silent, Louise gets settled on the couch. She lies that way several minutes, her weeping gradually becoming stronger. Still neither of us says anything. The days are long past when I'd help her get started; she knows the way, and she's doing her work without my help.

Finally, she reaches for another tissue and begins to talk. Her voice is scarcely audible, but it gradually gains strength.

"I'm so mixed up." Weeping more strongly. "I don't know how to say it all."

"Just as it comes. Don't try to sort it out yet."

"Well, after the group, I thought. . . . Or at the end of the group, I thought I was going to be all right. I mean, I thought I knew where I was. Then I got home and started to go to bed, and then all the awful things I'd said came back to me and . . . oh, I just wanted to die. I kept thinking of what I'd said to that poor woman who was hurting so much. And I thought you and the whole group must surely hate me. I didn't think I could ever come back here, and I knew I'd never dare go to the group again." She is silent, crying; sobs now starting to come.

"Mm-hmmm." Let her do it her own way.

"Then I thought I just had to call you, tell you I was sorry, find out how to get in touch with Jennifer, apologize to her. I almost called you in the middle of the night. But when I thought about Jennifer, my feelings began to change, and . . . and then suddenly I was mad. I was so mad, and I thought of a whole lot more things I wished I'd said to her, and I knew I couldn't really tell her I was sorry. That would be a lie. But then I thought how you and the others probably would hate me for being so. . . . Oh, I don't know. Because right in the middle of everything, I. . . . "

"You? . . . "

"I suddenly heard you asking me, 'Are you having the feelings I want you to have?' in that mocking tone of voice you use sometimes. And all of a sudden, I. . . . " She is silent, not crying.

"Mmm?"

"I said out loud to you, 'You can go to hell, Bugental! I'm mad, and I don't care who knows it.' And then I started laughing, right there in the dark in bed, I laughed out loud. But then you said — in my head, I mean — 'Are you being angry because you know that will please me?' and I didn't know, and now. . . . "

"Now?"

"Now, do you know?" Surprised tone. "I feel better. I mean, right now I do. I wish I didn't think at all about what you feel about all of this, but I do. And I hope you're not mad at me or disgusted with me. But I don't think you'll send me away even if you are, and. . . . "

"And? . . . "

"And, if you try to, I'll fight with you too! So there!" She turns and grins at me. I try to stop myself from grinning back, but I can't do it. So we laugh together.

Then I sober. "And so you've ended up pleasing me, eh?"

"Oh, darn you!"

Monday, May 22

Kate. The first thing that strikes me about Kate as she comes in is her appearance. She's wearing a bright floral pattern dress that just covers her knees (I don't think I knew she had knees), a playful necklace, stockings, and moderately high heels. I think if I saw her on the street I wouldn't recognize her. She looks so much younger! I realize that I had come to think her as much older, more like Billie, than the forty which, surprisingly, is her real age. She's an attractive woman!

She settles in the big chair, crosses what I discover are good-looking legs, and smiles expectantly at me. I ought to make her say it first, I suppose, but she is so eager.

"Well, Kate! You look splendid."

"Do you really think so? Oh, I'm so glad. I feel a bit . . . uh . . . shy, you know? It's kind of a surprise to me."

She wants more reaction. Well, damnit, she deserves it.

"Yes, it is a surprise, but such a nice one."

"Yes." She breathes the word, savoring her feelings. We're silent for a minute or so.

"Will you tell me about it?"

"Oh, yes! I want to very much. I was just collecting my thoughts."

"Take your time."

"Well, it was the group." She considers silently a moment. "Last time, you know, in the group . . . well, it was very power-ful—for me. Poor Jennifer, hurting so much, lashing out at everybody. I could just feel what it was like inside her. I've wanted to do that sometimes. I can't think when, but it was as though it was all familiar inside me."

"Mm-hmm."

"And Louise! Wasn't *she* splendid! She took it for a while and then she just reared up on her hind legs. And I don't know how to say it, but she was . . . splendid."

"Mm-hmm."

"And I went home quite shaken. I mean literally shaking inside. It took me quite a while to find out what was making me tremble so. I didn't sleep hardly at all Thursday night, and called in sick Friday. I wasn't sick. I just was too busy."

"Busy?"

"Yes, busy. I mean I realized I was shaking because I was seeing what a woman could be. Oh, that doesn't say it at all. Well, watching Jennifer and Louise, I realized they were strong women, having strong feelings, and letting them out, and fighting for their lives and claiming their lives. It was . . . splendid! They were splendid. And I . . . well, I was . . . sitting on the sidelines, is what people say. I wasn't even . . . Jennifer called me a 'mother' at one point; do you remember? A 'mother.' You know what that means to me." She waits as I nod, and her eyes fill briefly, but she is anxious to tell me more. And I'm anxious to hear it.

"Well, I'm not a mother. I'm hardly a woman. I think that ever since my mother reacted so badly . . . so sadly . . . for her as well as for me, when I had my first period . . . I think that ever since then I've tried to be more a man than a woman. Oh, that's too strong, but something like that. Men didn't seem to get hurt like women did, you know." She's weeping quietly.

"Yes."

"And I was shaking so because there was a woman inside of me who wanted to get out. I know that sounds fanciful, but that's just what it felt like. Can you understand that?"

"Yes, Kate," softly. I'm near tears.

"So I let her out!" She looks up with a great smile and tears running down here cheeks. "Here I am."

"Here you are indeed!" And my own tears come.

We sit for several minutes, yielding to the tears, smiling at each other. Shyly, she reaches a hand out to me, and I take it readily.

Then she stands — a bit unsteadily, I realize, on her heels. She holds her arms out a bit like a model and slowly turns around for my inspection. "You can see I'm a woman, can't you?"

"Indeed, I can."

"My name is 'Sunny.' That's what my dad used to call me when I was small. I think I'd like to be called 'Sunny' now."

"You look 'Sunny.'"

She sits down again and leans forward intently. "I watched Jennifer and Louise, and I thought, there are two women, and they are really hurting, and they are really mad, and they are . . . splendid! And I can be a woman and I can hurt and I can be mad and maybe even, I can be. . . . " She hesitates; I complete it.

"Splendid."

Thursday, May 25

Group Psychotherapy. Jennifer arrives first, quite early. When
I see her in the hall, she explains she didn't want to come into
the room and see the others all there looking at her. I let her
into the group room and go back to my office. When I come
back at 7:00, our meeting time, Frank and Hal are with her,
and Louise and Kate enter with me. Ben has called from the
east, where he has taken a new job. He won't be back to the
group.

There is none of the usual light talking. People are getting settled and looking around at each other, smiling rather
perfunctorily. As soon as we're seated, Jennifer speaks.

Jennifer: "I want to say something to all of you right
away." She pauses, gathering strength, looking directly into all
the faces turned toward her.

Frank: "Aw, you don't have to, Jenny."

Jennifer: "Yes, Frank, I do. Just listen now, please."

Frank: "Okay."

Jennifer: "Last time I behaved very badly, and—No, I
don't want to sound that way. Last time I blew my top . . . at
Louise . . . at all of you. I'm embarrassed, and I was terribly
ashamed. I say 'was' because I've done a lot of thinking . . . and
Jim's helped me . . . and I am really sorry if I hurt any of you.
Especially you, Louise," looking directly at her, eyes brimming,
hopeful smile.

Louise: "I understand." Her answering smile is cautious.

Jennifer: "I hope in time to show you that I am not just
the bitch I was last week. I'm finding that out myself. It's rough
to face how very angry and destructive I can be. I don't like
to see that in myself."

Hal: "It's against your rules?"

Kate: "That's mean, Hal."

Jennifer: "Ooh, that hurts. But, yes, you're right. It's
against my rules . . . or what rules I had. I want to throw that
rule book away, but. . . ."

Hal: "I'm sorry, Jennifer, that was a mean thing to say."

Jennifer: "No, I deserved it."

Frank: "Shit, don't go looking to get kicked. That'll just be another rule."

Wham! Right on target, Frank, I say to myself.

Kate: "What a shrewd observation, Frank! I never would have thought of that."

Frank (pleased): "Yeah, well. . . . "

Jennifer: "Oh, that's right, isn't it."

Louise: "I want to say something too. Last week I hit back at Jennifer as hard as I knew how, and then I went home and felt miserable. I was sure you all hated me."

Kate, Hal, and Frank start to protest, but she pushes past them.

Louise: "No, please hear me. I appreciate that you're trying to tell me that you didn't feel that way. But the point is I had to tell myself that first. And I think I did . . . at least partially. I had to tell myself that even if you did hate me, I was not going to let myself be abused anymore."

Frank: "Good stuff, Louise."

Hal: "Yes, good stuff is right."

Jennifer: "Oh, I'm so glad you did fight back at me, Louise. If you hadn't I would have . . . would have felt even worse . . . though I can't imagine how that could be possible."

The conversation goes on in this style for several minutes. Meantime, Kate-Sunny, splendid in her new attire, takes part, but I imagine she wishes she'd be seen. It's Frank who abruptly switches attention to her.

Frank: "Jesus H. Christ! Has anybody really looked at Kate? Wow, you look absolutely fucking great!"

The group's attention shifts at once. Kate flushes, pleased, embarrassed.

Louise: "You're right, Frank. Kate, you do look wonderful. What's happened?"

Frank: "Hey, and you've got great legs too."

Kate: "Thank you, Frank. I really like looking 'absolutely (ulp) fucking great.'—and I like it that you like my legs also." She actually pulls her skirt up just above her knees in a playful gesture.

Jennifer: "Kate, I can't believe it's you. How nice you look."

Kate: "I want to say something to you, Jennifer, and to you, Louise. I thought the two of you were . . . splendid! And I really want to say something to all of you: What happened here last week (pauses, swallows). Well, it was so helpful to me. Wait." The group has started to respond. "Let me finish. It woke me up to my life, and to my being a woman."

Thursday, June 22

Louise. There's a subtle sense that I think we all have but that we cultivate and value far too little. Watching Louise come in with a set face and rather stiff body, my intuition is that she's very determined or angry, but I'm equally sure it's not the fear and ambivalence that I've seen her wear other times.

She sighs resignedly, and I violate my own policy of letting the client speak first. "What is it, Louise?"

"Dr. Elliott has put out some new regulations that are just too much, too strict, too old-fashioned. I'm so scared, Jim. I'm not going to go along with him this time. I'm tired of trying to smooth things out between him and the students and the other staff. Oh, I don't want to have trouble. It just scares me so. I mean, I keep thinking of running away. I know it's silly, but I can't help it."

"You're starting to break faith with yourself, Louise."

"That's right! I hadn't thought of that. Well, I'm not going to do that." Her head comes up, her jaw juts out. "I want to make a joke about my getting mad, but I'm not going to. I am mad. I think Dr. Elliott's going to wreck a good program, a program I put a lot of effort into, and I'm going to fight him."

For a while she talks about this new-found determination, about the unreasonableness of the director's newest edicts (actually quite a startling attempt to turn the clock back, as I know from other sources), and about the fear she keeps feeling, which seems unreasonably strong.

"Jim, it's too much. I mean, I really find myself trembling inside when I think of telling him that I won't cooperate with these new regulations. It's as though he will literally kill me or do something else terrible. I know he might be able to get me fired. But I'm not sure he can even do that, at least not without an awful struggle. But this fear and trembling isn't just that I'll lose my job. It's much more, much, much more."

She sighs, swings her legs up, gets settled on the couch. In the process her skirt comes up, and she makes only a token gesture to put it back. Okay, I tell myself, I've enjoyed the view; now it's time to get to work.

Meantime, Louise has taken several deep, sort of shuddery breaths, and tears have started out of the corners of her eyes. Watching her, my mood changes, and I feel warm concern.

"Jim, I'm thinking of lying in bed with Don the other night. It was so sweet, so much what I've longed for for so long, so very long. I really don't give a damn about Dr. Elliott and his rules. I have been so lonely, so very lonely. It was so good to be with a good, warm, loving man. He was so kind, so kind, Jim. And it was so good to just make love without any restraint. I never knew it could be that way. Why have I waited so long? I am so glad we talked about sex and everything. I wasn't all tensed up, and I didn't just want to please him — but I did want to please him, and I did. I also discovered he wanted to please me! And that was so strange. He wanted to please me!"

"It's hard, even now, to think that someone wants to please you."

"Yes, and no. Both. I really am in love with Don, Jim." Her mood changes. "Are you jealous? I love you too, you know, but I'm *in* love with Don."

"I can hear that. And yes, Louise, I think I am a bit jealous, even though I'm a whole lot glad for you."

"Oh, that's nice." She is silent for a minute. Again her face changes. "Why does this darn fight with Dr. Elliott have to come along right now? I am so happy in so many ways, and then I think of him and I get that trembly feeling again."

"Just keep open and tell me whatever else comes along."

"I see my bedroom again. And that feels nice. And then I see clouds and a summery sky. It would be good to be outdoors and make love. Oh, that makes me think of New Hampshire and Mr. Colten. The poor old man! And poor Mrs. Colten too. I didn't know I'd ever feel that way about her."

"What comes next?"

"Oh, thinking about when Mr. Colten got me to take my clothes off, or at least starting to."

"Uh-huh."

"I had my clothes off last night. I liked that. But . . . but . . . oh, I got in trouble when I took off my clothes at the Coltens. And now. . . . "

"Go slow."

"I'm afraid I'm going to get in trouble now. That must be it! I took off my clothes at the Coltens and got in trouble and I took off my clothes last night and I expect to get in trouble."

"Sounds more like your mind than your guts talking."

"Well, yes, but no, not really. It's some of both."

"You know that just a good theory isn't going to do much."

"That's what you always say, but I'm not sure. After all, an awful lot of therapy values good theories. What makes you so sure you're right and they're wrong?"

"Touché. I do sound very sure, and I have to admit I do feel pretty sure, but . . . you go ahead and work with it if you feel it's useful."

"I don't know, but it's worth a try."

"Good enough. Go ahead. I'll help if I can."

She does think-feel her way along, exploring the link between being sexual and expecting punishment. Neither of us can tell just how deeply this insight goes, but it seems to help her feel she's done something about her excessive fear, and that's all to the good.

I also smile inwardly at her new ability to argue with me, not just pro forma, but because she has a genuinely different view.

Jennifer. A preoccupied half-smile, bright red and yellow, a light blouse (without a bra?!), capri pants, sandals — this is Jennifer today. She sits down, drops the sandals, lies back, musing without speaking. I wait.

"You just saw Louise."

"Mm-hmm?"

"I ran into her in the lady's room. She was . . . I don't know . . . she was friendly — although I can feel there's still a little wall between us. I don't blame her." She pauses, listens to her own words. "In fact, I'm tired of blaming anybody (pause), including me."

"So?"

"So Louise said something that kind of . . . well, I don't know exactly what she meant. She said I looked 'like orange sherbet, appetizing.' I think she meant it as a compliment, but there was something more."

"What comes to mind, without your figuring it out?"

"Why . . . why I feel a little shy to say this, but . . . but I think she meant appetizing to men." She giggles slightly.

"What does that trigger in you?"

"Just what I was going to tell you anyway. I have a date!" She pauses watching for my reaction. I smile and wait.

"Tonight I'm going to dinner with a man. And then, if he's real nice and if I feel like I do now," she pauses for dramatic effect. "If I feel this way, I'll invite him home to. . . . "

"To? . . . "

"To spend the night! It's Bert that I have the date with."

"Mmmm?"

"I called him yesterday and asked him to meet me at a restaurant for dinner and to talk."

"Uh-huh."

"I think I want to be 'appetizing' for him, but 'orange sherbet' isn't quite what I have in mind." She's going slow now, listening inside. "I think what I have in mind — I'm not sure about this yet (quickly). But I think I may want him to move back home."

"That's a big step, isn't it?"

"Yes, it is (pause). But no, in another way, it isn't. I've been getting ready for this for at least a month. He is so sad and says he's so lonely. And I'm sad and lonely too. So. . . . "

Hal. We've talked about today's session for over a week, and now it's here, and I'm reluctant for it to be here, and I think Hal is too. He comes from the waiting room with his hand on my shoulder, gives it a squeeze before sitting in the chair.

"Well, this is it, Jim," a sweet-sad smile.

"Yes, Hal." I'm emotionally full myself.

"I'm going to miss coming here and giving you a hard time."

"The same goes for me: I'm going to miss you and miss giving you a hard time too."

"Yeah, we traded a lot of punches, didn't we?" He grins. I wait. "But seriously, it's been very, very good. Funny, in a way so many things aren't changed; yet everything's changed. I had a blow-up with Tim just Tuesday, but it didn't have the old venom. I was sick and tired of my work one night last week, but then I had a session with Paul Kleiner the next day, and I felt lucky to be in this work. I feel scared to be stopping coming here, scared of endings, scared of dying." He stops speaking, reflects soberly.

Then his face changes. "Hell, Jim, I think I ought to start over right now."

"My god, Hal, I didn't know you had deteriorated so. Lie down at once, and come six times a week, and your fee is doubled."

"It's a deal!" Then he breaks into his big grin. "Jim, I can't tell you what our work has meant for me. You'll have to use that great intuition of yours to figure it out. No, I guess that's an oxymoron. You just use your intuition."

"I know, Hal. And it's been important for me personally as well."

"Yeah, I kinda figured that."

We sit for a few minutes grinning at each other and then get self-conscious.

"There's no real reason for me to prolong this. I'll be going now, but I'll see you tonight in the group. I want to tell them myself, and I want to say good-bye to each of them."

He stands and comes over to give me a hug that is all affection and awesome in its power.

Jim. Tonight I go for the first time to a small apartment I have rented. I don't know all that has gone into this decision, but I have moved out of my house on the hill, out of the home that it was so important to establish and make stable (unlike my boyhood homes). My wife is a very special person, and we have had many good things together for many years; yet increasingly we seem to be separate.

As I eat a solitary dinner in a coffee shop and then go to the coldness of these unfamiliar rooms, I feel as though I'm imagining what I'm doing, not truly living it. For more than twenty-five years I believed that my marriage was good and would last the rest of my life. I am shocked, unbelieving, that now I'm ending it.

For months I've been recognizing — reluctantly at first, but with increasing conviction — that I stay on the surface at home, that I avoid confrontations and conflict, that I feel unable to express what most matters to me. It is not my wife's fault; it is not my failing; it is something we've unwittingly brought about between us.

My teachers — Hal, Jennifer, Louise, Frank, and Kate — have shown me that change is possible when one musters the courage to confront life. It's a lesson I've helped them learn but one I've feared to take into my own being. Now I choose to accept and act on it.

Somehow it seems fitting that the end of my work with Hal comes this same day. He has struggled to find himself, and therapy has helped him. I struggled to create a self, and psychoanalysis helped me discover that a created self is an automaton, not a real person.

Eight years ago on the analyst's couch I discovered an image buried in my unconscious that was a powerful confrontation: My left wrist had been cut (a suicide symbol?), but instead of blood, tissue, ligaments, and bone, what was revealed was a metal bar and wiring. In that moment, I knew I was really an android, a made man, not a real person. With this recognition came the expectation that my analyst would say, in a sad but kindly voice, "Well, I am truly sorry, Dr. Bugental, I should have recognized this about you sooner, but obviously I cannot continue to treat you. You will have to leave now. We can do no further work here."

This conviction was so strong that I then realized that for some time whenever the analyst spoke to me I tried to capture and remember everything he told me — to remember it so that I could take it out to my car and examine it to see what might apply to the real me, for I was certain he couldn't know that creature, the real me.

I think from that incident forward I've been moving toward this evening of breaking with my past, trying to win free to be newly myself.

Fourteen

"There's a Riot in Me, Too."

Thursday, July 7

Frank. "It's a war!" Frank is excited. "The niggers are burning things up all over the damn country. More power to them, I say. They've been getting the shitty end of the stick for a long time. 'Course some of them are mean bastards, but a lot of them are really okay. I remember one who helped me out when I was really stony and so hungry I thought I'd eat the next dog I saw running loose."

I listen as Frank goes on, excited by the astonishing news of riots, looting, and burning that is going on everywhere. And I debate inwardly, what is my role? I'm pleased that Frank doesn't have the blanket prejudice that seems to characterize so many whites who are in the unskilled labor ranks. I understand their fears, but I think they're short-sighted. Yet I react with instant shock when Frank speaks of 'niggers.' I want to tell him that's a slur, and that I and others will find it offensive. Yet I don't think that would do more than provoke an argument. For now, I'll just be quiet; maybe I'll find a way to drop a suggestion in later.

He pauses, shifts his position in his chair. "Yeah, well, I didn't come here to give you a news bulletin." Then he grins, shifts in the chair again, and straightens his face before saying, "Well, maybe I did have a news bulletin for you: I got promoted."

"Hey, great! How about filling me in?"

"Oh, it's no national headline. But Gandowsky says I'm doing good work, and now I'll be one of the supervisors on the night shift."

"How is that for you, Frank?"

"What d'you mean, 'how is it?' Aw, wait. It's okay. I like it."

"Are you a good supervisor?"

"You do ask the screwiest questions."

"You didn't answer."

"Yeah, sure, I'll be the greatest supervisor in the whole fucking country." He pauses, looks uncomfortable. "I sound like a damned fool, don't I?"

"No, you sound like someone who's getting used to taking himself seriously and to talking candidly about what he thinks and feels inside."

"Hmmm. Yeah (pause). I guess you can say that." He chews on this silently. "You know, that's so, isn't it? I am just getting used to this whole shitty — no, it's not shitty — this whole way of being a . . . a . . . what the hell am I?"

"A pretty smart man, who's finding himself, who's risking new ways of being alive, and who has just gotten promoted."

"Whoa, not so fast." Again he takes time to assimilate what I've said. "Yeah, I guess that's right." Another pause while he gets set to deal with the loaded point. "Do you really think I'm 'pretty smart,' like you said?"

"Yes, Frank, I really do. You've done a remarkable job of taking hold of and changing your life. You couldn't have done this if you were a dummy."

"Yeah, I guess not. You know — I really appreciate your saying that."

"I do know it. And it's time you really knew it too."

I don't usually give clients flat-out, evaluative statements, but with Frank it's different. He hasn't had the usual experiences that would have provided him with the comparisons by which to assess his own place. If he had had such times, I would have confronted his unwillingness to make his own judgment. But as it is, he needs to have some estimate on which partially to base his planning now that he's taking hold in life.

Thursday, July 27

Jennifer. I almost don't recognize Jennifer in the waiting room. She is wearing quite short shorts, a halter top, and sandals. It's a hot day, but this costume is a real surprise. It doesn't fit the Jennifer I've known. She watches my face, and it's clear that she has anticipated some such reaction from me and is pleased.

"Well, what do you think?" She pirouettes playfully.

"You've got great legs; that's what I think."

"They are good, aren't they? You didn't mention the top."

I realize then that the halter appears better filled than I would have expected. "I don't know what to say."

"They're falsies! But it's fun anyway. I always wanted to wear them — well, not always, but a lot of times — anyway it seemed unfair or cheating in some way. Now, I want to thank you, Doctore Bugentalli (exaggerated Italian accent), for the great therapeutic triumph: I can now wear falsies and enjoy it." She's delighted with herself as she sits in the chair, grinning.

"There's nothing false about your pleasure or your attractiveness, Jennifer."

"Thank you, kind sir." Then her tone changes. "Jim, as you know, Bert is moving back in. We're going to try to . . . no, we're going to make it go this time. And we're going to have a second honeymoon. We've got tickets for Hawaii, and we leave this evening."

"How great! I'm truly pleased for you."

"Yes, it is great. I've heard that things aren't so great for you. I don't want to pry, but I do want you to know that I'm sorry if that's so."

"It is so, and thanks."

"The point of this is, I think I am ready to stop therapy now, Jim. What do you think?"

"First, what's your thinking?"

"Well, I think the biggest thing is that I'm really sick of blaming myself and everyone else all the time. I still do it, but usually I seem to be able to catch myself."

"That's no small thing."

"No, it sure isn't. And along with that, I'm trying to learn to balance between the rules and being human. That's hard,

and I sure haven't got it licked yet, but I know the direction
I want to go . . . or at least I think I do."

"Two big steps, Jennifer. Anything else?"

"Well, the whole new relation Bert and I are making. . . .
Oh, did I tell you? I had Frank come meet Bert the other day.
It was strange having them together, but I'd told Bert all about
Frank — even about my going to bed with him and wanting him
to make love to me. You know, it was really hard for Bert to
hear that. Isn't that something! After all he did. Well! I don't
have to do any bookkeeping on that now."

"How'd it go?"

"Oh, they were both very stiff at first, but gradually they
relaxed, and it went very well. I don't think they're going to
be best friends or anything, but I'd like to keep in touch with
Frank, and I'd like Bert to feel comfortable about it."

"Makes sense to me."

"So what do you think now?"

"It sounds as though you know what you're doing, and
if your judgment says now, then I think we should trust you
and your judgment."

"Oh! Oh, I remember when you first said we could trust
me. That meant a lot to me, Jim."

"I know."

I suggest that after she returns from Hawaii we have a
few interviews, to take a little time to think together as we end
such a major journey as we have had. She readily agrees. All
in all, though, this is essentially the end of Jennifer's therapy.

Louise. "Do you remember how I told you once I'd like to undress all the way and show myself to you?"

I am startled and suddenly alert. If she intends to do that
now, I'm not sure I should encourage it, but I also know I'd
really enjoy having her do so. These months of following her
erotic maturing with Don have been stimulating to me as a man
who cares about Louise, as well as significant to me as her therapist. I content myself with a nod and a few words, "Yes, I
remember."

"Well, uh, you know Don has this Polaroid camera, and we were fooling with it the other day, and he took some pictures of me. And, well, I thought maybe you'd like to see them. You know, this really embarrasses me, and I didn't think it would." Pause. "Do you want to see them?"

"Of course, Louise."

She hands me an envelope. I hold it, but make no move to open it. "What's happening in you right now, Louise?"

"Oh, darn you. I might know you'd make me recite!"

"You're being so very appealing and flirtatious that I think to myself, 'Oh, don't be such a spoilsport; you know you want to see the pictures and she wants you to see them.' But Louise, I don't want to see them as much as I want to help you keep faith with yourself right now."

Suddenly sobered. "I know. I really am embarrassed. I can't take my eyes off that envelope in your hand, and I think I must be crazy. I can't be showing you pictures of me naked. The next thing. . . . And I want you to see them, but. . . . "

"The 'next thing? . . .'"

"Heavens knows what will be next!" Laughing, flustered.

"What do you think might be next?" Smiling, insistent. I'm getting aroused by this game. She's teasing me; yet I don't think she is conscious of doing so.

"Who knows what will happen after you see the pictures of me naked?" Laughing, too much, forced. "You might get so wild you'd tear my clothes off." Abruptly, the laughter stops. She's frightened, embarrassed.

"Tell me what's going on now, Louise." My own voice sober, still supportive, insistent. Want to put the fun back in, the tease, the implicit sexual chase, but even more I want to help her confront her fear.

"It just changed. I don't feel so funny, but. . . . "

"I think you frightened yourself when you said I might tear your clothes off."

"Yes. I don't know why I said that. I'm sorry."

"It sounds as though you feel you've done something bad."

"Well, I don't know. I just wish I hadn't said it."

"Louise, you're in flight from yourself and from me now.

You've forgotten the happy, stimulated self you were a minute ago. You've forgotten who I am. You've forgotten what our relationship is. You're back to being a frightened schoolgirl, and you're making me into a punishing parent."

"No. Yes. I mean, yes. I don't know. I'm confused. Are you mad at me?"

"Your question even sounds like the child in you is speaking. How do you read me, Louise? Really look at me right now. Take charge of your life in the now. Can you?"

She looks into my face like someone peering through a fog. Her eyes are swimming, but she is bringing her awareness into the moment. Rather quickly, her expression changes. The smile starts in the corners of her mouth and breaks out into a delighted chortle. "Wow! I sure do it to myself, don't I?"

"Tell me."

"I mean knock myself out of what is going on right now. And then I feel like I'm a child again and back in the past. I can't believe how just a minute ago I was sure I would find anger or disgust in your face. I mean, I really expected to see you hating me."

"And now?"

"Now, I think you like me, and. . . . Oh! There I go again! I started to say that you liked looking at me, and right away the fear came in. I can't be so presumptuous. And besides, right there in your hand you have pictures that will prove how bad I am. Well! I just don't believe it. That *is* the past. Will you look at the pictures?"

"I'd like to." I open the envelope and suddenly feel my own erotic heat. Louise and I are so close emotionally as we struggle with her fears; and now, here she is quite naked in the pictures. "You are a very lovely woman, Louise."

She draws in her breath sharply. "Oh, it's hard to stay here right now. I want to make a smart remark or to take the pictures back. Yet I really love watching you look at me. Do you know, Jim. . . ." She pauses, and suddenly I sense she is close to tears. "I've never before been proud of my body or really enjoyed it as a woman? Never!" She weeps quietly and then reaches out and takes my hand, squeezes it. "Thanks." Whispering. "I'm so glad I found my body before it was too late."

We sit silently for several minutes, both busy with our own thoughts but still in communion. The buzzer signaling the arrival of my next client and the end of Louise's hour catches us both by surprise. We stand; she comes toward me, and I hold her in a warm embrace. Her body yields against mine in a way it never has before, and my own pulse becomes more insistent. I would like to kiss her, and I know she is waiting for me to turn my head to her. For some reason, I hesitate, and then decide against it. Giving her a little extra squeeze, I pull back and turn toward the door. "See you next Monday."

Jim. Terrible race riots are raging across the country. I feel a nagging in me. I should be doing something. What can I do? That's a cop-out. That's reality. Why can we humans never make major social changes except with blood and destruction? It's so hard for us to let go of the familiar because someone else says they want some of what we have . . . and maybe we won't have as much if they get some. This feeling isn't just about tangible things; it's very much about subjective and intangible values — like respect, opportunities, and appreciation for what we are.

There's a riot in me too. Louise's pictures of her lovely nude body come at a time when I'm hypersensitive to such things. There's no doubt about it, I'm jealous of her Don. I'm not sure I keep my emotional balance when she brings these pictures. In fact, I know I don't. On the other hand, I don't go overboard either. I know of two therapists who've been having sex with their clients, and both are sure it's been a positive thing. I don't know. I just know I'm not ready for that.

Well, I read my paper that told of the unorthodox extremes experienced therapists could conceive in their practices — chiefly involving partial or complete nudity and allowing sexual stimulation — before the psychiatric association and I published it in a journal. I expected explosive reactions. I've heard practically nothing about either one! Have I been so conventional while others were more daring? Have I so shocked my colleagues that they dare not speak of it? I don't know what to make of this nonresult.

So much pain and confusion about being separated. My wife is hurting terribly; my children are upset. Is it worth it to inflict all this anguish on those I care so much about? It's a question I confront over and over again. I hardly feel I'm really choosing. It's more something I am just doing — whatever that may mean.

Ten days ago I started therapy again. I'm hoping this will help. My wife and I go to couples therapy also. I wonder whether I really commit to it. Only time will tell. Meantime, my new therapist, a woman, is going to help me deal with more of the residue from the analysis. I'm glad she can be both very feminine and very strong. I need her to be both. We never get to the bottom of the barrel, do we?

Monday, August 2

Louise. Louise, a study in contrasts, sits on the couch. Her face and manner are tight, strained, unhappy. Her costume is light, bright, summery — and, for Louise, brief: short halter dress, bare back, deep V front. She takes off her sandals, pauses, then lies down, sighing, adjusting the brief skirt, and then crossing her arms over her chest. Another sigh. She looks both frightened and stubborn.

I'll just be quiet. She's struggling with something in herself, and she knows how to do the job. Her arms tighten, then slowly relax. From the corner of each eye, a tear silently slides. Then more tears. Slowly the tightness subsides. Probably five minutes have passed; neither of us has spoken. Good work is going on.

Another sigh. "I'm so messed up inside. I want to tell you about it, but . . . but every time I start, more thoughts and feelings get in the way. I've fought this fight too many years, damn it."

"Tell me what you can," very quietly.

"It started after last time. No, wait! Don't ask me. I'll do this. Last time I showed you pictures Don took of me when I was naked. I showed you pictures of me naked. There!"

"Mm-hmm."

"And I . . . I liked doing that (pause, quick breath). And I think . . . well, I thought. . . . No! I believe you liked seeing them (defiantly)."

"I did."

"Yes. I was so mixed up I couldn't remember very well all that happened (pause). Don't say anything — please." Tears flowing again. She reaches for the tissues. For a full minute she is silent, and I feel a kind of loving admiration for her courage and determination.

"I kept thinking about it . . . about you looking at the pictures and about Mrs. Colten and Aunt Julie. Sometimes I would feel that I was shameful and you probably hated me and would tell me not to come back anymore. Sometimes . . . sometimes I knew that wasn't you . . . and I wasn't . . . hadn't been bad."

Again she pauses as the tears flood her. This time she sobs quietly for a bit. "I don't know why it hurts so much, but it really does. Well, I guess I do know some about it: I've been realizing how much of my life has slipped by without my being aware of it, with my double-crossing myself again and again. I'm forty years old this year! I don't like to think about that, but I'm going to. I'm going to think and think about it. I don't want any more of being . . . being dead and not with myself. And then today . . . or yesterday actually, I —" She stops, and it's apparent she is fighting another battle.

I take in a breath to say something, but she catches it and speaks first. "No, Jim, don't say anything. I've got to do this myself . . . and in my own way."

"Today," she continues, her voice conveying a mobilization of her resolution, "I got this crazy idea that. . . . No! It's not a crazy idea. I know. I started to break faith with myself. It isn't a crazy idea, but I want to reject it and the me who had the idea."

Once again she is silent, struggling. I have to remind myself that she is demonstrating she needs no help now. Shut up, Bugental!

"It hurts! It hurts physically. In my throat and in my chest (pause). I don't want to go on. I want to talk about the power of the emotions to do things, to be abstract, and to get away from. . . ."

"From?" Had to say something, didn't I?

"From what I thought I wanted to do. I'm afraid you'll . . . it's as though you could destroy me or . . . or at least send me away."

We're silent again. I want to point out that she's making me into her rejecting uncle, but this time I'm able to stop myself. Why do I have to continually prove to myself and to my patients how much they need me — when, as now — it's obvious they need only my silent presence?

Suddenly, she gathers herself and speaks in a clear voice. "I thought today I would come in here and take all my clothes off and not use the cop-out of photographs." She is silent, holding herself very still, waiting. I am also silent, but inside I hear a clamor of voices: "I mustn't let her do that. I'd really like to see her naked. It's clearly unethical; I'll get in big trouble. It's not unethical if I don't touch her. I'd like to touch her. No way! Stop this whole thing right now!" And then I let it all go and just wait.

"Jim, tell me frankly, if I did undress here, would it be hard for you? I don't want to make you hurt. . . ." She stops and looks at me in surprise.

I've begun to chuckle. A minute before I was concerned about legality, and here she is concerned for me, the person. Then her unwitting pun. My tension comes out in the laugh.

"I'm sorry to interrupt you, but your unconscious just tickled me with a pun. You asked whether your undressing would make it *hard* for me. The answer is, probably so."

"Oh, oh, I see. Oh, that embarrasses me, but that's silly. Yes, I hope it does make it hard for you. Oops! I'm not very used to this kind of talk, but I like it too."

"Louise, I hear your concern for me, and I value that. If you were to undress, I'm sure I'd react emotionally and physically, but it would not be a serious hurt."

"I've always heard that if men get excited and then the woman doesn't . . . doesn't want to have intercourse. . . ."

"That's male propaganda. If a man finds it uncomfortable to have an erection, he can certainly do something about it. Men continually seek out ways of getting sexually excited where no completion is possible. They do it because they enjoy it. No, Louise, my concern is not about possible physical discomfort."

"But you are concerned?"

"Yes, in two ways: I know many of my colleagues would be shocked and critical if they knew I let you undress. 'Words but not actions'—that's our policy. I don't always agree, but that is one concern that I have."

"I don't want you to get in trouble. Let's just skip the whole thing."

"No, Louise, you're letting the outside make your decision. I'm affected by the traditional way we think about these things, but I am not totally controlled by it. It has much that is good in it, but is not divine edict. You and I need to think about such matters carefully and then to choose responsibly how we act."

"I'm concerned about you, though."

"That means a lot to me, but it's not the only consideration. My other concern is whether you've thought about what would happen once you were naked here with me."

Her quick intake of air is almost answer enough. She looks startled and then laughs. "Yes, I have, and I thought it would be very nice."

"Put it in words."

"Well, maybe then you'd hold me and maybe . . . you'd take off your clothes too. . . . Oh, this is harder than I thought it would be (pause). Then maybe . . . maybe we'd make love." She gulps but meets my eyes smilingly.

I'm the one who needs to take a big breath. But, in a way, it's simpler for me now. "You are very attractive and very desirable, Louise, and what you suggest is extremely inviting. But for many reasons—some having to do with us here, and some related to other parts of my life—I will not have intercourse with you; so. . . ."

"Oh, I know (hastily). I mean you asked, and so I. . . ."

"Louise, you're making my answer into something it is

not. You are hearing me as reprimanding you, and you're ignoring what I said — in real sincerity — about how nice the idea
of our making love was for me."

"Yes, I suppose so (sadly). Well (pause), well it's probably better this way anyway." She pauses, thinking, uncomfortable. "It's probably better too if I don't undress, don't you think?"

"You sound as though you're passing the choice back to
me."

"No. I mean, yes, I started to. Well, I came here to do
it; so unless you insist I don't do it, I will do it!" Tone defiant.

"It sounds very nice, Louise."

She is silent, motionless, collecting herself. Inside my own
head, I am surprised to be calm. I know I should have thought
of many more points to raise. There's still the question of possible scandal if anyone found out. Oh, nuts, I'm tired of being
careful and denying life. Louise is showing me a more courageous way. Sit back and enjoy her honesty and her body.

Slowly, her hands come up behind her neck and work
with fastenings under her hair. Still slowly, they come back
down, bringing the straps with them so that now she is peeling
down the halter top of her dress. Hesitantly, her hands move
lower, and the tops of her breasts are bared. Then, abruptly,
she stops and sucks in her breath as she clutches her hands to
her chest.

We are both silent as she lies tensely, the tears rolling
down her cheeks unheeded. Her whole body is so tense that it
is on the verge of shaking convulsively. I find momentary disappointment as my excited anticipation is replaced by warm
caring for what is obviously her pain.

"What is it, Louise?" My voice is a whisper.

"I'm sorry, Jim." More crying. "I'm really, really sorry."
She cries with such clear sadness.

"Tell me."

"I'm sorry. I know how much you want to see me. I really
can feel that. I've been feeling it since I showed you the pictures. And I want to . . . wanted to show you me. I have for
a long time. Ever since the day I opened my blouse. And now. . . ."
Again she cries. I wait. This isn't what I thought at all. I thought

she was embarrassed at her sexual excitement, but I sense now she's weeping for me. For me!

"I still will undress. I mean, I really will, because I know you would like that, but I have to tell you — oh, darn it, I don't want to say this — I have to tell you. . . . "

"Tell me, Louise." Softly.

"I'd be doing it," whispering, "mostly to please you. Oh! That's not all so. I'd enjoy doing it, but somehow, since I have Don — it wouldn't be the same. I mean, oh, I don't want to make you feel bad. I really care about you, Jim, you know that. I really love you. But not that way anymore. I mean, after I showed you the pictures the other day, I suddenly knew that it wasn't really for me anymore. Well, it was for me. I really get kind of excited; aroused, I mean. But then in another way, I guess, I was doing it chiefly for you. Like I knew you'd like it. And I liked your liking it. And now, now, I really would enjoy seeing you see me, seeing you enjoy looking at me without any clothes on. It would be scary, but it would be exciting too. And. . . . "

"And?"

"And, I want to do it for you . . . and for the looking at you looking at me. . . . " Her hands start to pull the halter down again.

"Wait, Louise." The hands stop, but no longer clutch at her. The upper surfaces of her breasts are bared, and I feel again the swelling wish to see her whole exciting body. "Wait, Louise. You're saying something very important. Important to you and important to me."

"I don't want you to think I don't care about you, Jim. You've saved my life. I mean, I really would do anything for you. And I really mean anything."

"I know, Louise, but I think you're in the middle of doing something even more important than taking your clothes off for me. You're right. I really would like to see you naked, but that isn't what I want most. Right now, you are also offering me something even more precious — your trust in me to be with you even if you don't do what I want or what some part of me wants."

"I know it, Jim. I started to take off my dress, and suddenly I knew that I wasn't keeping faith with you or with me. Before Don and I became so close—I mean, both sexually and emotionally—I would have loved to take all of my clothes off in front of you just for me. I know, because I thought of it lots of times. But now, just now, when I started to take off my dress, I knew it really wasn't for me but because I knew how much you would like it. I was making you old Mr. Colten, I guess, and just trying to be pleasing. And I don't want to do that to you or to me, Jim."

"And you knew that down under my sexual excitement I really don't want that either, Louise. I really value your keeping faith with me and with you."

After Louise leaves I sit for several minutes, tired and dispirited. There is no doubt that she was right in her reading of me—and right in her decision to stop undressing. I was so caught up in the delight of her emerging sexuality, her greater freedom with her body, and her always powerful eroticism that I lost track of what was her motivation and what was my yearning. Ruefully I appreciate her courage in confronting me. It's time to recognize that we're entering a new—and probably final—stage of our work together.

Thursday, August 5

Louise. Subdued, her face sober and inward, Louise sits in the big chair rather than lying on the couch. "Jim, I'm having. . . . Ever since I left Thursday, I've been battling inside myself."
       "Tell me."
       "Oh, there's so much going on. One minute I'm pulling away from myself, telling myself how presumptuous I was to. . . . And then I suddenly feel that I missed my chance to have something . . . something special with you. Then I get mad at myself for thinking you'd . . . for wanting to. . . . Then I get straight for a minute and think what a good thing Thursday was, but right away, I start to lose that and. . . . "

"I've thought a lot about Thursday too. And the main thing I end up with is deep appreciation for your guts in keeping faith with yourself . . . and with me."

"Sometimes I wish I hadn't."

"I know. So do I, at times. But mostly. . . . "

"Mostly I'm glad it went the way it did."

So the hour goes. We've warm appreciation for each other, and implicitly we know we've passed some point of no return.

After she leaves, I have time to reflect about Louise and our work together. This once frightened, desirable, conflicted woman is now emerging as a person of strength and self-direction. My own wantings might have obstructed that growth; perhaps they did in some ways. Still, in other ways, those same subjective responses to her were important to the evolution of her growth. I could never have planned a strategy such as the one that unfolded. (For that matter, I can't consciously plan strategies for any of those with whom I work.) Maybe I lost perspective for a while with her — maybe I lost perspective more often than I like to know — but in our depths (my clients' and mine) resides the potential to reinterpret what occurs and to make it serve our truer intentions. If only we keep aware. What a big "if"!

Jim. Would I like to be a part of a research project on the future of education? Good question. Not something I've ever thought of doing. Sounds interesting. But that would mean moving north and stopping practice for a year or possibly even longer. What about my patients? I can't leave them when they're in the middle. Have to wait until they're in better places to be interrupted. And when will that be? Always some are just beginning, more are in various middle stages, and a few are finishing up. There'd never be a right time for everyone.

These and other thoughts are triggered by an invitation from a very creative man who was in one of my Esalen workshops and who has read some of my writings and, evidently, liked them. He heads a research project that seeks to anticipate the changing needs of education in the next twenty to one hundred years. He'd like me to join them for a year at least.

Isn't this a fortuitous time to make a change — at least for a while? I've gotten in up to my neck (but not over my head, I insist) with Louise. I'm tired of my little apartment and semi-bachelor's existence. I am pretty sure I'll never be returning to the house on the hill (oh, I choke up when I think that).

Well, let's write for more information and tell him I'll need at least six months between the time we agree — if we do — and my showing up for work. Maybe that will kill it. Maybe not.

Monday, September 11

Louise. "I'm pleased, frustrated, relieved, and annoyed!" She sits on the couch, her face mirroring the play of the contradictory feelings. "You'll never guess what happened."

"I'm sure I couldn't."

"Oh, you can be annoying sometimes! Well, I'll tell you anyway. Dr. Elliott has resigned!"

"I can understand why you'd be pleased and relieved, but I gather that's not the whole of it."

"No, it's not!" She stops, makes a wry face, then shrugs helplessness. "I talked to him last week and told him flatly that I would not go along with his new regulations. They were crippling a program our whole staff had invested a great deal in, and they were also destroying staff morale."

"You said that to him directly?"

"Yes, almost exactly those words."

"Quite a step!"

"Yes, it was, and I felt very good about it. He was surprised. I guess I've always been so agreeable. So he said he'd have to think about it, that he had some other issues that were taking all of his attention right now so he couldn't give me an answer right away."

"An answer?"

"Yes. I forgot to tell you. I told him that I was going to file a formal protest with the board if he persisted in his plans."

"You really let him have both barrels."

"Do you think I was too . . . no, I wasn't. I was polite and yet I let him know exactly where I stood."

"Mm-hmm."

"So he was to give me his answer today. Instead there was a notice on the bulletin board that he had submitted his resignation. And it makes me mad in a way. I finally got my nerve up to fight him, and—"

"And he's left you with no one to fight."

"That's right! It's not fair. Oh, I know that's silly, but that's the way I feel."

"'Silly,' huh?"

"Oh, I'm not really putting myself down this time, I just mean that it's paradoxical."

"Uh-huh."

"Oh, I've got another thing to tell you. Don's invited me to come live with him."

"And?"

"And I'm going to do it. I'm going to love living with him and loving him."

"Great."

"We talked about getting married—it was scary and exciting for me—but we decided we ought to be together for a while first and see how we do on a day-to-day basis."

"Makes sense."

"I want to tease you and ask if you're jealous, but I know you're not in a very good place in your own life; so I don't want to make you feel bad in any way."

"I think I am a bit jealous, Louise, but I'm also very glad that you have someone special and that things are getting so well for you."

Jim. I am pleased for Louise—and jealous. But tonight I am so caught up in the news that I don't think very long about her.

Yesterday we put a camera on the moon! What an incredible thing. I understand that fact, but I can't really grasp that we sent some machinery up through the air, through space, all the way to that familiar moon and that the pictures we see in the paper today were really taken way up there.

What a wonderful species we are! I'm a species chauvinist. How amazing the things that we can do! We ought to all be dancing in the streets — not just in the USA, but all around the world — to celebrate this achievement, celebrate ourselves.

But just last month we were bombing Hanoi, killing soldiers and civilians. Last month too we sent another huge bunch of our troops over there. What a terrible species we are!

I believe both are true. We are terrible. We are wonderful. How lucky I am to work with such terrible wonder!

Fifteen

"We Had an Affair."

Monday, October 9

Jim. I've decided to accept the research consultancy offer. It sounds very interesting, I'll like being in new surroundings, and I'm flattered that they — particularly Bill, the director — think that I have so much to offer them.

I took a quick trip up there this past weekend, and "the Peninsula," as they call the area south of San Francisco, is very appealing. Although I've lived in the L.A. area for many years, much longer than in any other, it still doesn't feel like "home." It's too big, too scattered, too impersonal. The Palo Alto area is more manageable in size, more beautiful in natural ways, and promises to be more stimulating to me, at least right at this point in my life.

I have a dear friend with me now, and if this develops well, she will go north with me next year. Like Louise and Don, we're going step by step. The wisdom of this is demonstrated when Louise tells me today that she and Don are having trouble making their relation work and so are going to live separately again. She was disappointed but not seriously upset.

Monday, October 23

Kate. On a bright fall day trailing memories of the summer's heat, Kate comes in wearing a more colorful dress than I've seen on her before. Her hair has had professional attention, and altogether she contrasts markedly with the gray, prim woman who first entered this office more than eighteen months ago. There is a lift to her chin and a tempo to her speech that express her growing participation in life and her emerging hope for herself. Her face has little of the granite tension, and her step no longer mechanically moves her from place to place.

Yet I watch Kate get settled on the couch with apprehension. For two weeks I've been dreading this day, postponing what I must do. Now I can delay no longer: I must tell her today that I will be leaving next year. It is well over six months before that time, but it is too soon for Kate's stage of progress. I've talked to Al Lasko, my closest friend and colleague, and he's ready to begin seeing Kate in concurrent sessions when she's ready. That should ease the transfer to him when I leave.

All of these thoughts do not quiet my misgivings, my self-blame, my guilt. I shouldn't leave. I can't do this to Kate, who suffered so from being abandoned when she was young. I'll have to withdraw my acceptance of the appointment, go next year. But what then of Lillian or Steve, who are just beginning to work through their hesitation to trust? I know, in a real way, that there is no right time.

All this has been going through me before Kate comes in, and it descends on me again as I look at her and hear her begin to speak.

"I've been thinking about what Larry said in the group last. . . . "

"Kate." Abruptly, in the middle of her sentence. "Kate, I'm sorry to interrupt you, but I have something I need to talk with you about. It is important, and I want to have plenty of time for us to think it over together."

She turns on one elbow, looking up at me, troubled, questioning.

"In brief, it's this, Kate: I'm going to be away for a year starting next July. I've accepted a research consultant position up north and. . . . " Her face is unchanging; perhaps the eyes are set a little too fixedly, but I can't tell. My words won't flow easily. I'm scared, guilty. "Well, I've talked to Dr. Lasko, and during the six months before I leave, he will work with us from time to time so that when you feel ready you can continue with him. And besides. . . . "

"When I feel ready? I'm afraid I don't understand." Her tone has some of the old formality, distance. Even so, it's a relief to hear her speak, to deal with a detail.

"Well, I mean we can arrange for you to transfer more to him whenever you like in the next six months." I'm fumbling, don't like the flavor of what I said.

"I see." Quiet, unemotional, controlled. I think she's frightened.

"And besides, I'll be coming back down here from time to time so that we can keep in contact in any way that seems useful." I still feel wooden, self-conscious. The tone is saying that it is all mechanical, impersonal; that's what wrong. Quick relief at identifying the problem, that's something I can deal with.

"Yes, I'm sure we can do that." She's withdrawn, impersonally meeting my impersonality, escalating the detachment.

"Kate, I feel a lot of feelings right now. I feel troubled to be leaving at all. I feel guilty for hurting you. I feel awkward in trying to express my concern and my wanting to do everything possible to make this a positive experience for you."

"Of course, I understand. It's really quite all right. I certainly understand your wish to advance your own career, and I'm sure Dr. Lasko will be very helpful should I need to continue in therapy next spring."

All so smooth. It's too smooth, but there are no obvious places to take hold. "Kate, I think this has more impact for you than you're letting yourself know. I appreciate your reassurance, but I'd like to help you get in touch with your deeper feelings about my going away." I'd guess she's clamping on controls to head off panic.

"Yes, well, it does come as a surprise. I hadn't really thought about the possibility before. But really, I don't think you need trouble yourself so much. Six months is a long time, and I'm sure whatever needs doing can be done in that time. Don't you agree?" Pleasant, distant, formal. Too pleasant, too formal; she's turning herself off.

"No, I'm not sure I do, Kate. Your being so agreeable and so distant right now really feels bad to me. Lately, we've been able to talk with each other in a much more straight way than this. I think, I'm guessing, that you're hurt and probably angry. Can you find any feelings like that?"

"No, I don't think so. I am simply aware of needing some time to think over what you've told me, and feeling a bit of annoyance that you always seem to make things into Greek dramas. Really, I don't feel that distressed." Evenly, reasonably. Have I underestimated her progress? True, she's pulled back a bit, but isn't that appropriate? Do I need her to be so attached to me that my leaving would be a major trauma? Or do I want to believe she's handling it well because it's too heavy to fight through her wall again?

"Well, Kate, we have plenty of time yet today. Why don't you do that, think over what I told you, and do it out loud so that I can listen in and be of any help I can be?"

But there is little need for me to do anything. The hour goes quietly; Kate talks in even tones, keeps a careful distance emotionally. I try — do I really try? — to penetrate the polite wall, to get back the closer working relation. She is pleasant, detached, and quite unwilling to remember any other way of relating. I think: She needs time, just as she said; it is normal, even healthy, to get a bit of space when something unexpected comes. She's handling it very well, all things considered. But then I think: She is walling off; we're losing the ground it took us months to win; she'll retreat so far that she won't ever risk coming out again. I feel hopeful, troubled, expectant, unhappy. Her brightly colored dress seems mocking and sad. Her face, although not apparently troubled, certainly no longer accords with her dress.

Frank. "I got promoted again! How do you like them apples?" Frank has never been one for consciously joking, but he's high with pride and pleasure. It's a balm for my troubled emotions, having just come from telling Kate my plans. And he's an astonishing sight when I think of how he looked for so long. He's wearing a new suit, clean shirt, neat tie, and — wonder of wonders — he's clean shaven!

"What's your magic, Frank, getting promoted twice?"

"Aw, it's just. . . . You know, this makes me kind of un-comfortable or embarrassed. Shit, I haven't any magic, as you know, but mostly the people I supervise are . . . well, like I was for too long. You know, unskilled and not very dependable. The thing is, I've been there every damned day and on time and looking halfway decent. It's a cinch to look good when those other jokers. . . . Well, they're doing the same thing I did."

"What's that?"

"Setting themselves up to lose. Goddamn, I know that route too fucking well — uh, too well. Gandowsky says I got to clean up my language too."

"What do you think of that?"

"Oh, it's just like the other things. I don't have to cuss all the time; I just got to break the habit."

"And you want to now."

"Right. I do. But Jim, there's a couple other things I got to talk with you about."

"Shoot."

"I think I'm ready to stop coming here, if you agree."

"I thought you were about ready."

"Hey, great! I hoped you'd say that."

"You know where you are and what you need now, Frank. What's the second thing?"

"I talked to Mr. Gandowsky and told him I wanted to go to college, and we worked out a deal. You know, he's really a great old guy, kinda odd some ways, but just the same really neat." He pauses, grins reflectively. I've never seen Frank smile so much.

"So?"

"You still got your 'sos,' haven't you? Well, anyway, we worked out a deal. I'm going to live on half what he pays me, and bank the rest. Then, if I do a good job, next year I'll start to college, and Gandowsky says he'll keep me on half-time, and I figure that way I can go full-time to school and make it financially."

"Sounds very good."

"You bet it is." He pauses, suddenly uncomfortable. "There's one thing though."

"Uh-huh?"

"I want to go all the way . . . for a doctorate."

"Yeah, I know. It sounds good to me."

"In clinical psychology, Jim." This is what's scaring him.

"Frank, that's great. It really gives me a good feeling that you want to come into my field."

"Yeah (sighing). I didn't know whether you'd feel that way or not. I hoped you would, but I thought maybe you'd laugh at the idea."

"I'm not laughing."

"Wow! I'm really glad you feel that way. I just decided that I wanted to go for the whole shit and kaboodle!"

And Frank's unconscious has the last say.

Tuesday, October 24

Kate. I'm waiting somewhat anxiously to see just how Kate will be today. But 10:00 comes, and Kate doesn't arrive. I wait. Still no one in the waiting room at five after. Ten minutes later I ask Phyl to check with the answering service, but they are holding no calls for me. I'm restless, guilty, self-blaming, anxious.

Usually I don't pursue clients when they miss their appointments. It's important for them to feel that it's their responsibility and their loss if they don't use the time I reserve for them. I do charge when people fail to cancel twenty-four hours in advance. All this is beside the point. Where is Kate? How is she?

At 10:25 I call Kate's apartment. No answer. I call her office, and she is there! Relief, uncertainty. She comes promptly to the phone, is businesslike. She forgot, got engrossed in her work. No, it doesn't have any particular meaning, so far as she is aware. Thank you, no she doesn't want another time today. She'll see me on Thursday as usual. Thanks for my call. Careful, polite, out of reach.

Thursday, October 26

Kate. The waiting room buzzer announces that Kate is on time, exactly, to the tick. The vibrations of her anger greet me as I open the door. She does not respond to my greeting, does not meet my eyes, does not look right or left, marches into the office, takes the straight chair, stares directly in my face.

"I have been thinking about your plan to leave and the unilateral way you announced it to me, and I have concluded that you are high-handed, irresponsible, and completely deceptive." Tough, hard, letting me have it right between the eyes.

I feel the impact. This woman isn't playing. She's mad, and she's determined to let me know it. I want to protest, to explain; but back of that I feel a kind of pride in her. She's not going to take it lying down. This is a gutsy thing to do. And I feel some relief.

"You are very angry." Quietly, wanting to be very straight now.

"I want to ask you if you think that you have the right to invite people to begin work with you, to encourage them to put their trust in you, to insist that they regard this psychotherapy as the most important event in their lives, and then to announce, 'Well, I feel like going away for a while now. Somebody else will take care of you.' What gives you the right to treat people that way?" Her eyes are fierce, her voice tight, controlled, and forced through jaws that do not open very wide.

"Kate, I really feel your anger with me. You are just furious, and it's coming over like a solid force." Ugh! What a stupid, shallow response to her! I want her to know that I still value her, that I think she's great right now; and I don't want to be patronizing or to pull back from her in any way. Yet my answer is stilted, and it's not really an answer. The force of her feelings joins with my own self-blame, and I'm on the defensive and talking in a forced, self-conscious, clumsy way.

"Are you going to answer my question, Dr. Bugental?" Coldly, intently. The question is unimportant; asserting her identity against me is everything. She will not accept "therapeutic" responses. Yet I'm reluctant to confront her fully, to give her the only real answer.

"Kate, I've been wrestling with that question daily for the past two weeks and even before that, and I still don't know whether I have the right. I try to tell you and the other people I see that they must know and respect their own needs while trying to be responsible in relation to the other people in their lives. That's the code I have for myself too, and. . . . "

"And you have decided it is responsible to go away because it suits your convenience now, I gather." She is slightly less intense, but her manner shows no relaxation of the vigilance with which she eyes me. I feel like she has me pinned at the point of her sword and at any sudden move she will run me through.

"I've tried, Kate. Tried to think about the needs of each of the people I see, and tried to think about my own needs. How well I've done, I really don't know. I do know that you are shocked and furious with me."

Oh, bah! I still sound so stiff and tight. I am tight, tight with worry and guilt and ambivalence. I'd really like to keep Kate's feeling for me, but even more important I'd like to help her hold on to the gains she — we — worked so damned hard to make. It could all be shattered now. Hell, I wasn't trained to be personally involved with patients. I shouldn't let my own feelings get in the act and be so needful myself. But I am. And I'm dodging with Kate. Have to. I don't want to have to point out the difference between her needs and mine; it will sound too rejecting.

Kate has been silent, watching me intently. "Yes, I am shocked and, I suppose, angry with you. I had thought you might be more responsible than it now appears you are."

"Kate, you're mad as hell, and I can't say that I blame you a damn bit. That's the way it is, isn't it?"

"How is it, Dr. Bugental, that last year when I wanted to go to a meeting that would have taken me away from therapy for a month, you objected and insisted that it was more important to me to be here? How is that? Was it more important for me? Or was it more important to your bank account?" Coldly, ready to destroy any response, well prepared to fire round after round. She's unconsciously pressing toward the answer I'm reluctant to give.

"I really believed that it was the best advice I could give you."

"How is it that I could not be away a month and you can

go for a year?" That's it. She's laid it bare. There's no honest alternative; I must say it straight, without cushioning.

"That's a hard question, and the answer is even harder: It's that your therapy must be the most important thing in your life, but it's not the most important in mine." There, that's the core of it, so stark, so bitter, so true. I half-wish the words back, to say them in some other way. Although I feel strangely good to have said it so straight, I am also frightened. Did I need to strike back?

Kate sits quite still, looks at me very intently, considers, then nods. "Of course, that is so. I have been quite silly, haven't I?" She gathers her purse close to her, rises abruptly, and starts toward the door.

"Kate, where are you going?" I am on my feet.

"Don't trouble yourself." She has the door open.

"Kate, come back!"

No answer. She is into the hall, heading for the outside door.

"Kate, I'm going to keep your time tomorrow for you."

"No." She pauses, half turns. "No, that won't be necessary. I will call Dr. Lasko or someone else if I need to discuss anything with anybody."

"No, Kate, I won't stop this way. I'll keep your time tomorrow for you, and I hope you'll come."

"Suit yourself." She is gone.

Friday, October 27

Kate. She isn't here at her appointment time. I'm not surprised, but I am disappointed. More than that, I'm worried. Once again the debate about calling her. If I seem to pursue her, will she need to fight me? Will she be afraid to call me if she really needs to? If I don't try to reach her, will she think I have crossed her off, will she feel it proves that I'm uncaring? Back and forth, yes and no. No resolution. Her time passes. I see two more clients, but my mind keeps going to Kate. I call her apartment; no answer. I call her office at the laboratory. Dr. Margate called to say she would not be in today. Any message? No.

During dinner, the phone rings. My phone exchange has a Mrs. Cudahay on the line. She is anxious to speak to me about Dr. Kate Margate! A chill down my back, take a deep breath, tighten my grip on the phone.

"Of course, put her on, please."

"Dr. Bugental? I'm a neighbor of Dr. Kate Margate. I hope you won't mind my calling, but I thought I ought to let you know, or somebody. I didn't know who to call. She gave me your name last month when I was feeling nervous, and so I thought. . . . I mean, Dr. Margate doesn't seem to have many friends; at least I haven't seen many people going into her apartment. She lives in the next apartment to ours. Not that I watch who goes in and out of her apartment, of course. She can do anything she wants. You know what I mean; I'm not one of those nosy neighbors. But I did think I ought to tell you or someone; so I hope you'll forgive me for troubling you. You see, we've lived next door to Dr. Margate for three years and. . . . "

Impatient, but know she's trying to be kind, to do something; so few people risk getting involved. Don't blast her just because I'm anxious. "That's all right, Mrs. Cudahay. What is it you wanted to tell me?"

"Well, it's nothing really. At least, I don't think it is, but it just isn't like Dr. Margate to go off and leave her apartment door wide open, and she's been gone over an hour now. Do you think she's all right? She stopped at our apartment to give me a package from the May Company that had been left with her. I mean the package was for me. And she just looked awful. So I said, 'Are you all right?' and she said she was, but she sure didn't look it. Her eyes looked like she'd been crying, and her clothes were kind of all mussed up. I asked her to come in, but she said no she had to go out and then she just walked out, didn't even go back and shut her door, just walked out. And I don't know whether to shut it or not or whether she has her key. I don't think she had her purse with her. So if I shut it, she won't be able to get back in, but I don't like to leave it open that way. I mean, just anybody could walk in. I've been keeping my door open so I could try to watch that nobody goes in her apartment; though I don't know what I'd do if they did. I mean, I'm all alone here. Do you think I should close the door? But I'm almost sure she didn't have her purse and then she wouldn't be able to get back in. . . . "

"Mrs. Cudahay," I cut in. "It's very good of you to be so concerned. Is there a manager in the building who could let Dr. Margate in if she came back without her key?"

"Well, there's supposed to be, but lately nobody's there much. So I don't know whether there's anybody there or not. I just don't like leaving her door like that though. Why, only last week there was a robbery over on Allen Street. They just went in and cleaned out the whole apartment of an elderly couple while they were out to the grocery. So I keep worrying that. . . . "

"Would it be too much trouble, Mrs. Cudahay, to check whether the building manager is in this evening and would be there to let Dr. Margate in if she didn't have her key when she came back?"

"Oh, no, not at all. That's a good idea. Hold the line — I'll be right back. It may take a minute, because if Mrs. Hennessey is there she's such a talker that it's hard to get away from her. But," laugh, "I guess I'm that way too, huh? My husband's always saying that when Betty and I get together it would take thunder and lightning to make us stop talking. Well, I'll go see if anybody's there. I'll be right back."

I manage several bites of cooling supper while waiting for her return; meantime, my mind is busy: Where is Kate? Was it a simple oversight that she left her door open? Is she suicidal? Possibly, but probably not. I don't like the thought of her wandering around, not taking notice of where she is, what she's doing. What could I have done? What can I do? What about that damned apartment door? Should I tell Mrs. Cudahay to close it? If Kate comes back in a low state, will she think to ask the manager for the key? I can't be her nurse, yet I can't ignore her need. I helped to put her into whatever she's in. I had to consider my own needs too, but I could have handled it better. The food is hard to swallow. Should I try to find Kate? What's the matter with me that I'm so involved? Would Kate be apt to get drunk? I don't know; doubt it, because drinking is linked with her mother. But maybe that would make it more likely. I don't know anything about her or about people. She's right to be mad at me. Oh, this is ridiculous.

"Doctor? I talked to Mrs. Hennessey, and she'll be in all evening. So I shut the door to Dr. Margate's apartment. Believe me that's a relief to me. Doctor, do you think she's all right?" A lot of genuine concern mixed in with the need to be involved and to know.

"Well, I can't really say much right now, Mrs. Cudahay, but I'm sure that Dr. Margate will appreciate your concern for her and your keeping an eye on her apartment. That's very thoughtful of you." Want to express appreciation but not get caught in another long monologue or in fending off questions about Kate.

"Oh, it was nothing, really. I just like to be a good neighbor, you know. Doctor, what could I do to help her — Dr. Margate, I mean? What do you think would be good for me to do? Do you think I ought to have her come over for dinner or something? She's not a great one for socializing, if you know what I mean, but she's really very nice. And she's so smart, being a doctor and all."

"Mrs. Cudahay, I think you're being a very good neighbor. Now, I wonder if you'd excuse me? I'm right in the middle of dinner, and. . . . "

"Oh, my goodness, yes, of course. I'm sorry. I didn't know."

"That's really all right. Thank you for your concern. Good night." Relief; hope I didn't sound too abrupt. Dinner cold; no appetite to make it worth heating up. Where is Kate?

Sunday, October 29

Kate. I hoped all yesterday, Saturday, that I might hear from Kate, but there was no word. Same through most of today. Now, after dinner, the exchange calls — Dr. Margate is on the line. Put her through!

"Kate?"

"Dr. Bugental, this is Kate Margate. I hope I didn't inconvenience you by not coming for my appointment Friday?"

"No, no, Kate. Are you okay?"

"I'm sorry not to have come on Friday. Have you filled my Monday time with someone else?"

"No, Kate, I've held it for you. Kate, tell me how you are."

"Then I'll come in at ten o'clock tomorrow morning. Thank you."

She's hung up!

Monday, October 30

Kate. Kate is rather pale, and sits hunched in the waiting room. Coming into the office, the old gray clothes, her manner careful but not exaggeratedly stiff. She sits on — not in — the straight chair. Eyes downcast, both hands on her purse, lips closed. I wait.

Have I done this to this woman? No, it is her own emotional distress. I should have foreseen better. But there is no way to foresee better. That's the myth of omniscience. I did the best I could. It wasn't good enough. Could anything be? Something needed to be.

"Kate, can you tell me how you are this morning?" Easy, kindly, concernedly; don't push the tenderness; she can't handle that now.

No movement of head, eyes still down. Lips move. "I'd rather not talk right now."

"All right, Kate, let's just sit here together for a bit. When you can, though, I'd like to know something of what's going on in you." Sit back. Seek a comfortable posture; none lasts more than a few minutes. Kate, on the other hand, is unmoving . . . carved of granite, again.

And so the whole hour goes. She barely moves, says nothing. Gradually I settle down, deal with my own contending feelings. There is a kind of companionship, a kind of shared pain, even a shared separateness. At the end of the time, actually past the end, for I'm reluctant to let her leave knowing no more than I do, I say softly, "Our usual time tomorrow, Kate."

She rises, goes out; no words, no acknowledgment.

Jim. Since I made the decision to move north next year, I can't take on any new clients for long-term therapy. Nevertheless, I am gradually having time freed up as my present clients finish their work, and — since I need more than ever to earn — I'm taking short-term referrals and consultations in which I see someone a few times to make recommendations for treatment or for similar reasons.

Two of these consultations have had particular impact for me. The other day I saw a colleague who had been referred by our association's ethics committee. According to him, he had done no more than kiss a client several times, and then she filed charges against him. The ethics committee evidently judged this not serious enough to warrant more than requiring him to talk with me a half-dozen times about his relations with his clients.

He's a very sincere person, much troubled by what he sees as the potential disgrace of this situation, and very anxious to cooperate with me. In fact, he's so anxious to do so that he has great difficulty in really exploring his own thoughts and feelings. But his plight sends a tremor through me as I think of my experiments in unorthodox procedures with Louise.

The other consultation that is curiously pertinent right at this time is a young woman in her early thirties whom I saw today because her parents in the east have been disturbed by the irrationality of her letters and phone calls to them. She came in late this morning for our interview.

Pippi, as she says she is called, was dressed in a fashion I would think more typical of someone half her thirty-four years: miniskirt, bobby sox, saddle shoes, and tight-fitting blouse that draws attention to her high, firm breasts. She was pleased to be here, she said, and at once launched into an account of a failed love affair, which, smiling, she said left her with a broken heart. Almost without pausing and still smiling, she then told of another relation that had ended when her lover told her to "get lost" because she was too "heavy" (which I took to mean too serious or sad, not overweight).

I tried to find out some details about Pippi's current life, but she was anxious to talk more about how badly she did in any relation and how she just didn't "make it" with people. When I asked why she thought that might be, she grew excited, said it was because she was a "phoney" and no good really. Then even more excited, "You see my figure? It's great, isn't it? Nice big boobs, huh? Well, they're phoney, just as I am." And to prove her point she pulled her blouse over her head and confronted me with her bare breasts, which clearly looked quite unnatural. (Oh, come on, ethics committee, I didn't ask for this.)

I told Pippi firmly to put her blouse back on, and she did and then apologized and said that just proved again how no good she was. I said I wanted her to stay in her chair for a minute while I talked to my secretary. She said she would. Quickly, I told Phyl to arrange for Pippi to be admitted at the local psychiatric hospital, with which we have a loose connection. Also I asked Phyl to cancel my next three appointments and intercept any of those clients who might not get the word.

Then I went back and found Pippi sitting demurely in the chair—except, I discovered, she'd pulled her miniskirt up around her waist so that she was covered only by a wisp of lace. Again I told her she must restore her clothing; again she did so readily, pointing out how bad she was. Now, I explained, I was going to take her in my car to a hospital where they would help her and be kind to her. To my surprise, she readily agreed, and that's what we did.

Pippi's ready acceptance of hospitalization taught me again that there is, even in someone who has lost usual control, another part that strives to bring the person back to normalcy. Were the circumstances different, I think I could have helped Pippi. I hope the hospital will. That same ready acceptance of hospitalization reminded me also, however, of how inviting it can be to have someone else take over your life.

Visiting the hospital—even briefly, and even such a well-managed and humane institution—confirmed my feeling that if at all possible I want to help Kate avoid having to be hospitalized. The impact of entering an institution is powerful — large buildings, many people busy with other matters, mostly professional rather than personal interest, standardized procedures, smells of disinfectant (and of urine on some wards), and all that makes one into an object. I don't want that for Kate. It's better than letting her suicide or going so far emotionally that she might have trouble ever getting back, but she doesn't require that now, and I hope she never will.

Tuesday, October 31

Kate. Today is the same as yesterday. To my early question as to how she is feeling, she answers only that she doesn't want to talk today. Again, we sit in silence through the hour. I decide against offering her a special Wednesday appointment, feeling she would experience it as crowding her. I mention our Thursday appointment time, and she leaves.

Thursday, November 2

Kate. Five minutes after the hour, Kate arrives. I am relieved; then I see her, and my chest tightens. She walks stiffly into my office, sits on the chair, shoulders and arms pressed tightly to her sides, head held stiffly. When she speaks, her voice is thin, strained.

"I realize I am overreacting to your decision. I find it very difficult to deal with it right now. Or with most everything. Mostly I just walk. Every day I walk. I need to walk. Sometimes I just wander. Sometimes I walk down to the ocean and back. I haven't been taking care of things at the office. I just walk."

The walk to the ocean is, I estimate quickly, at least ten miles each way, probably more. She is drugging herself with fatigue. "Kate, can you talk about what's happening in you? Let's see if we can't help make things a little less painful."

"I think I am just very sad. I know it's out of proportion.

You've certainly tried to be fair, and you've done a great deal to help me. I'm sorry not to be able to deal with things better."

"You're very sad, Kate. I feel sad too. But together I think we can make it different." Earnestly, hoping to reach her, wanting her to know I haven't withdrawn, not wanting to frighten her.

"I don't know how much I can tell you. I know you want to help, but much of the time I don't know it or believe it. I want you to help me, and *eughh!* there, just like that, I hate you! I said I want you to help me, and now I hate you and I want to scream things at you, horrible things. Don't come near me." She is fighting a miserable battle within herself right now. I can see how much she wants to be helped and yet how strong her impulse is to attack me or to leave.

"I won't come toward you, Kate, but I won't go away either." Quietly, firmly, without pressure.

We sit silently for several minutes, but it seems to me I can hear silent screams from Kate as her inner struggle goes on. I feel such sympathy for her, but I know how important it is for me not to crowd her in any way right now.

Finally she speaks, and her voice is colder and more controlled. "I think it is all right now. I don't hate you now." There is some kind of a spasm within her. "But I hate myself. When I feel like this at home, I really frighten myself. Last night, yesterday, sometime, I was looking in the mirror to comb my hair, and suddenly I realized I was just standing there looking at myself and hating myself. I wanted to smash the mirror and then use the pieces to cut myself, my face and . . . and other parts of me. Just slash and tear myself. I got so frightened; I just went out and started walking right that moment."

She stops talking, sinks into herself. I am busy with my own thoughts. She really could do it. She could kill or mutilate herself. People really do those things. Should I let her leave? Am I being irresponsible by not hospitalizing her? I should see that she is protected against herself. Also, she's in real danger walking the streets in this condition. She could walk in front of a car or truck and never know it or perhaps intend unconsciously to do it.

Kate looks up as though sensing my thoughts. "I don't

think I'll do it." Her voice is low, from deep within her, only partly a communication to me; the rest is simply saying out loud her inner thoughts. "I don't think so. Some part of me wants to live. Sometimes I hate that part, too. I don't want to want anything. Nothing! *I will not* want anything or anybody!"

Once again she falls silent, but it is enough for me. I'm going to back Kate's bet on her own life. To take the choice from her, to put her in the hospital might save her physical life, but it would very likely end lastingly her struggle to have a more vital life. But the minute I decide, I feel scared and want to back down.

For the rest of the hour, we sit mostly in silence. Occasionally, Kate provides a scrap of information about how she lives these days — the endless walking, the brief visits to her office only to leave almost immediately, the irregular bits of food half eaten, the drugged sleeping. She cannot tell me much of her inner feelings and thoughts. Clearly, she feels she must keep them shut off. Nor do I press her for self-exploration. She must resist right now to hold herself together. I know, as Kate does not, that if only she can hold on, the same inexorable changefulness that she so deplores will help her come through.

Friday, November 3

Kate. Kate is not here at her appointment time, and my heart falls. But, within a few minutes, she is on the phone. She's at her laboratory, working. There is so much to catch up on. She can't come in today, but she thinks yesterday's visit helped. She will be here at her usual Monday time.

Relief, doubt, hope, apprehension.

Louise. Two weeks ago, Louise brought up the possibility of our ending our work together. We agreed to use some time to think through what she'd accomplished and what remained to be done — as though there ever is an end to such work! That review has gone as well as usual, which is to say with an uneven objective and explicit product, but a constructive subjective summarizing and reinforcing effect. Today, we have agreed, is to be our last session.

She is dressed brightly, attractively, as for a celebration — which I suppose this should be — but her face and manner don't accord with her costume.

"You put the wrong face on to go with this happy outfit."

"Yes," she is near tears. "Yes, I wanted this to be a party. I planned to get some balloons and bring a cake and maybe some wine. But then this morning when I started to come here, I just didn't have the feelings for that. I'm really sad that I won't be seeing you after today." Now the tears do come.

"I feel very much the same way. I'll miss seeing you."

"I'm glad you said that."

"We've had quite a journey together, and it's been very meaningful for me personally as well as professionally."

"Good! I never felt you were just a cold professional."

"I don't see how you could have." We grin as we look at each other with fond eyes, and the silence stretches out. Finally, I say, "We like each other, and this is our last time together, and it seems that we should be saying profound things to each other, but we have a short supply of profundities."

"I do have some news for you. Two weeks ago, I told you that Don and I agreed our living together wasn't working out well so we'd separate for a while. We were still friends, but we kept having disagreements. I guess I learned too well how to not be pleasing all the time."

"I remember."

"Well, last night we were together again, and this morning we agreed we'd rather fight together than be lonely separately."

"I think that's a decision only mature people can appreciate. When we're young we expect to find someone with whom we'll always feel good. When we grow up or older, we do well to choose a partner we can trust to fight with."

"Why didn't you tell me that sooner?"

"I'm only really finding it out myself."

"Oh. How does your relation go, Jim, if you don't mind my asking?"

"No, it's fine for you to ask. It goes well, which means I'm not avoiding conflict the way I always have before."

"You too?"

"I too."

"But I haven't told you the best news yet. We're going to give it six months' trial, and if we both feel then as we do now, we're going to . . . to. . . . " Suddenly her eyes are swimming. "We're going to get married."

"I do hope that works out for you . . . for you both. Your tears tell me how much that means as if I didn't know already."

"It really does, Jim. Thanks to you, though, I'm not going to sell myself out to make it work."

"Thank yourself. You worked hard and went through torment to make that so."

"Yes, I do thank myself, but you were crucially important."

"Good. I like having a part in it."

"And Jim, I have one other request."

"Yes?"

"Will you be my maid of honor?"

We had an affair, Louise and I. We didn't go to bed together; does that make it less an affair? We didn't take off all our clothes. We didn't have sexual intercourse. So, it would be said, we didn't "consummate" our affair. Nonsense. There was more of a consummation to our relation than there is in many a heavy breathing, genital congress.

In fact, I also had an affair with Jennifer, and I'm having one with Kate. And with Frank and Hal. And all were consummated. All led to a completion, a fullness of being with each other, and the production of new life — new aliveness for both of us.

There are other clients, of course, for whom it didn't work out so well. I regret that and intend to grow to reach others better each year.

Monday, November 6

Kate. Our 10:00 appointment time comes and goes. No Kate. I should have made her come in Friday, or given her a Saturday appointment. Or I should have hospitalized her. Am I failing her? Then the phone.

"Dr. Bugental, I'm in Santa Monica. I've been walking."

"Yes, Kate. I'm glad you called. How are? . . . "

"I can't get to your office in time, and I. . . . "

"Do you want to come in later today? I can make time for us at. . . . "

"No, no, that won't be necessary. I will come at my usual time tomorrow."

"Kate, how are you? What's happening?"

She's hung up.

I worry well into the afternoon. Dr. Taylor, Kate's physician to whom I referred her, calls. He and I have worked together with several patients. He's concerned because a pharmacy just called him for approval for a refill of Kate's sleeping pill prescription. It was filled just last month. Should he okay it?

"Len, she's in a very rough place. I can't be sure, but I think it's best to give her the pills. If she decides to kill herself, she'll find a way. The pills won't make the difference."

After a brief discussion, we agree that he will go along with Kate's request, though he'll authorize only a small number of pills.

Have I done the right thing by encouraging him to put those potentially lethal pills in her hands? I don't know. I really don't know.

Tuesday, November 7

Kate. Again she's not here! And no word. This is wearing me down. I feel angry with her. What right has she to put me through all this? I've really tried to take care of her needs. She ought to just grow up and know that other people have needs too. I can't be her mother, her nursemaid. I'm worried. I want this nonsense to stop and to stop *now!*

Twenty-five minutes into her hour, as I'm sitting at my desk ruminating, sweating it out, despairing, the phone rings. It's Kate. All the other thoughts drop off.

"Kate, where are you?"

"I'm sorry, Dr. Bugental." Her voice is slurred; she sounds groggy. Has she been drinking? "I've just awakened. I took some sleeping pills last night because I was too tired to walk. I must have been more fatigued than I realized. I slept right through my alarm."

"I understand. Would you like to come in tomorrow? I can make a time for you."

"Thank you, no. I am still trying to catch up on my work at the laboratory, and I really must get in there today and tomorrow. I will see you Thursday." She hangs up.

I can't really judge how she is. So many of the cues I would get in person are lost on the phone. It's clear that she is still very formal, distant, but she is making a consistent effort to keep in touch. That's all to the good.

I'm tense, irritable, worried, sad, hopeful. Well, not truly hopeful; more, wanting to hope.

Thursday, November 9

Kate. Again, Kate is late in arriving—such a contrast to her former precision. As she sits down, she is shocking to see. Her clothes are carelessly arranged and ill-matching. She has not made up her face nor fixed her hair. She has been walking again, she tells me. She worked Tuesday and thought everything was going to be okay. Wednesday she left work after less than an hour and began walking. As on so many nights, she only went back to her apartment when she was too dazed with fatigue to keep on her feet any longer. She had a can of soup and fell into bed. But she only slept an hour. She cannot stand being awake at night, and so she takes too many pills to ensure that she will sleep through till morning.

"Kate, I'm concerned about the pills. You take too many."

"I have to sleep. I must have them."

"Yes, Kate, I know you want the sleep, the shutting out of awareness, but. . . . "

"I have to have them. I simply have to have them."

"Can you ration yourself better, Kate? Being as tired as you are from your walking, you could easily take too many by mistake."

"I've got to have them. I'll get them some way."

"Kate, you don't have to threaten. I'm trusting you. But I'm concerned, and Dr. Taylor called when you got the refill the other day, and he's concerned too."

"I'm not going to kill myself. I have thought of that many times, but I am not going to do it."

"I believe you, Kate, but I'm worried about a mistake."

"I've got to have them."

But she never takes an overdose. Something within her is fighting for her life.

Wednesday, November 10–Wednesday, November 30

Kate. For thirty-five days Kate travels in hell, on the brink of disaster, but never giving in to the pull of the pit. Somehow she maintains, keeps going, sometimes working, sometimes walking. She comes to at least one session each week; although she can seldom use them verbally. Still, I think she finds my constant availability an anchor to keep herself from drifting too far, a reference point to relocate herself, and a promise of ultimate reconciliation—with herself, even more than with me.

The sleeping pill prescription runs out again, and Dr. Taylor calls. He suggests strongly that we should hospitalize Kate. I am tempted, and it is hard to make my case to him that this would be a failure of trust.

"I truly believe, Len, that to take over responsibility for her life now would very likely end her chances to ever reclaim it. She's fighting for her life."

"I hope so, Jim, but I want to protect her life too, you know. I want to back up her fight for her life."

"I know you do, but we can't. There's no way we can get in on that fight right now. You see, she's fighting what within herself seeks to destroy her. For us on the outside, it feels as though she's fighting us. I think we are incidental."

"Maybe. I hope you're right."

"So do I (fervently). Before God, I do hope so. But see
it this way, Len: It's her struggle, and we have to respect how
well she's carrying it out. She hasn't suicided. She hasn't over-
dosed. She has made it to work sometimes. She has come here
some. We tend to see the ways she isn't fitting the 'normal' pattern and overlook the many ways she has maintained herself
in the usual world despite a tremendous pull within her to let go."

"When you say it that way, I have to go along with you."

"Good. Thanks, Len."

I hang up and think again how uncertain I really feel and
yet how — no matter how I rework my thoughts — it always comes
out, she deserves this chance. Too many Kates learn to let go
of choice, of responsibility for their own lives when they are put
in a hospital against their wills. Then they label themselves and
are labeled by others "sick" or "emotionally disturbed" and never
fully break out of the category cage.

Thursday, December 1

Kate. Finally, it is over.

Today brings Kate on time for her appointment and
manifestly emerging from her trial. Her wall is lower, but she
is not as open as she was before I told her of my plan to leave.
Yet, it is apparent, she is back within herself and in charge of
herself. She knows it too.

"I think I'll be all right now. It's as though I've had a bad
fever and been delirious, and now the fever's gone. I still feel
weak, but I know that I'll get stronger."

"Yes, Kate." Warmly, feeling emotionally full myself.
"Yes, I can sense that the fever has broken too. It's good to see
you again."

"Oh," a quick intake of breath, "go slow, please. I am so
afraid of my feelings still. When you are warm toward me, I
want to run away or lash out at you. But you know that isn't
all, don't you?"

"Yes, I do know that, Kate," voice carefully neutral.

"Sometimes I didn't think I'd ever be like this again—ever again." She stops as a wave of feeling washes through her. "And sometimes I wanted to come here and kill you. I mean, really *kill* you. I even thought how I would do it." She sinks back, exhausted by this confession.

"Your anger just wanted to get rid of me, destroy me." I say it calmly enough but realize I hadn't thought of the danger to myself. Of course, it makes sense. If there's ever a next time, I don't want to be so naive.

"And other times, I wanted to run in here and throw myself in your arms and say take care of me and forgive me for being so much trouble."

"It must have been very lonely for you these weeks, Kate." Another sudden recognition: How terribly alone she must have felt. My words reach straight to her feelings. She drops her head, the tears stream down her cheeks. She does not sob, but cries quietly and steadily. I lean toward her but keep from crowding her. She cries in this way for several minutes, then shyly her hand comes groping out toward me. I take it eagerly and hold it as she continues to cry. My own eyes swim in empathy with her and in relief that the trial seems over.

"Do you know what helped a lot?" She looks up at me with her face dripping but with an excruciatingly sweet expression of appreciation and shyness.

"Two things I believed—still believe—you felt about me. I said them over to myself again and again. First, I believe you took me very seriously. You really knew what I was struggling with and let me struggle with it. And second, you trusted me. Dr. Taylor said you didn't let them put me in a hospital and that you told him to give me the pills. Sometimes I hated you for one or both of those, but mostly I . . . mostly I . . . mostly I loved you for them."

"Yes, Kate." I say it softly, cherishing the gift of her trust and faith.

Although Kate and I work together another five months, this is the climax of our journey. She uses these months to consolidate the genuine gains from her time of agony—and there are very real gains: more readiness to invest in relationships, more acceptance of her own flowingness, more trust in her inner awareness.

Monday, December 16

Jim. Christmas — birthday — again. Each day of living is a day closer to my death. No matter what my age. Yet each day is a new birth, brings new possibilities. My companions on these intimate journeys have taught me much, but one lesson underlies all the others:

There is always more.

When Jennifer came to me, she saw only two choices, murder or suicide. Frank believed it was a dog-eat-dog world in which he must be constantly alert to avoid being destroyed. Louise found only inner hollowness when she wasn't pleasing others. Hal compulsively raged at his son, and all Hal's reason and love were impotent to stop his tirades. Kate, granite Kate, rejected the very notion of changefulness, dreading any closeness with another person. Prisoners all. Prisoners of confining, painful, unsatisfying worlds.

Therapy did not change those worlds. I did not dissuade Jennifer from her fury with Bert or call on Hal to recognize his son's feelings or supercede Frank or Louise or Kate in their governance of their own lives.

Therapy demonstrated how we all imprison ourselves by the ways we define ourselves and our worlds. When this recognition is deeply experienced, the world is already beginning to change — since the crippling element in these definitions is the certainty that things are — and can be — only the way one sees them at the time.

The other side of that recognition is a subtle time-bomb. Ultimately, the world is made up of possibilities far more than of certainties. Ours is the task of selecting from among the possibilities latent in any certainty. Unwittingly, we often choose those which limit and cripple our lives. Yet always other possibilities await our discovery, our creativity. Too often we fail to recognize that potential and mistake a possibility for a certainty.

- The head of the U.S. Patent Office announced that everything that could be invented had already been invented — in 1899!
- The four-minute mile was once widely recognized as a physiological limit, impossible for any human to run faster.
- An English scientist with an international reputation solemnly assured the world in 1895 that heavier-than-air flying machines were impossible.
- In 1923, after careful study, a U.S. Nobel laureate in physics pronounced impossible the notion of harnessing the power of the atom.
- Frank, Jennifer, Louise, Hal, Kate, and Jim have all been sure they knew their important life situations were absolutely unchangeable.

The gift above all others that my clients have given me is the conviction that there is always more; that courage, persistence, and determination can always open possibilities where none has seemed to exist.

We cannot do everything, but we can do so much more than we usually do. It is tragic how little we recognize this. It is breathtaking to recognize how much more is possible.

Postscripts on the Clients

Jennifer

Jennifer and Bert got back together and had a wonderful two years. Then, as she sees it, Bert's wandering eye returned, and he had another affair. They discussed this and agreed to try having an "open marriage." Bert evidently found this very much to his taste; but Jennifer, after a single venture, decided it wasn't for her. They separated and divorced.

In the meantime, Jennifer had taken a second master's degree, this time in English. She left the dean's position and is now happily teaching composition and grammar. She dreams of writing a novel but so far has not begun it. She has a new love relation.

Frank

Frank earned his doctorate at a good school and landed a job on a hospital research team. He lives in the Southwest and has been married twice. The first try was evidently a miserable experience, but the second marriage seems to be going well. His wife is a coprofessional, and he has three children.

Frank still tends to enjoy adversarial discussions, but he is seldom assaultive. He is richly imaginative in his writing.

Louise

Louise and Don married. Shortly thereafter, they moved to the Pacific Northwest, where Don heads a small clinic in which Louise is the director of social work. They have one child, who is the focus of both their lives. She says they may adopt another, since she is now too old to have a second natural child.

Louise is no longer devoted to pleasing. In fact, she has become somewhat militant about women's rights.

Hal

Hal gradually changed his professional life so that he could devote full time to his private practice. He is particularly interested in the transpersonal aspects, and has written several papers about this field.

Several years after our work together ended, I was encouraged by my therapist to enter a therapy group. The coleader of that group was Hal! Thus, contrary to usual doctrine, we reversed roles. It worked out excellently, and I will always be grateful for Hal's warm support of me in a time when I deeply needed it.

Kate

Kate married a professional in another field, and for some time devoted herself to being a housewife and stepmother. Then she began what has been a fascinating journey through various subfields of contemporary culture — astrology, massage, the Tarot, feminism, and so on.

Jim

My move to Northern California was a change in more than geography. My dear companion and I married, adopted a wonderful young person to be our daughter, and have made our home in this beautiful area. For some years, Elizabeth and I had psychotherapy practices, but we have now retired from that work. I devote myself to teaching and writing; she to writing.

I have had an unusually good life. I know it, and I feel very fortunate. Many factors have contributed to making this so. One of the foremost has been the patient teaching of my clients — teaching that confronted me relentlessly with my compromises, encouraged me repeatedly to risk changes that seemed threatening, and always held up the reality of the endless possibilities open to me and to all of us.

Lessons Clients Teach Therapists

Lessons About the Nature of Being, of Life Itself

The miracle of all miracles is the fact of being. That miracle is only discovered through its other facet, the miracle of awareness. Thus the duality of objectivity and subjectivity is the foundation of all else and permeates all else.

Living is the fundamental business of life. We all do it only partially. Being alive is a matter of degree; not an either-or proposition.

Possibility is literally infinite, but conscious life cannot cope with that emptiness. We conduct our lives through the self-and-world construct system that each of us has — and, in one sense, is.

Each person's self-and-world construct system is unique. We create/discover it out of our original endowment, our experiences, and how we work with these materials to make the life we live.

Lessons About the Individual's Life Direction and Experience

We live in the world as we perceive it. The size of our life is the size of our perceived world.

Who and what we are is a part of how we see the world. Our identity is not a given but a continual creation-discovery.

Our true identity is a process, not a substantive thing. Thus we are continually changing. The effort to remain unchanging is crippling and results in a smaller life.

Lessons About the Place of Psychotherapy

The self-and-world construct system makes life possible, but it also limits our lives. The work of therapy is to help clients become aware of how they limit their own self-and-world definitions and thus limit their lives. Emotional distress is not an illness, it's a perceptual problem.

Psychotherapy is one of the ways we try to be more alive. The need for psychotherapy arises from our being caught in ways of being alive that are too cramped or distorted.

The most frequent way we cripple our lives is through making ourselves objects and thus being cut off from awareness of our unique individual experiences, needs, and intentions.

Our current cultural teachings encourage us to treat ourselves as objects. There are, of course, many places where the ability to do so is useful; the crippling occurs when this perspective is the chief or only one in life.

Psychotherapy often has as its first task countering the destructive overemphasis on objectifying ourselves. Only when we have greater access to our subjectivity can we make lasting and significant life changes.

There is no "how to" in the subjective life; only intention. Trying to make ourselves do or not do things is splitting ourselves into slave and master, and is usually futile and often mutilating in the long run.

Lessons About the Conduct of One's Life

Our inner flow of awareness is essential to our self-care, our self-direction, and our living fully. Most of us are at least partially blind/deaf in our capacity to use that inner flow.

We need to recognize and respect our needs, emotions, anticipations and apprehensions, and our sense of concern. To recognize them is not the same as being dominated by them.

To take responsibility for what we do and do not do is to take power; to avoid responsibility is to make ourselves victims, objects.

To have choice is to have power; to be choiceless is to be a slave, an object.

We are always limited. Ambiguity, uncertainty, incompleteness are part of life; to try to avoid them is to try to avoid living. Perfectionism and either/or thinking are diseases that cripple life.

We need relationships, the sharedness of being. Trying to be totally self-sufficient is a perversion.

Relationships are frightening, because the other person is always and ultimately uncontrollable and unpredictable. Paradoxically, that very quality adds to the richness of relating.

Our embodiedness is a given of our being but is not the whole of our being. We transcend the merely physical with our emotions, our aspirations, our intelligence, and our spiritedness.

Our sexuality is a powerful, creative, and enlivening part of our embodiedness, but it can also be wounding and destructive. It can bring us to intense experiences of our relatedness, our separateness, our capacity for ecstasy, our capacity for emotional pain and despair.

Unless we invest in life, make commitments to what we do and to those with whom we relate, we remain outside of life and feel empty and unsatisfied.

Relinquishment, losing in some form, is always a part of every life. It is not, in itself, a sign that something has gone wrong.

Laws, rules, folkways, mores, and the like have grown out of shared human experience and are worthy of our respect and attention. They are not, however, absolutes, and they need to be continually reexamined and revised.

Index

A

Abandonment, feelings of, 86–89
Acceptance, of human imperfection, 78
Acknowledgments, xv–xvii
Activities, relating to people through, 39
Aging, 83, 199; self views of, 12–13
Agreements, therapist-client, 34, 196, 197, 203–204
Alcohol, suppression of feelings with, 89–90
Alive, being, 20; self-awareness and, 21–22; self-worth and, 200
Allegory: climbers on the mountain, 225–226; East Coast power failure, 2; flowing river, 228–229
Ambiguity, 170; rules and, 123
Analysis, outcomes of traditional, 56, 98. *See also* Psychotherapy; Therapeutic practice
Anger: at disagreement, 70–71, 228; at others' expectations, 208–211; at therapist's leaving, 300–303, 311; at wasted living, 237–239; as defense, 38–39, 149–150, 150–152, 173–174; denial of, 39; in group, 251–256, 268; helplessness and, 149–150. *See* Rage
Annoyance, at needing psychotherapy, 16–17
Answer, the, xi, 28

Answers, having the, 222
Argument, client-therapist, 101–102, 104–105, 142–143
Assumptions of psychotherapy. *See* Psychotherapy
Attention, paying, 41–44
Authority, 73, 187–188; human needs and external, 119–123, 123–124, 222–224
Awareness, inner. *See* Inner awareness

B

"Balancing pole" defenses, 106–107, 181–182
Bathing habits, client, 98–99, 103
Being, the nature of, 325
Betrayal: by infidelity, 32, 122, 247–248; in childhood, 86–89; vulnerability and, 97
Bindrim, Paul, 165
Blame: concentration on, 70–72, 251–257; guilt and, 73–74; pattern of, 46, 279
Breakthroughs: emotional, 98, 238–239, 251–257; from old patterns, 239; to subjectivity, 129–130, 263–264, 267

C

Calling the therapist: emergency basis, 24–25; fear of, 18–19

Centeredness, subjective, 27–28, 136. *See also* Inner awareness; Intention

Change: client's need for, 58; client's power to, 56–57, 320–321; feelings regarding, 83, 170, 182–184, 320; time needed for, 178, 180–181, 317–318; working-through process and, 125

Chatter, inner, 113–114

Children: disappointment of, 86–89; tenderness towards, 175–178

Choice, existential: power in life and, 89, 150, 318, 320–321; responsibility and, 73–74, 224. *See also* Crisis, existential; Intention

Client behavior: avoiding therapeutic work, 112–113; challenging the therapist, 101–102, 142, 146–148; confused feelings and, 191–193, 203, 259–261; in crisis, 28–34, 317–318; feeling stuck, 179–180, 198, 234–236; gift-giving, 168–169; inappropriate prompting, 138; missing appointments, 300–306, 310, 312, 314–318; reciting facts, 29–30; revealing themselves, 127–128

Clients: distressed *vs.* sick, 56–58; expectations by, 66, 112, 209–210; lessons from, xi–xii, xvi–xvii, 111–112, 239, 320–321, 325–328; well-analyzed but unchanged, 56, 98

Closeness, fear of, 147–148, 163–164, 230, 243–244

Commitment, and investing in life, 328

Companion, life, longing for a, 83, 164, 273, 293, 313

Concerns, life issues and, 113–114

Conflict: father-son, 9–10; of inner self with outer authority, 123; self, 310–312, 314–318

Confusion, 203, 259–261; period of therapy, 191–193

Consistency, rules and, 121–123, 170

Control: fear of losing, 94–96, 97; need to be in, 52–53, 62

Couch, therapist's, 11, 51–52, 109, 187; sleeping on, 54

Courage of clients, xi, 170, 285, 290, 321

"Crawl psychology," 11

Crisis, existential, 198; clients in, 28–34, 309, 310–318. *See also* Choice, existential; Suicide

"Crutch I have to bear, the," 144

Crying, 135–136, 177–178, 195, 239, 256–257, 319; self-conflict and, 31, 247, 264, 288

D

Daughter-mother relationship, 43–44

Deadness feelings, 234–236

Death, 204–205, 212; of parents, 5–6

Dependence: fear of, 38–39, 88, 90, 97, 152, 262–263, 318; on pleasing others, 6, 74–76, 123–125, 132, 189–192, 212–213, 223, 264–265, 288–290

Depression, the, 1, 192–196, 196–198, 199

Destiny, 90

Detachment: problems with therapist's, xii, xvii, 137–138; rationalism and, 55

Disappointment, 181; childhood, 86–89

Distress, psychological: nature of, 56; persistence of, 56, 98

Divorce and separation, 30–31, 284

Doctor. *See* Psychotherapist

Doodling, by the therapist, 2–3, 124

Dress, personal: messages of, 150, 229–230, 242, 265–266, 269–270, 272–273, 279–290, 295–296, 298–299, 308–309, 316; therapy and disrobing, 24, 140, 157–160, 161–164, 174, 281–283, 286–290

Drinking, suppression of feelings with, 89–90

E

Emergency help concerns, 25, 315, 316–317, 319

Emotions: deadness of, 234–236; difficulty of exploring, 94–96; fear of positive, 231, 262–264, 277, 318; feeling better, 249–250; frozen, 89, 91, 176–178, 185, 297, 307–308; having *vs.* being dominated by, 115; hollowness of, 4–5; "nothing to say" about, 91–92, 179–180, 307–308, 310, 312, 317; phobia of, 97; rejection of, 94; relationship of reason to, 65–67, 133–136; suppression of, 89–90, 310, 312, 316–317; thinking and, 26–27

Erotic attitudes. *See* Sexuality

Esalen Institute, 13, 140

Existential psychology. *See* Psychology, existential

F

Fairness in life, wanting, 32–33, 72, 119–123, 253–256

Father-son relationship: conflict, 9–10, 49; loss of, 135–136

Fatigue, self-drugging with, 310, 312, 316–317

Fear: of calling the therapist, 18–19; of closeness, 147–148, 163–164, 169, 230, 243–244; of group therapy, 152; of losing control, 94–96, 97; of losing the therapist, 298; of needing other people, 38–39, 88, 90, 97, 152, 262–263, 318; of sexuality, 281–283; of therapy, 18–19, 170–171; of vulnerability, 97, 126

Femininity, awareness of, 4–6, 266–267, 270, 282–283

Frank, 18–19, 98–102, 103–107, 126–128, 141–144, 145–150, 200–203, 229–232, 233–234, 242–244, 248, 252–257, 260, 261–265, 277–278; first interview with, 37–39; joining group, 150–153, 173–174; last visit of, 298–300; postscript, 322

Fred, 35–36, 55, 77–78

Friendship, lack of, 17, 103, 141, 170, 207

Fromm-Reichmann, Frieda, 55

G

God-feeling, 210–212, 220–222, 224

Grief for lost living, 89, 133, 177, 198, 239, 249, 285

Group psychotherapy, 233–234, 245–246; after an upheaval, 268–270; assistance through, 205–206; departures from, 139–140; entry of new members to, 59–61, 81–83, 150–153, 214–217; exercises in, 139; involving a member in, 67–69, 173–174; purposes of, 47, 59–60, 149, 208; resistance to joining, 47, 208; struggle in, 250–257; time commitment to, 149, 217

Guilt, blame and, 73–74

H

Hal, 25–27, 47–55, 108–111, 116–118, 128–132, 133–136, 182–184, 192–196, 196–198, 203, 208–212, 217–218, 218–222, 224–226, 234, 234–239, 249–250; first interview of, 9–11; last visit of, 273–274; postscript, 323

Hating life, 38

Hemlock Society, 204

Hippie, son as a, 9–10

History, collecting client, 15, 65, 111. *See also* Reporting on oneself

Hollowness feeling, 4–5

Honeymoon, therapy, 185

Hospitalization, psychiatric, 309–310, 317, 319

"How to" and intention, 129–132, 326

Human beings, pride and despair in, xi, 12, 171, 293–294

I

"I-ness," 76, 219; as center of life, 27–28

Ideal, discrepancy of reality and the, 78

Identity: basis of, 199–200; as process, 326

Individuality and feeling special, 199–200, 211–212

Infidelity, issues of, 32, 34–35, 247, 251–257

Inner awareness, 113–114, 327; aliveness and, 20–21; breaking through to, 117–118, 129–131, 190–192; difficulty understanding, 26–27, 50–51, 116–117; disbelief in, 54; eruption of, 218; rationalism and, 55; readiness for, 178; thinking about oneself *vs.*, 48–49, 133, 189–192

Intellect, primary reliance on the, 17

Intention: no "how to" in, 129–131, 326; self-direction and, 131–132, 133–136. *See also* Choice, existential
Intention, subjective, 326
Internal chatter, 114
Interviews. *See* Sessions
Involvement. *See* closeness; Other people
Isolation as refuge, 95

J

Jealousy, about a client, 283, 293. *See also* Infidelity
Jennifer, 40–46, 69–74, 119–123, 179–182, 187–189, 207–208, 214–217, 246–248, 259–261, 272–273; emergency call by, 24–25; first interview of, 28–34; lashing out in group, 251–257, 268–269; last visit of, 279–280; postscript, 322
Jim, 1–3, 9, 11–15, 19–22, 22–24, 25, 27–28, 35–36, 38–39, 46, 65–67, 72–74, 76–78, 88–90, 102, 106–107, 110–111, 118–119, 123, 131–132, 133, 160–161, 164–165, 171–173, 198–200, 203–205, 214, 293–294; career of, xix; changes in life of, 274–276, 283–284, 291–292, 295, 308–310, 313–314, 320; on the nature of psychotherapy, xii–xiii, 54–59, 111–114, 137–138, 184–185, 224, 308–310, 314; postscript, 323–324; purpose for including story of, xi–xii, xvii. *See also* Psychotherapist
Job: getting a new, 242–243; identity and a person's, 20, 199–200; interviewing for, 229–230; losing a, 205–206
Justice. *See* Fairness of life; Punishment

K

Kate, 62–65, 81–90, 91–98, 114–116, 167–170, 175–179, 226–229, 265–267, 295–298; in distress and missing appointments, 300–307, 310, 312, 314–318; first interview with, 16–18; postscript, 323; recovery, 318–320
Killing: of possibility, 165–166; threat of, 30–34, 256, 311–312, 319
Known, being, 19

L

Language: of clients, 242, 261, 269, 299, 300; psychotherapy terms and, xi, 14–15, 113. *See also* Restatements
Life-conduct lessons, xi–xii, xvi–xvii, 111–112, 239, 320–321, 325–328
Life-growth consultation, 115
List-making, 40–42, 44–45
Listening: difficulty in, 40–41, 43; to yourself, 53. *See also* Inner awareness
"Listening I/eye," 27–28
Loneliness, 244, 319
Louise, 22, 74–77, 123–125, 132–133, 153–160, 161–166, 174, 189–192, 212–214, 222–224, 240–244, 251–257, 264–265, 270, 272, 280–283, 284–290, 290–291, 292–293, 295; first interview of, 3–9; last visit of, 312–314; postscript, 323
Lying to oneself, 108–109

M

Marriage, rules of, 122
Masturbation, 156
Maturation, therapy and, 15
May, Rollo, 90
Meaning, lack of, 5. *See also* Crisis, existential
Medication, authorization of, 315, 316–317, 319
Melodrama, emotional expression as, 147
Memories, solitary *vs.* discussed, 97
Menstruation, first, 84–87
Misery, giving up, 103–106
Motivation: difficulty of exploring life, 94–96; to enter therapy, 114, 138

N

Neighbor, concerned, 304–306
No, saying, 213–314
"Nothing to say," 91–92, 179–180, 307–308, 310, 312, 317
Nudity, 165; bathing, 13–14, 140; venturing, 160. *See also* Sexuality

O

Objectification of oneself, 17–18, 111, 133–135, 171–172; overemphasis of, 326; restatement and, 116–119
Objectivity, xii–xiii; subjectivity duality with, 18, 325
Office environment (psychotherapist), 1–3
Openness, 278; and subjectivity in group, 216–217; to life, 113–114
Ortega y Gasset, Jose, 36
Other people: allowing involvement with, 248, 260–261; anger defense from, 149–150, 173–174; being with, 38–39, 233–234; blaming, 46, 70–72, 251–257, 253–256, 279; dependence on pleasing, 6, 74–76, 123–125, 132, 189–192, 212–213, 223, 264–265, 288–290; desire to punish, 32, 251–257; fear of needing, 38–39, 88, 90, 97, 311–312; focusing on, 74–76, 123–125, 132, 189–192, 212–213, 223, 264–265, 288–290; pride and despair in, 171, 293–294; projections of, 245–246; relationships with, 327
Outward Bound, 204

P

Pain. *See* Crying; Emotions; Grief
Partnership, therapy as, 15, 138
Patterns, life: essentiality of, 106–107, 181–182; intention and, 131–132, 133–135; psychotherapy as review of, 56–58; self-limiting, 22, 66, 320–321; working through, 125, 185–186, 239
People. *See* Other people
Physical presence: of female clients, 4, 245–247, 272–273, 279, 280–283, 385–290; of male clients, 10, 37, 98–99. *See also* Dress; Sexuality
Pippi, 308–309
Pleasing others. *See* Other people
Potential, human, 12
Power in life, 172–173; anger and, 149–150; existential choice and, 89, 150, 318, 320–321; intention and sense of, 131–132

Presence, 113
Present, being in the, 44, 76; avoiding, 47, 112–113; in life-changing therapy, 65–66, 113
Protection patterns, breakdown of, 93–94
Psychologist as a client, 9, 11–12
Psychology: behaviorist, 11, 107; existential, 12; experimental, 11
Psychotherapist, the: absent clients and, 303–306, 310, 312, 314–318; client suicide threat and, 31, 33, 34, 194–195, 258–259; differences from the client, 137–138, 184–185, 302–303; discrepancy between vision and personal life of, 78, 214; doodling by, 2–3, 124; effect of clients' emotions on, 184–185, 209, 226–227, 238–239; evaluative statements by, 278; impatience with client by, 100–101; lessons clients teach, xi–xii, xvi–xvii, 111–112, 239, 320–321, 325–328; modeling by, 115; power of, 9, 153; resistance to matching client by, 126; sexual feelings of, 4, 7, 9, 14, 22–24, 77, 157–160, 165–166, 189, 214, 240–242, 280–283, 286–290, 308–309; in therapy, 284, 323; weight of responsibility of, 194–195, 209–210, 217–218, 224. *See also* Jim
Psychotherapy: assumptions and rethinking of, 56–59, 98; client motivations for, 114, 138; depth, xvi–xvii, 56; educative process of, 111–114, 228–229; inner readiness and, 178; lessons about the place of, 326; media view of, 98; medical model and, 56–57, 111, 318; nude, 165; stages of, 185–186, 198, 225–226; terminology of, xi, 14–15, 113; whodunit view of, 98, 178
Punishment, desire for other's, 32

Q

Question, the, xi

R

Race riots, 277–278, 283
Rage, 39, 149–150. *See also* Anger

Rationalism: controlling emotions with, 10, 17, 28, 113, 227–229, 286; as substitute for living experience, 62; unreasonable use of, 55

Readers (of author's books): personal interaction with, 77–78; responses by, 36, 55, 291

Reality, existential, 240

Reasons people seek psychotherapy, 57–58, 66, 112, 209–210

Recalling past emotional experiences, 65, 84–87

Relationships. *See* Clients; Other people; Psychotherapist, the

Reporting on oneself, xii–xiii, 17, 29–30, 32; with lists, 40–41, 44–45; with stories, 65, 103, 141, 175–179, 201–203

Resistance: seeing one's own, 67; to change, 58–59

Resistance. *See also* Change

Responsibility: guilt and, 73–74; of life, 219–220; as opportunity, 73–74

Restatements: by the client, 40–41, 116–119; by the therapist, 17; and twisting words, 146–147

Restatements. *See also* Talking

Rogers, Carl, 186

Rules and mores, 208, 253–254, 261, 268; ambiguities of, 123; human needs and external, 119–123, 279–280; the place of, 328

S

Sarcasm, 146, 187, 245; therapist's, 100

Screaming, 238–239

Seductiveness. *See* Physical presence; Sexuality

Self: as subject or object, 17–18, 111, 116–119, 133–135, 171–172, 326; unified, 76, 109

Self-and-world construct system: essentiality of, 106–107; lessons about, 106–107, 325–328

Self-awareness, and being alive, 20–22, 275–276

Self-awareness. *See also* Inner awareness

Self-criticism: blame and, 46, 110, 251–257, 259–261; vs. life authorship, 18

Self-deception, disunity of, 108–109

Self-determination, 250, 265–266, 270–271, 287–288, 290–291, 292–293, 301

Self-evaluation, of life's progress, 13, 291–292. *See also* Reporting

Self-interruptions, 69–70

Self-mutilation, threat of, 311–312. *See also* Suicide; Violence

Self-worth, basis of, 199–200

Selfishness, 28

Sessions: frequency of, 11, 79–81; portrayal of, xii, xvi–xvii; undress during, 24, 140, 157–160, 161–164, 174, 281–283, 286–290

Sexuality, 23, 327; emotions of, 154–160, 201–202, 235–236; experiment with, 154–160, 162–164; love and, 251, 273; self-image and, 245–246; shame and, 7–8, 156–157, 163–164; therapist-client relationship and, 4, 7, 9, 14, 22–24, 77, 157–160, 165–166, 189, 214, 240–241, 280–283, 286–290, 308–309. *See also* Nudity

Sixties, the, xiv, 160–161

Sleeping client, 54

Slowing down, impatience and, 41–42

Specialness. *See* Individuality

Spontaneity, 76

Stein, Gertrude, 28

Stevens, Barry, 186

Subconscious processes, cognitive interpretations of, 3

Subjectivity, human: coping with new insight of, 184, 197–198, 217–218; duality with objectivity, 18, 325; as the enemy, 169–170; no "how to" in, 129–132, 326; objective grasp of, xii–xiv, 128–129

Suicide, 204–205, 258–259; threat of, 31, 33, 194–195

Suppression of emotions, with fatigue, 310, 312, 316–317

Suppression of feelings, with alcohol, 89–90

System, fitting into the, 122

T

Taboos, cultural: psychotherapy relationship and, 240; sixties' changes in, 160–161

Talking: about the subjective, 3, 118, 216–217, 278; objectification and, 118
Talking. *See also* Restatements
Teaching, during therapy, 228–229
Teilhard de Chardin, 126–127
Temper, ungovernable, 10
Therapeutic practice: as an affair, 314; appropriate limits of, 165–166, 239–240, 283–284, 287–288, 308–309; availability to clients during, 24–25; commitment and obligations of, 137–138, 217–218, 224, 291, 308; composite subjective experience of, xii; couch use in, 11, 51–52, 54, 109, 187; detachment and, xii, xvii, 137–138; ethics of, 308–309; fees and, 18–19, 202–203, 300; first-name basis in, 114–115; helping clients be present in, 66, 111–114; interruption and transfer of, 296–298, 301–303; medication and, 315, 316–317, 319; outcomes of traditional, 56, 98; purposes of, 14–15, 112–114, 225–226, 291; short-term referrals and consultations of, 308–309; sources of stress during, 35
Therapist. *See* Psychotherapist
Therapy. *See* Psychotherapy; Therapeutic practice
Tillich, Paul, 172

Transference, 93
Trust, 32, 247, 280, 289, 313, 319

U

Unconscious, conscious control of the, 63–64

V

Victim role, 72, 101–102
Vietnam, 12, 229, 294
Violence, threat of, 31–35, 256, 311–312, 319
Visits, client. *See* Sessions
Vulnerability, fear of, 97, 126

W

Waiting to speak, 41–42
Wallenda, Karl, 106–107, 181–182
Ways of living, outgrowing, xii, 15
"Whodunit psychotherapy", 98, 178
Woman, emergence as a, 266–267, 270, 282–283
Work. *See* Job; Therapeutic practice
Working through. *See* Patterns, life
Writing on psychotherapy, xii–xiv, 36–37, 118–119; and readers, 35–36, 55, 77–78